TABLE OF

HISTORY AND CULTURE

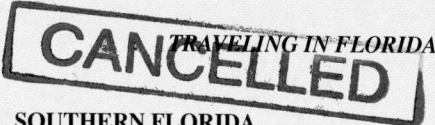

~~TRAVELING IN FLORIDA~~

CANCELLED

SPECIAL TOPICS

FEATURES

GUIDELINES

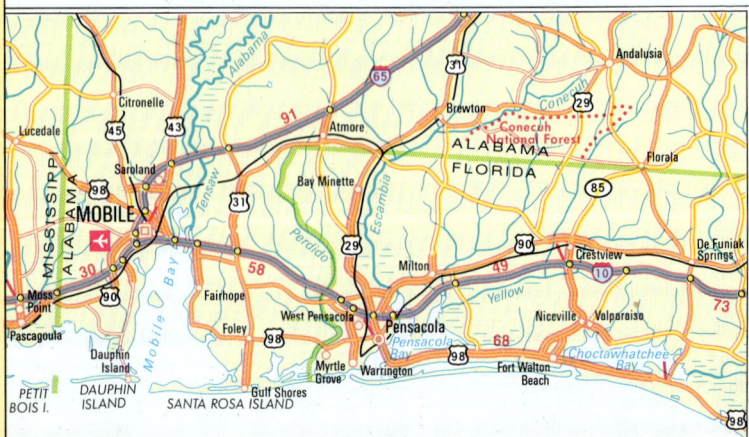

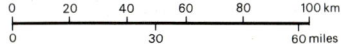

LIST OF MAPS

Haines City
Cypress Gardens
er Haven
Singing Tower
Lake Wales

Melbourne
Palm Bay

441
192

Lake
Kissimmee

Lake
Marian

104

60

Blue
Cypress L.

Gifford

Vero Beach

A T L A N T I C

Avon Park

84

Sebring

441

95

Fort Pierce

HUTCHINSON
ISLAND

27

98

70

Port St.Lucie

L. Istokpoga

Okeechobee

70

Stuart

St.Lucie Inlet

L. Placid

O C E A N

98

Brighton
Seminole
Indian
Reservation

L. Hicpochee

Lake
Okeechobee

Pahokee

St. Lucie C.

98

441

Jupiter

1

Settlement Pt.
West End
Settlement

F L O R I D A

hatchee

La Belle

80

Clewiston

Belle Glade

North Palm Beach

Riviera Beach

West Palm
Beach

Greenacres
City

West Palm Beach

Lake Worth
Lantana

Freeport

Immokalee

The
Big Cypress
Indian Reservation

Boynton Beach

441

42

Delray Beach

95

Big
press

29

Tamiami Canal

93

84

75

Miccosukee
Indian
Reservation

Boca Raton

Deerfield Beach

27

Coral Sprs.

Margate
Sunrise

Pompano Beach

U N I T E D   S T A T E S

B A H A M A S

swamp

Big Cypress

Everglades

National

Preserve

Plantation

Pembroke Pines

Miramar

Carol City

FORT LAUDERDALE

HOLLYWOOD

Hallandale

North Miami Beach

Alice Town

NORTH BIMINI

BIMINI

SOUTH BIMINI

land

glades City

OUSAND
SLANDS

Miccosukee
Indian Reservation

41

HIALEAH

Kendall

North Miami

MIAMI BEACH

MIAMI

Coral Gables

NORTH CAT CAY

ISLANDS

Everglades

National

Homestead

Cutler Ridge

Biscayne
Bay

Biscayne
National Park

Whitewater
Bay

CAPE
SABLE

Park

1

KEY
LARGO

SOUTH
RIDING ROCK

East Cape

Flamingo

Key Largo

Florida Bay

Key Largo

of

Florida

Marathon

133

1

F L O R I D A

K E Y S

ORANGE CAY

Straits

of

SOUTHERN FLORIDA

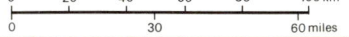

| 0 | 20 | 40 | 60 | 80 | 100 km |

| 0 | | 30 | | 60 miles |

FLORIDA'S HISTORY

So you're going to Florida! Say hello to the Sunshine State: a brassy blend of Mickey Mouse, beach parties and *Miami Vice*, of antebellum plantations and mangrove swamps, where you can fish, swim or go diving along the Florida Keys, or simply relax on the beach, gazing out across the vast, azure ocean.

Culture is also well-represented here, whatever your interests: whether you like Delius and Bach, or jazz and reggae, you will be sure to find the right music festival. Museums and collections display a broad spectrum of art, from prehistoric finds and ancient Chinese porcelain to Art Deco, Dalí and Tiffany.

Cape Canaveral brings us a little bit closer to outer space, while the Carribean influence on Florida's cuisine provides a few earthly pleasures.

Paradise for Retirees

Even with a map in hand, it's difficult to realize that Florida is almost as wide as it is long – about 450 miles from the Georgia border in the north to Key West in the south, and about 350 miles from Jacksonville in the east to Pensacola in the west.

Florida has a total area of 58,560 square miles, making the state larger than England and Wales. It is larger than the states of New York, Massachusetts and Rhode Island combined – yet no corner of the state is more than an hour's drive from the ocean.

Preceding pages: Cypress Gardens Recreational Park. Neptune Beach near Jacksonville. Beach at Key Largo. Left: In the Miccosukee reservation, Everglades.

The state is dotted with 7,712 lakes of ten acres or more, threaded with 34 rivers, and rimmed by almost 2,300 miles of tidal shoreline containing around 663 miles of beaches. Its southern tip is closer to the Equator than any other point in the continental United States.

At the turn of the century, the richest community in Florida was Key West, which then, after the Great Depression and the hurricanes of the 1930s, suddenly found itself in one of the poorest regions in the state. These days, Key West is a magnet for tourists, yuppies, artists and drop-outs of all ages.

Because it was the last area of the continental United States to rise from the ocean, Florida is America's youngest state, geologically speaking. And, because the median age of residents is 34.7 – and over 50 in some counties – it's also the nation's "oldest" state. In Sarasota, for example, senior citizens make up 30 percent of the population. Of all Americans over the age of 60 who choose to move, 25 percent of them move to Florida. When senior citizens' groups, such as the Silver Hair Legislature, or the Grey Panthers, or the American Association of Retired Persons, speak, Florida politicians are all ears.

Florida has nearly 350,000 lodging units, from hotels and motels to bed and breakfast inns. There are more than 100,000 campsites throughout the state. No part of Florida is more than 60 miles away from its famous beaches. Florida even managed to take six places on the list of the nation's ten most beautiful beaches. Year for year, tourism continues to grow in Florida, with nearly 43 million visitors having made their way to the Sunshine State in 1996.

The Many Faces of Florida

Florida has many facets. To capture the true essence of Florida is to travel from the frosty winters of Tallahassee to the

17

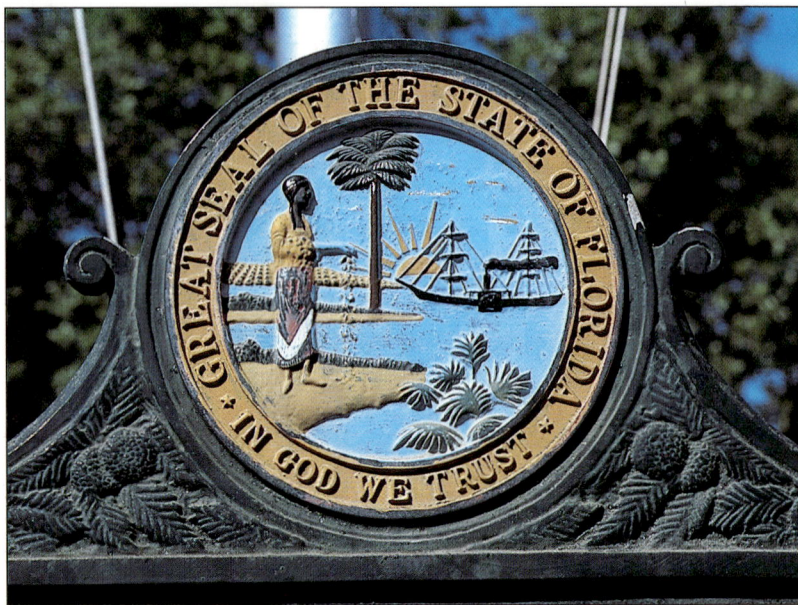

steamy swamps of the Everglades; to sample the blaring hustle of Miami Beach; to walk barefoot along Miracle Strip beaches as white as salt.

When you stop at a quiet country church to pump a glass of cold water from the well outside, the cities seem to be far away indeed. Then there is the countryside, with endless acres of orange groves and field crops, rich ranches and hard-toiling farms. Florida pine lands border farms bristling with sugar cane or dusty phosphate mines.

Some Florida communities are strictly Dixie, with attitudes and accents of the Old South. And the state has its share of solid, small-town American communities, not very much different in temperament from those in Ohio or Nebraska. Scattered throughout are pocket communities sheltering relative newcomers

Above: The Seal of the State of Florida celebrates a scene from the time Florida was admitted into the Union in 1845. Right: This engraving depicts an early native ceremony.

from Cuba, Mexico, Nicaragua, Jamaica, Haiti or Southeast Asia. A number of Arabs and wintering Canadians are also attracted to Florida to build first or second homes.

Florida is a modern hub of state-of-the-art commerce; an American model in areas of tourism development and tourist services, not to mention international trade and banking which flourish here.

How it All Began

About 130,000 years ago, a giant ground sloth slithered into a slime pit in what is now Daytona Beach, where its remains lay for millennia while the history of Florida took shape. Today you can see the sloth's massive skeleton, the most complete ever found in North America, at the Museum of Arts and Sciences in Daytona Beach.

A remarkably complete mastodon skeleton has recently been uncovered in the same area, another clue to the world of dark, primeval Florida prehistory. The

R. Saturioua

II.

scene must have been much the same near Tallahassee, where another mastodon skeleton was found. It is now on display in the Museum of Florida History in Tallahassee. Partial skeletons of mastodons and saber-tooth tigers are constantly turning up in the phosphate mines, as well as in excavations made by developers. A turtle skeleton was found in an oil well 9,000 feet deep.

The scene now shifts to about 12,000-10,000 B.C., when an ancient, unknown people spread through the state, living on harvests of shellfish, acorns, and small game. The massive shell mounds at Crystal River mark the oldest site continuously occupied in the present-day United States. Two cultures, Weedon Island I and Weedon Island II, were unearthed and named in the 1920s in Pinellas County. Separated by distinct layers of dirt showing that there had been two periods of migration, the digs reveal a settlement that probably began with a group akin to the Muskogees or Muskohegean, who had brought with them

objects typical of the Amerindian cultures of Georgia, probably acquired during their trek to Florida.

Another rich and interesting archeological discovery was made on an island not far from Naples, where wooden Calusan artifacts were perfectly preserved in mangrove swamps. In the 1980s, the oldest canoe ever found in the western hemisphere was fished out of De Leon Springs.

By the time the Spanish arrived in the 16th century, the Apalachee Indians (from Apalachee Bay in northern Florida) were knowledgeable and talented gardeners, and were soon supplying the Spanish in St. Augustine with food. Tequesta Indians lived in the Palm Beach area, the Ais near Cape Canaveral. Timucuans, who had been in Florida since at least 300 B.C., occupied an area stretching from Tampa Bay to Jacksonville. The Jeaga Indians dwelled in the Keys, and the Mayaimi and Calusa in southern Florida. So fierce were the Calusa, who were accomplished sailors and

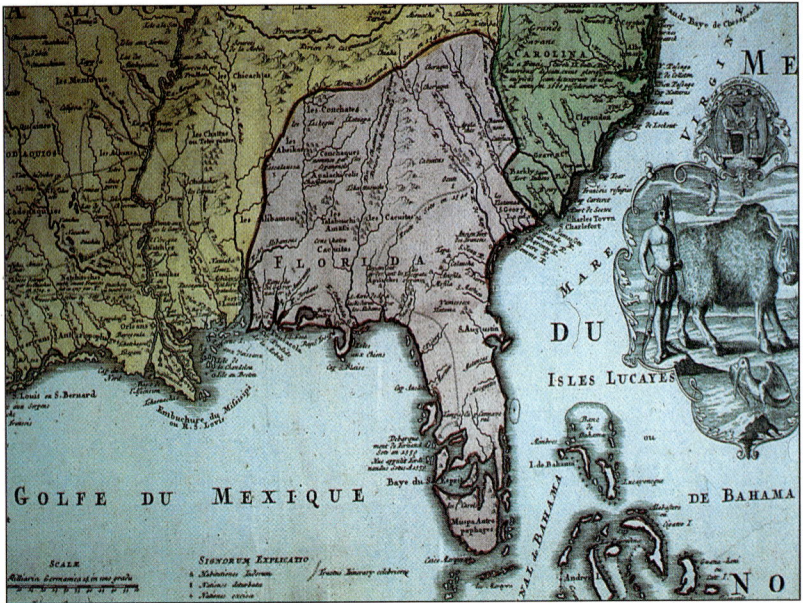

believed to be related to the man-eating Caribs, that the Spanish never did get a foothold in southwestern Florida.

Before the coming of the white man, the Indian population of the state was thought to be about 10,000. The various tribes grew crops, including corn, a food new to the Spanish. They had working systems of irrigation, which also included digging elaborate coastal canals. Pottery-making, forming flint into arrowheads, hollowing hardwood logs by burning and shaping them to form long-distance canoes, and basket-weaving were practiced.

Early explorers' accounts include reports of tattooed aborigines, self-mutilation, and fingernails grown long and filed to sharp points. These early Florida residents wore deerskin clothing and antlers to help them sneak up on deer during a hunt. They used to adorn themselves with beads, rattles and inflated fish bladders.

As a sacrifice to their sun god, in hopes of a better harvest, parents might club a firstborn child to death, and prisoners were brutally tortured. However, the natives were not cannibals. As archeologists unearthed many skeletons with missing or displaced bones, researchers jumped to the conclusion that the human flesh had been eaten. It is now thought that bodies may have been left exposed to the elements prior to burial.

An aboriginal widow cut her hair short to symbolize her grief. When it grew down to her shoulders, the mourning period was considered over and remarriage was permitted. As was common among pre-Columbian Indian cultures, inheritance and power were held by men, but were passed on through the female line. A chief's death, for example, meant the succession of the son of the dead man's sister, not of his own son. Although women controlled their own spheres of power as producers of chiefs, they seldom ruled, although some studies have shown evidence of female leadership in certain instances.

Elders met in tribal councils. Chiefs and priests built their lodges high atop square mounds. Evidence of the way these early Floridians lived can still be seen today, most notably in the Indian mounds at Crystal River, and lodge excavations in and around Tallahassee.

European Settlement

Modern Florida history began in the 16th century, when Spanish sailors first noted on their maps a land near the Bahamas blessed with "the waters of eternal youth." The legend persists to this day, with some saying that the Fountain of Youth is located in St. Augustine, and others pointing to De Leon Springs west of Daytona Beach.

The Spaniard Juan Ponce de Leon, who had been aboard Columbus' second voyage to the New World, brought his own expedition to Florida at Easter time in 1513. He named the place *Pascua Florida*, Spanish for "Flowery Easter." De Leon's crew spent only a few days exploring the area that was to become St. Augustine.

Spanish influence spread throughout the region through the establishment of forts and missions, intended primarily to curtail the ambitions of the French and British. By the time Sir Walter Raleigh and the first colonists arrived in Virginia, the Spanish had already established more than 200 settlements. Hernando De Soto was sent by Spain's King Charles V to explore and conquer the New World. He is said to have found a handful of pearls when he landed near Tampa Bay in 1539. His quest for exclusive riches would take him more than 4,000 miles through territory that had never before been seen by white men.

Leading an expedition of more than 1,000 men, De Soto spent his first winter at Tallahassee, which was already an advanced settlement of Apalachee Indians. The band then pushed into the Carolinas and Tennessee, then on to Alabama, where they were attacked by Mobile

Indians. In a further search for gold, survivors crossed the Mississippi River, reaching as far as today's Arkansas River before returning to the Mississippi, where De Soto died.

The great Spanish explorer was buried somewhere along the "Father of Waters." A stone monument five miles west of Bradenton marks the spot where De Soto landed, powerful and hopeful, four frustrating years before his death.

The first Spanish settlement was made at Pensacola in 1559, only to be abandoned after two turbulent years marked by illness and Indian attacks.

St. Augustine, orignially protected by a wooden fort, was founded by the Spanish admiral Pedro Menéndez de Avilés in 1565. The settlement endured fire, disease, flood and battle to survive today as America's oldest continuously-inhabited city. Just one year earlier, in 1564, French Huguenots established Fort Caroline at the mouth of the nearby St. Johns River, but they were attacked and massacred by the Spanish, leaving the entire region securely in Spanish hands.

The Castillo de San Marcos in St. Augustine, a stone fort built by the Spanish, has walls 16 feet thick and a moat 40 feet wide. It was unconquerable in its day. Over the centuries the old fort changed hands many times for many reasons, but it was never broached in battle.

By 1622, gold-laden galleons were sailing past Florida's southern tip ferrying treasures plundered from Central and South America back to Mother Spain. One of their ships, *Nuestra Señora de Atocha*, sank off Key West and was not seen again for 350 years, when Mel Fisher and his team of treasure hunters began salvaging her rich cargo of jewels and precious metals. Some of the booty that made millions for Fisher and the state of Florida is displayed in Fisher's Museum in Key West.

An early and unwilling Florida tourist, Jonathan Dickinson landed in the region

when he was shipwrecked off what is now Hobe Sound in 1696.

Dickinson's diary was published after he and his family survived starvation, Indian attacks, disease and near drowning. It detailed their early days of barefooted and nearly naked trekking, before eventually finding their way home to Pennsylvania. The adventurous book fascinated the gentry of the time. The popular author Dickinson went on to become mayor of Philadelphia. Copies of his book, a riveting account of his escape, are still available, providing an intimate look at the Indians of that place and period, vivid descriptions of the problems faced by travelers in a land without roads, and a tribute to the courage and grit of an early American family.

In the Treaty of Paris of 1763, the British received Florida in exchange for

Above: It was patience that brought gold worth millions to Mel Fisher. Right: Dozens of shipwrecks containing gold are thought to still be lying offshore.

Cuba. In the Treaty of Versailles of 1783, the British had to return Florida to the Spanish. In return, Britain won possession of the Bahamas and Gibraltar. Florida's Tories (British Loyalists), who had fled to Florida to escape the Revolution in the colonies to the north, now set sail for the Bahamas or other British holdings in the West Indies, seeking yet another homeland where they could remain loyal to the Crown.

Until into the 20th century, remote corners of Florida, such as Key West, had closer cultural and economic ties with Nassau than with the fledgling United States. Some of Key West's finest homes were prefabricated in the Bahamas of wood cut in the forests of Great Abaco. These houses, and subtle nuances in the accents of native-born Key Westers, remain today as reminders of the days before the 1930s, when the Keys, like the nearby Bahamas, were not yet a major destination for tourists.

Florida's history is threaded with pirates and plunderers, duels and derring-

do, and the swashbuckling of cocky opportunists. Despite Florida's family attractions and its placid retiree communities, the state is as much a magnet for adventurers as ever – immigrants, refugees, retirees, drug dealers, deadbeats, beautiful models and starlets, runaways, teen surf bums, time-share sales reps and developers – lots of developers – American dreamers all. The result is a colorful and charged mixture of cultures, lifestyles and views.

In 1812, a group of so-called Patriots got fed up with constant Spanish-British wrangling over Florida and proclaimed their own republic. The Patriots' flag was raised over Fernandina Beach on Amelia Island, which became, for a time, an independent republic. A few years later, the fort there was wrested away from a Scottish soldier of fortune, Gregor MacGregor, by a Mexican named Luis Aury, who raised yet another flag over little Fernandina. American forces were in control again by 1817, just in time for the Seminole Wars to begin.

The Seminole Wars

By the late 1700s, most of Florida's native inhabitants had disappeared. A Spanish visitor reported after a trek from St. Augustine to the Chattahoochee River in 1719 that he had not seen a single Indian along the way. Many had been sold into slavery; thousands more had died of European diseases against which they had no immunity, such as measles, the pox, venereal diseases, or even the common cold.

Scores of Timucuans died in an uprising against the Spanish in 1656. Carolina governor James Moore lead an attack against the Indians in 1702. Some Indians, probably a very small number, were assimilated into black or white families. A colony of surviving Indians was taken to Cuba by the Spanish when they lost Florida to the British in 1763.

Stragglers who had managed to escape into the wild eventually united with northern Creeks who had begun migrating south from Georgia. The resulting

23

groups became the Seminoles and Miccosukees, tribes which still survive today on reservations in southern Florida, where they make their living selling cigarettes and running bingo parlors.

A series of bitter guerrilla attacks began in 1818 and continued for some 40 years. Known as the Seminole Wars, the period is a fascinating footnote in American history. A truce was finally signed in 1934, followed by another treaty in 1937, thus ending the longest war in United States history.

The Seminole Wars included the massacre of Major Francis L. Dade and two companies of U.S. Army troops on a lonely plain near Bushnell. Some consider the ambush as shocking and tragic as Custer's Last Stand. Yet the Dade Massacre did not take a Custer-size place in American folklore because the nation

Above: Invitation to the instructive Seminole Museum near Destin. Right: Pioneer days are commemorated at Orlando in a larger-than-life fresco.

was more fascinated by the Wild West than by happenings in the muggy heat of the Florida territory.

Northern newspapers gave it little notice. The Seminoles, whose name means "separatist" or "runaway," were mainly a ragtag confederation of renegade Indians from a number of different tribes who were joined by freed and escaped slaves. Seminoles were fierce fighters who could disappear into the swamps and savannahs, then survive for months until it was time to emerge and strike in a new surprise attack.

Against the Seminoles fought the likes of future U.S. presidents Zachary Taylor and Andrew Jackson – "Old Hickory," as he was known – who also served briefly as governor of Florida before his time in the White House. In banishing eastern Indians to the Oklahoma Territory along what became known as the Trail of Tears, where many Indians died, Jackson presided over a shameful episode in American history. It was against this mass expulsion, and other land grabs by

Washington, that the Seminoles fought almost to the last man.

The greatest of the Seminole heroes was Osceola, grandson of a Scotsman, stepson of a white trader, and son of a Red Stick Creek mother. Osceola's chief, Micanopy, caved in to demands of the white man to sign over more territory. Osceola – who apparently hated whites because his wife, who had a trace of Negro blood, had been captured and charged as a runaway slave – slashed the treaties with his knife and went on the warpath. Osceola led his people on hit-and-run raids that were considered the start of the Second Seminole War. Eventually captured, he died in prison in South Carolina. Seminole ranks were seriously decimated when new leaders were persuaded to migrate to an Indian territory in Oklahoma. In 1842, about 3,000 Seminoles were driven west.

Approximately 150 Seminoles resisted the transfer. Led by Billy Bowlegs, who would later start another Seminole war, they disappeared into the Everglades. Al-most all Florida's Indians today trace their ancestry to Bowlegs and his band. The Seminole Wars surface time and again for the Florida tourist who seeks out historic sites. The ruins of sugar and indigo plantations burned by the Seminoles can be seen at Flagler Beach, New Smyrna, Port Orange and Homosassa. The Dade Battlefield is a state historic site.

City names including Fort Lauderdale, Fort Pierce, Fort Walton, and Fort Myers remain long after the actual forts, built for defense against the Seminoles, have been forgotten. The war saw the building of dozens of forts and fortified posts, some of them now buried under great cities, and others, such as Fort Ann, Fort Armstrong, Fort Casey, Fort Wacahoota and Fort Chokonikla, forgotten sites in a forgotten war.

Indian Key, near Islamorada, is being restored to the way it looked in 1840, when the tiny, ten-acre island was the seat of Dade County. At the time, Key West had a monopoly on the lucrative

25

salvage business in the Keys. So rich were the cargoes and so hazardous the reefs, that an industry grew up around the salvaging of goods. Salvager Jacob Housman was soon tired of jostling for a place at the trough in Key West, which was then the center of the recovery industry, so he decided to buy Indian Key, which was closer to the reefs. The Key became a busy port with 50 or 60 inhabitants, shops, homes, warehouses and a thriving botanical experiment in which Dr. Henry Perrine grew tea, coffee, bananas and mangoes.

The prize was too tempting for the Seminoles to ignore. On one August morning in 1840, a force of 100 Indians attacked, killing at least seven people and burning the settlers' village. The actual death total was never known because inventories in those days sometimes listed

Above: The other side of heroism – a cemetery in Pensacola. Right: Heading for the New World – the figurehead of the rebuilt Bounty. Far right: Marquis de Lafayette.

slaves as chattels rather than persons. Today, nothing remains but ghosts, foundations, fragments, and wild descendants of Dr. Perrine's beautiful botanical gardens. The island can be visited only by boat.

Altogether, American forces lost a total of about 1,500 men against the Seminoles. The last massacre occurred in the Everglades in 1855, when a group of surveyors was butchered by Seminole braves under their last war chief, Billy Bowlegs. This was the last straw: the government offered bounties on Indians, who were then hunted down like animals. Bowlegs and some of his men surrendered and were sent west. Remaining Seminoles, without a leader, retreated so deeply into the Everglades that the bounty hunters eventually gave up. From this small number of survivors descended today's Seminole community.

Unrelated to the Seminole Wars, but an interesting, sad incident in American Indian history, was the coming to Florida of the great Chiricahua Apache brave,

Geronimo. After his surrender in the west, he was sent to Fort Pickens in Pensacola and imprisoned there from 1886 to 1888. Although some reports say he was put on display and was an object of scorn and derision, others say he was a popular prisoner, known as His Medicineship. Three wives and his children joined him at the fort, and one wife who died there is buried at Barrancas National Cemetery. Later transferred to Fort Sill in Oklahoma, Geronimo died there in 1909, at the age of 80.

Florida becomes American

Spain finally provided official title to Florida to the United States in 1819, in a deal in which the U.S. gave up its claim to Texas, while Spain relinquished its claim to the Oregon Territory. By 1822, Florida had a governor and a legislative council, and by 1824 the territory had a log cabin capitol near the present Capitol Building in Tallahassee. The old site lies miles from the beaches and today's popu-

lation centers. It was chosen because it was halfway between the state's two major settlements, Pensacola and St. Augustine.

The American Revolution had been won decades earlier, but it wasn't until 1825 that Congress got around to rewarding the Marquis de Lafayette of France, who had sided with the Colonies. He was granted $200,000 and a parcel of land near Tallahassee. Although he never saw the area, he sent a colony of Norman peasants to plant grapes, olives and mulberry trees. On the same site today, Lafayette Vineyards produces grapes for local wines that are gaining more and more international notice.

The Civil War Era

Florida became the 27th state in the Union on March 3, 1845, at a time when Florida was populated by an unkown number of Indians, approximately 58,000 whites, 25,000 slaves working on approximately 300 plantations, most of

When it was connected to Fernandina Beach by railroad, Cedar Key became a haven for blockade runners, and it was a prime target for Union forces who captured it early in the war.

Although many white Floridians remained loyal to Washington, and many free blacks went north to fight for the Union, 15,000 Florida volunteers served on the side of the South. The state also produced beef, pork, naval stores, and other products for the Confederacy. Inland Florida remained fairly aloof from the war compared to other states deep in Dixie, but its well developed coastal fort system was targeted by both sides. Immediately after war was declared, the Florida militia took control of several forts, including St. Augustine and Amelia Island, while Federals held on to forts at Key West and Fort Jefferson in the Dry Tortugas.

It was in this remote brick fortress that Dr. Samuel Mudd was imprisoned. Unjustly convicted as a conspirator in the assassination of Abraham Lincoln for setting the broken leg of assassin John Wilkes Booth, Mudd was imprisoned for years after the war at "Devil's Island."

Today, the island fort, with its ghosts and legends, can be visited by boat or seaplane. Campers who want to stay overnight must supply their own drinking water.

Each side held one of the two forts that guarded the narrow entrance to Pensacola's harbor during the Civil War. According to local legend, an entire night was spent firing at each other, but distances were too great and every shot fell short. By morning, both forts remained undamaged, but the waterway between them had a new artificial reef formed of cannon balls.

One of the South's great victories occurred at the Battle of Natural Bridge, saving Tallahassee, which was the only Confederate capitol east of the Mississippi that did not fall into Union hands.

them cotton farms in northern Florida, and 1,000 freed slaves.

Florida's first Congressman sent to Washington, D.C., was David Yulee, a St. Thomas-born Portuguese Jew who served until secession. The ruins of his sugar plantation can be seen near Tampa. Near Crystal River, at the Gamble Plantation, which is open to the public, the Confederate Secretary of State, Judah Benjamin, was hidden in canefields after the Confederacy collapsed. Florida played a dramatic role in America's Civil War, losing at least 5,000 men between 1861 and 1865. By the time the war ended, more than $20 million in property lay in ruins.

Salt, produced at Cedar Key, was an important food preservative in pre-refrigeration days. Now a tiny community clinging to a little island at the end of a miles-long causeway, Cedar Key was once one of the state's busiest ports.

Above: Andrew Jackson, "Old Hickory."
Right: Scene from the Civil War.

28

Still, the Union prevailed. By May 1865, the Stars and Stripes once again flew over the Capitol. And, by 1868, voting rights had been granted to all Floridians, regardless of race. By 1877, the much-hated Yankee "carpetbagger" government was gone, and a golden era of development began. By 1880, the state's population was 270,000; double what it had been at the onset of the war.

Except for a cross-Florida railroad that had been built from Fernandina Beach to Cedar Key in 1860, there was almost no overland access to the state. Steamships ran the St. Johns River from Charleston to Sanford three days a week; all other commerce called at ports along the ocean, gulf, and navigable rivers.

Two railroad magnates are credited with bringing the state out of the swamps and into the locomotive age. Both were given enormous land grants in exchange for laying rails through a wet wilderness that was alive with mosquitoes and alligators. The precedent is carried on in modern Florida with the zoning and envi-ronmental concessions granted to developers such as Disney, the company that turned thousands of acres of central Florida scrub into the most successful theme park in the world.

Henry Plant's line stopped in Tampa. To lure wealthy northern tourists, Plant built a flamboyant hotel. It was so big that guests were trotted through the halls in rickshaws. Today, the ornate, minaret-topped relic is the Henry Plant Museum, part of a bequest to the University of Tampa.

Henry Flagler built a railroad running down the state's east coast, confirming his position as one of the titans of Florida development. He wanted his railroad to outshine Plant's and to lure greater numbers of tourists to the Atlantic side. This was accomplished by building lavish hotels from St. Augustine to Key West, transforming insect-ridden pest-holes into plush winter havens for wealthy northerners.

Surviving Flagler hotels, as luxurious today as they were in their heyday, include the Casa Marina in Key West and the landmark Breakers in Palm Beach. Another Flagler hotel, the Ponce de Leon in St. Augustine, is now part of Flagler College. The Flagler mansion, Whitehall, in Palm Beach, ranks with the most extravagant stately homes of Europe, and is open to the public as a museum.

In the winter of 1894/95, northern and central Florida suffered a severe frost that destroyed the orange groves. Up until this point, a plucky Miami pioneer named Julia Tuttle had been campaigning unsuccessfully to get Flagler's railroad to come as far south as Palm Beach. Seizing the opportunity, she reportedly dispatched a messenger by boat to carry a fresh boquet of orange blossoms to Flagler, a fragrant reminder that Miami's oranges had survived. The message was acknowledged, and the Florida East Coast Railroad continued south. However, the effort to extend the railroad beyond Miami and through the Keys proved Flagler's undoing. A hurricane in 1926 and the stock market crash of 1929 ended a dizzying real estate boom in southern Florida.

The state was flattened by the Labor Day Hurricane of 1935, one of the most intense tropical disturbances ever recorded. It smashed through the Keys, carrying away Flagler's railroad, much of the roadbed, engines and rail-cars, as well as more than 400 human lives, countless cattle and wildlife. The railroad was never rebuilt, although its remains became part of the Overseas Highway, which at last linked Key West to the rest of the United States.

Cigars and Pirates

The spectacular Cuban immigration following the Castro takeover was not the state's first migrant wave: at Key West, at the turn of the century, Cuban cigar makers were turning out 100 million stogies a year. Their simple, three-room "shotgun" houses were so named because you could shoot from the front door through to the back without hitting anything. Examples of these old houses still remain today.

With labor problems deepening in Key West, Vincente Ybor moved his cigar works to Tampa. Restored and transformed into shops and restaurants, Ybor City today is a tourist attraction where hand-rolled cigars can still be purchased. Ironically, they cannot be smoked in the historic Columbia Restaurant, which these days is entirely smoke free.

The cigar industry brought waves of new Cubans into Tampa, where they were spurred on by local speeches by José Martí, as well as by the inspired presence of Theodore Roosevelt and his Rough Riders. They worked feverishly to fund the revolution against Spain.

The battleship *Maine* called at Fort Jefferson for fuel, and proceeded to Cuba where it was blown up. The Spanish-American War thus began, its soldiers exhorted to "Remember the *Maine*," as they charged up San Juan Hill. Military tent cities sprang up in Florida. Clara Barton set up a Red Cross station. The British press sent a young and unknown reporter named Winston Churchill to cover the war from Tampa.

It was during this same era, just after the turn of the century, that one of the state's most colorful festivals was founded: Gasparilla Days, held in Tampa each February, was named for pirate José Gaspar. He was one of several pirates who reportedly found shelter, and possibly safe burial sites for gold booty – most of which remains unrecovered – in Florida coves and lagoons.

During this splashy event, pirates land in Tampa Bay, parading, shouting, shooting and swashbuckling. Locals and tourists alike make merry, to the delight of Bay Area cash registers. Pirate legends

Right: Catching up on a little history.

THURSBY HOUSE
HISTORIC SITE
THURSBY HOUSE IS RESTORED TO THE
WAY IT WAS IN THE EARLY 1880'S –
THE GOLDEN AGE ON THE ST. JOHNS
RIVER-A TIME OF GREAT ACTIVITY
AT THE STEAMBOAT LANDING HERE
AT BLUE SPRING.

pop up in almost every coastal community, but so elusive were the likes of Gaspar, Anne Bonney and Blackbeard, that it has become impossible to separate truth from the elaborate myths that have grown up around their names.

Jean Lafitte may have kept his headquarters in New Orleans, but his colorful career began at Pensacola. During the war of 1812, he was offered $30,000 and a commission in the British Navy to betray the United States. Loyal to his American homeland, he went instead to the governor of Louisiana to warn him about British ambitions.

Ironically, his roguish reputation preceded him, and his story was not believed. At the Battle of New Orleans, Lafitte fought alongside the Americans. Eventually, he and his buccaneers were granted pardons by President James Madison. Their honor then reinstated, they returned to pirating with a proud new vigor.

Sanctioned salvagers as well as home-grown pirates were the plunderers of Key West, where the recovery of shipwrecks was a legal and very profitable enterprise. Some of today's Key West fortunes had beginnings in the days when tall ships were driven onto the treacherous reefs of the Straits of Florida.

Treasure by the ton, from mahogany pianos to linens and crockery – some of it on view today in Key West museums and private collections – found its way into Key West homes. Local legend has it that whenever business slowed, false lights were hung to lure ships to their doom. Whether this is true or not will probably never be known.

Real Estate Madness

Most of the gold-rush-like madness of Florida's current real estate boom is simply a continuation of the state's favorite pastime: real estate speculation. The bubble has burst time and again as land values zoom during good times and plunge after a freeze or war or crop failure or hurricane.

31

Central Ave. looking West.

The end of slavery spelled the end of the plantations with their palatial manor houses. Lands that had sold for as much as $12,000 an acre in Confederate funds sold for $1 an acre in gold. An article in an 1870 issue of *Harper's Magazine* told of a farmer living in a Florida paradise for which he had paid a nickel an acre.

The coming of the highway system meant the beginning of the end for some riverside developments whose economies were based on steamboat traffic. The decline of rail traffic led to the abandonment of settlements along useless tracks. Still today, the beat goes on as populations shuffle and shift, and grow, grow, grow.

It was after the Spanish-American War that one of the most colorful boom-bust eras occurred. Soldiers returning from Florida told stories of moist, moonlit nights on Tampa Bay, and oranges free

for the picking. Railroad transportation was in its heyday, and the state had begun a massive road building system; reaching Florida no longer involved a long sea voyage. After mosquito control programs brought an end to the yellow fever epidemics that for years had raged through Florida's coastal settlements, the health-promoting merits of sunshine and fresh air became marketable.

Rash speculation was the religion of the 1920s, not just in real estate, but in a soaring stock market as well. The American dream was going daffy. Addison Mizner moved to Boca Raton. Determined to make Palm Beach look beggarly, he built a highway 20 lanes wide, and hired his brother Wilson as a publicist. The clever motto they came up with was "Get the big snob and the little snob will follow."

Land sales averaged two million dollars a week. "I am the greatest resort in the world," blared newspaper ads run by the Mizner Development Corporation in 1925. Potential customers were invited to

Above: Who says "St. Pete" hasn't changed much? Right: Bridges near Jacksonville.

call Miami Beach 888. Detractors pronounced Mizner's Boca Raton as "Beaucoup Rotten," perhaps rightfully so, as the financier's whiz-bang maneuvering displaced the Finnish farmers who had originally settled the area.

Starting in 1915, Carl Fisher dredged and filled to turn the swampy farmlands of Miami Beach into a grid of high-priced lots. Sites in Coral Gables, the nation's first fully-planned community, sold like hot cakes, thanks to the persuasive, early-celebrity endorsement of famed orator and one-time presidential candidate William Jennings Bryan.

Excess became commonplace. Barron Collier sailed into Useppa Island in Pine Island Sound, built lavish "cottages" for his winter visitors, and awarded Tiffany diamond stick-pins to winners of fishing tournaments. John Ringling, best known as a circus showman, was also responsible for real estate developments in Sarasota that forged his fortune.

The wildest stories were carried north to a limitless list of eager buyers. A barber had turned $80 in tips into a million dollars overnight. St. Petersburg developer Walter Fuller wrote a book revealing how he had bought $50,000 worth of land and sold it for $270,000. Unfortunately, most of the wealth was on paper – mortgages and options – including deeds for worthless swampland, and $3,000-a-week salaries that were spent on more paper.

The boom slowed when hit by a series of natural disasters, including a freeze and a hurricane. Soon the pool of buyers began to dry up. The stock market crashed, the Depression dug in to stay, and the looniness of an era depicted in the Marx Brothers' movie *Coconuts* came to a close.

Of Wings and Wheels

During the 1880s, roads were still so rare in southern Florida that mail was delivered by a barefoot mailman. He walked a regular route, on the beach, between Palm Beach and Miami. It took

33

three days down, a day for rest, and three days back. At the time, the only other way to post a letter between the two communities was to put it on a schooner to Key West. From there it went to New York via Cuba, and back south via railroad and riverboat. By the beginning of the 20th century, good roadbeds were still rare, so when automotive pioneers looked for places to set speed records, the endless miles of hard packed sand at Daytona Beach beckoned them.

Today's space events at Cape Canaveral are a direct descendant of a love affair with gallantry and speed that began on those tide-flattened sands, where records were set by such greats as Barnie Oldfield and Sir Malcolm Campbell, starting in 1903, when Alexander Winton set a 68 mph world record here. Florida's automotive racing heritage has resulted today in the Daytona International Speedway, with its world-famous events.

The state's aviation history goes back to 1911, when the first night flight in history was made over Tampa. In 1914, the world's first scheduled airline carried one passenger at a time across Tampa Bay. An exacting, full-scale replica of the tiny Benoist seaplane used in the project is now on display at Heritage Park in Largo. Pablo Beach, south of Jacksonville, was the take-off point for Jimmy Doolittle when he set a transcontinental speed record in 1922. He made it from Florida to San Diego in 24 hours. By 1929, commercial flights operated between Key West and Havana, a forerunner of what would become Pan American World Airways. America's first scheduled jet service linked New York and Miami.

It was the beaches that were Florida's first runways and race tracks, and Florida weather that has kept the state in the aviation spotlight for as long as airplanes have been flown. Clear weather year-

Above: This is something most northern drivers are unprepared for – ships have the right of way! Right: Inside the Naval Aviation Museum at Pensacola.

round has made Florida an important training area for pilots since World War I. Today, the state is dotted with very good, paved, private airports that were built during World War II to train pilots by the hundreds. One trainee was movie star Clark Gable. Quiet and overgrown, once-busy bases house flight schools, sightseeing rides, soaring, skydiving, air shows, aerobatics, and other airborne activities, thus making Florida a mecca for aviation buffs from all over the world.

Pensacola's Naval Aviation Museum is the largest of its kind in the world. The Valiant Air Command Airshow held each March in Titusville is the largest all-war-plane show in the nation. Funds are being raised to create a year-round VAC museum here. A large collection of vintage fighters, bombers, and aviation memorabilia is housed in the Flying Tigers Warbird Air Museum in Kissimmee.

In 1950, when a German V-2 rocket carrying a WAC missile was launched from Cape Canaveral, Florida entered the space age. From Canaveral, in 1958, the first U.S. space satellite, Explorer I, was launched. In 1965, Major Edward White became the first American to walk in space and, in another 1965 mission, a successful space rendezvous was made between Gemini 6 and Gemini 7. In 1969, Apollo 11 blasted off from the Cape for the moon. Canaveral remains the focus of international attention as its space probes come and go from the Kennedy Space Center.

Despite the U.S. space program's first tragedy, which occurred in 1967 when three astronauts died in a fire aboard Apollo I, two years later men walked on the moon. After the Challenger tragedy in 1986, in which seven astronauts died, shuttle flights again resumed with new resolve. Visitors are often surprised to find that, in addition to highly publicized shuttle launches, there are equally spectacular launches of communications,

weather and experimental vehicles that get little national media attention. The local newspaper, *Florida Today*, is the best source of launch information. On any day, the Kennedy Space Center Visitor Complex is a top sight, and the fourth-largest tourist attraction in the state.

Florida's Tourism History

Tourists first came to Florida via steamships and sailing ships, before railroad days, when some of the state's most extravagant resorts flourished. As roads were built, people began driving down in their Oldmobiles and Packards, pitching tents because there were too few hotels. Locals called them Tin Can Tourists and set about finding ways to fleece them.

In 1925 alone, in the last insane madness of the real estate boom, more than 400 hotels and apartment complexes were built in Miami. By the end of World War II, the state was attracting 2.5 million tourists a year. Polls of Florida visitors show that 97% of them want to return, and state tourism promoters spend $7 million a year to tempt them to do so.

No matter how extravagant the numbers, however, every influence pales when compared to the impact of Walt Disney World, which covers 43 square miles and attracts millions of people from all over the world. Although Disney does not reveal its gate counts, it admits to hosting more than 35 million visitors each year. The 100-acre Magic Kingdom opened in 1971, the 260-acre Epcot in 1982, Disney-MGM Studios in 1989, and Disney's Animal Kingdom opened in April 1998. Recent growth has been giddy, including several new resorts, a wedding pavilion and Disney's World of Sports complex, with facilities for 30 different sports. Almost every county and community in the state lists tourism among its biggest industries. Some of New York's biggest public relations agencies represent Florida clients.

While the beaches and theme parks steal most of the thunder, a quiet explosion has also been going on in the state's cruise ports. Three million cruise passengers a year pass through the Port of Miami. New super-liners, carrying more than 2,000 passengers, are being added each year to a list of ships that includes the fabulous 2,284-passenger *Sovereign of the Seas* and the 2,600-passenger *Ecstasy*. In Miami alone, nine ships are taking on passengers on one side of Dodge Island while four more megaships are loading or unloading on the other side. A new, five-lane bridge had to be built to accommodate the constant flow of cars, chartered buses, cabs and food trucks.

Fort Lauderdale's Port Everglades is another leading cruise port. Tampa hosts such ships as Holland America's *Nieuw Amsterdam*. Port Canaveral is home port

Right: The Flamingo Hotel, Miami Beach, 1923 – holding a party.

to Premier Cruise Line, and Disney's new cruise line set sail in July 1998. Some ships even call at little Key West.

A Look Ahead

In recent years Florida's taxes have risen faster than those of any other state. Although some believe the most rapid growth rate has leveled, the population is still swelling by hundreds of families per month. Roads and other vital human services can be badly out of sync with the needs of a rocketing citizenry.

The Everglades, once thought to be a worthless swamp ripe for draining and development, are now known to be the source of drinking water for all southern Florida. Yet encroachment has been escalating since as early as 1898, when a contract was given for the draining of eight million acres. Now reduced to half the area they enclosed before developers arrived, the Everglades continue to be threatened by man and nature.

Some environmentalists say it is already too late, and that southern Florida will eventually have to be abandoned for lack of drinking water. Others who warned that a major hurricane could devastate heavily populated regions were proved right when, in August, 1992, Hurricane Andrew, the largest natural disaster ever to strike the U.S., left a multibillion-dollar trail of destruction in the cities of Homestead and Florida City, barely sparing downtown Miami from the worst. Doomsday events aside, there is much in Florida that is bright, that is happening now, and that bodes well for a shining future. Talk of a bullet train that will link the major cities and relieve highway congestion is heard more often these days. Environmental legislation is taking hold.

Alligators, once hunted close to extinction, are once again so abundant that they can be harvested legally for meat and leather. Pelicans, which suffered greatly

before DDT was outlawed, have made a successful comeback. Plumed birds, nearly wiped out by hunters who took only their feathery topknots and sold them to milliners for the making of elaborate hats at the turn of the century, are again nesting safely in rookeries. There is also hope for the tiny Key deer, and even a faint hope that the Florida panther and the manatee may endure. Best of all, thousands of unspoiled acres are already set aside as parks, wildlife refuges, state and national forests, and pristine wetlands in which life struggles to go on in harmony with the human population.

Timing Your Own Florida Visit

Arriving at the right part of Florida, at the right time of year, has been a large part of historic success or failure for visitors to Florida long before people came here for vacation.

Let's explode some myths. Although Florida is still called the Sunshine State, it has an annual average rainfall of 50 to 65 inches. During a hurricane, 30 inches or more may fall in a 24-hour period. During the summer rainy season, there is a 50-50 chance of rain every day.

October is the driest month in northern Florida; one of the wettest in the Keys. Never forget the distances mentioned previously. Florida spans from subtropical to tropical climate zones, which means that it can be snowing in Tallahassee while people are basking on beaches in Fort Lauderdale. Yet in summer, when it is peak season at steamy Panhandle beach resorts, it may be a few degrees cooler in Miami, where hotel rates are chopped in half. If you want to save money, go to southern Florida in summer, where 100-degree temperatures are almost unknown. Record highs in New York, Rome and Athens average higher than those in Miami.

Weather is one thing and costs are another. If you're looking for rock bottom rates, go to southern Florida and to the Keys in summer and to the Panhandle in winter. In other areas, rates rocket up and

37

down according to other factors, such as school holidays, when family tourist traffic is heaviest, special events such as the races at Daytona or the Gator Bowl in Jacksonville, and big conventions that can fill a city to overflowing.

If climate is your most important criterion, south is best in winter. During brief but bitter cold snaps, Miami temperatures may fall into the 30s, while Key West's overnight lows remain in the 40s. February and March are warm, breezy, flower-filled months in central and northern Florida. Generally, cities that face the Gulf are muggier during the warm periods, while the Atlantic beaches are cooled by ocean breezes. The hurricane season, with humid heat and flooding rains, runs officially from June through October, and storms are likeliest to occur in August and September. But the chance of your being involved in a hurricane is rare; the chance of heavy rain and almost unbearable humidity during these months is very good.

Beating Florida's Bugs

Although the state has ambitious and effective mosquito control programs, mosquitoes remain a problem in some areas. Avoid the Everglades in summer, and have repellent with you when venturing outside cities. Big, biting green flies are a scourge in late spring; sand flies or "no-see-ums" give nasty bites on still days in sandy areas. "Love" bugs collect in spring and fall on warm highways where they are smeared thickly onto speeding cars. Inexpensive protective netting can be purchased for vehicles.

Living History Re-enactments

History comes alive all over Florida. Living history exhibits have always been

Right: A reminder of the pirates' heyday in Florida.

popular with visitors. Among the major historic reenactments on view is **Fort Foster**, which recreates the installation built here during the Seminole Wars. Tours leave from Hillsborough River State Park on weekends and holidays.

Fort Clinch State Park. Although this massive brick fort saw service in a number of events, its living history interpretation is that of 1864, when the fort was occupied by Union troops.

Kissimmee Cow Camp. You should always keep in mind when you talk to the men here that, to them, the word "cowboy" is a derisive term. These are men who happen to be cow hunters, and don't you forget it. Brought to Florida by the Spanish in 1521, cattle thrived in the Florida scrub and roamed freely until they were rounded up each spring by these cow hunters. Their tools were the whip, the cow dog, and the lariat. The year is 1876. Tours are provided on weekends and holidays at the camp 15 miles east of Lake Wales.

Dade Battlefield. Each year on the scene of the massacre at Bushnell, the Seminole attack on Major Francis Dade and his 108 officers and men is reenacted on the Saturday nearest December 28. Half the men fell when the Indians fired their first rounds in an ambush. Survivors of the first attack hastily cut trees and tried to built a breastwork, but were cut down by deadly fire. Only two soldiers made it back to Fort Brooke to tell their story.

Battle of Natural Bridge. At the battlefield six miles east of Woodville off US 363, this Confederate victory is replayed on the Sunday closest to March 6 each year.

Battle of Olustee. On the Sunday nearest February 20 each year, Florida's biggest Civil War battle is reenacted by men in authentic blue and gray. The original battle was a Confederate triumph. The site is located only two miles east of Olustee on US 90.

FLORIDA'S SPICY
CULTURAL MIX

If the beaches get monotonous and the theme parks seem too superficial, reach out into Florida's neighborhoods and savor the spicy flavor of the state's population mix. It is no surprise to see black beans and rice on the menu of a Chinese restaurant, or to see bearded Hasidic Jews in frock coats on the same Miami beaches as young European sunbathers wearing tiny string bikinis.

Key West has a highly visible and vocal homosexual community; Jacksonville has one of the largest Arab communities in the United States; Jamaican music rules the airwaves on Saturday mornings in the little college town of De-Land, where the owner of your motel may well be a Pakistani.

Almost every community has at least one Spanish-language radio station, and most cities have one or more Spanish-language TV channels.

Almost every hamlet in the state has at least one Spanish-language church, and many have a Spanish church for each major denomination. A Cuban-born Floridian represents Miami Beach in Congress. Even English-language stations broadcast certain commercials, as well as public service announcements, in Spanish.

No longer is Miami the only center of Hispanic culture in Florida, and no longer do Cubans have a monopoly on Florida's love of all things Latin.

Florida residents now include Puerto Ricans, Mexicans, Panamanians, Costa Ricans, Nicaraguans and Hondurans – plus pockets of Argentinians, Brazilians, other South and Central Americans, and

Left: Greetings from Ybor City – rum, reggae and cigars.

even the occasional family from Spain. In some neighborhoods, especially in Miami, it can be difficult to find anyone who can give you street directions in English, understand that you need extra towels in your room, or take a complicated restaurant order.

So thoroughly Latin has Miami become that many travelers feel a real culture shock when they arrive. Those hotel workers who aren't Hispanic could well be Creole-speaking Haitians.

On sunny days in Tarpon Springs, men hunch over coffee and speak spiritedly in Greek. In Surfside or Daytona Beach, French Canadian newspapers are sold on every corner. On Indian reservations, school lessons are taught in the Seminole language.

In Miami Beach, Yiddish is the everyday language of the many old-world Jews who continue to winter here. In the fields, the melodic English of Jamaica is spoken by seasonal workers who are brought in on a contract basis. Many of the state's nurses are well-educated Jamaicans, speaking their own, highlands-tinged Caribbean patois as well as English.

The New Smyrna Colony was founded in 1768 by a group of southern Europeans who set sail from the Spanish island of Minorca led by a Scotsman, Dr. Andrew Turnbull. He named the new community after the birthplace of his Turkish wife. Menorcan Easter cakes, called *fromajardis*, are still served in New Smyrna homes. It is believed that the fiery hot datil pepper also arrived with the Minorcans. It is now a staple ingredient in the cooking of some Florida kitchens.

In Volusia County, acres of ferneries are worked by Mexicans who impart their own brand of the Hispanic culture to that area. Ordinary supermarkets sell rice by the 25-pound bag and jalapeño peppers in five-pound packages.

Proud, hard-working men bring their wives and babies to share the spectacle

and ritual of shopping for food in a land of plenty. The slap-slap sound of women making *tortillas* by hand is commonplace in migrant housing complexes.

Florida's Immigrants

Ever since the earliest explorers, Florida has been a refuge for the stateless. Hounded from their homelands during the religious wars of the 16th century, French Protestants settled near present-day St. Augustine. British Loyalists escaped to Florida rather than fight against the Crown during the American Revolution. José Martí, leader of the Cuban war of independence against the Spaniards, took refuge in Tampa.

Today's refugees come from Haiti, Panama, Nicaragua, Cuba or Southeast

Above: Besides existential anxiety, Latinos also brought their cheerfulness – Hispanic Festival in Miami. Right: Florida's black population fought long and hard for rights.

Asia. There are more Nicaraguans in Miami than in any other city except Managua. In 1980, 140,000 Cuban refugees were absorbed into southern Florida.

Others here are escapees from the cold northern winter: Midwestern retirees, New York vacationers, Canadian pensioners, European beachgoers, and families from everywhere whose kids want to meet Mickey Mouse.

The result is a mix of all ages, hues, religions, languages, customs and habits. The state's calendar is peppered with ethnic events. Miami's carnival has all the glamour of Rio de Janeiro's. The St. Patrick's Day mayhem in Pensacola rivals New York's. Vizcaya, an Italian Renaissance villa in Miami, is the scene of an Italian Renaissance festival. Teenage boys dive for a golden cross which is thrown into the waters at Tarpon Springs on Epiphany, recreating events from a Greek fishing village.

So numerous are the Britons who have bought motels in the state that they have formed their own British Motel Owners'

Association. The Cape Coral German-American Club even sponsors its own *Oktoberfest* during the last weeks of October.

Florida's Black Culture

Florida's black communities have an especially rich heritage that combines influences of descendants of the earliest slaves with newcomers from the North and the Caribbean. In Spanish times, blacks mingled and married with whites and Indians alike. Until the Civil War, most of Florida was a haven for escaped slaves, many of them allied with the Seminoles. Other blacks were purchased by the Seminoles, who incorporated a version of slave society in which servants were required to give only token service.

Although Jacksonville remained a hotbed of contraband slave trading, even after slavery was outlawed, the state granted blacks freedoms that were denied in other parts of the South. During some antebellum eras, blacks could vote and serve on juries. The census of 1860 listed 61,000 slaves in the state, but also a total of almost $100,000 in properties owned by free blacks.

Badly outnumbered, white plantation owners became increasingly afraid that their slaves might rise up en masse. By the 1840s, laws regarding blacks became ever tighter. Freed men had to have white guardians; visiting ships were not even allowed to put black crewmen ashore.

When Florida joined the Confederacy, 1,200 blacks went north to join Union forces. After Reconstruction, the state had 19 blacks in its legislature, and a black secretary of state was appointed in 1868. Still, strictly-enforced racial segregation became acceptable practice in Florida, where it lingered as firmly as in any other Dixie state. Drinking fountains, hotels, restaurants and schools were segregated. Blacks were not allowed on the island of Miami Beach after dark, nor

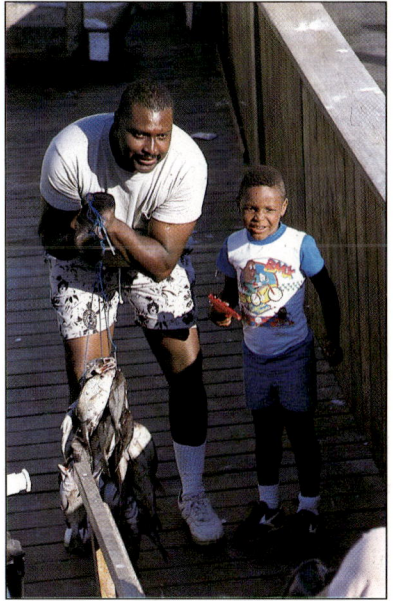

were they allowed to swim in the sea near Palm Beach.

True emancipation didn't come until the 1960s, with the passage of the Civil Rights Act. Eatonville, a town near Orlando that was incorporated in 1888, was probably the first black community in the nation. At Daytona Beach, black education pioneer Mary McLeod Bethune lived and worked until her death in 1955. Her spacious home, filled with memorabilia, including the room where Eleanor Roosevelt slept while visiting here, is now open to the public on the campus of Bethune-Cookman College.

Also in Daytona Beach is the home of Dr. Howard Thurman, who was named by *Life* magazine in 1950 as one of America's ten most-celebrated 20th-century preachers. Author of 14 books, professor of systemic theology at Howard University, and Phi Beta Kappa, Thurman was the principal contact in the United States for Mahatma Gandhi.

Jackie Robinson, the first black to play major league baseball, played his first

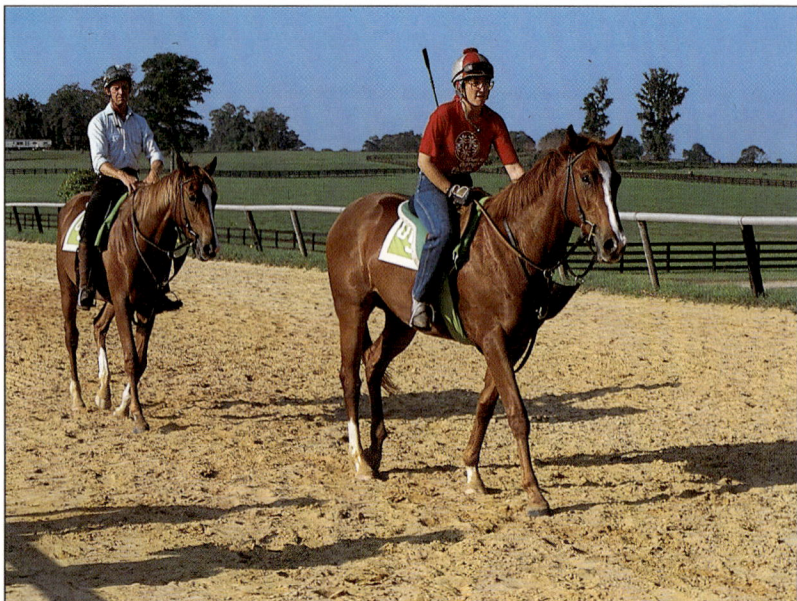

spring training game with the Montreal Royals at Daytona's City Island Park. Recently renamed Jackie Robinson Park, the site of major league baseball's first integrated game is marked with a large bronze statue of Robinson.

Black Music Month is celebrated each June in Miami with jazz, folk, gospel and rhythm and blues, and with Caribbean and Afro-Cuban entertainers. The headquarters for the festival is Model City Center.

On the first Saturday of February, Black Awareness Day in Boynton Beach includes a beauty contest, dancing, a parade, an oratorical contest and theater. Among legendary black musicians born in the state, and surely inspired by Florida's unique pleasures and cadences, is Ray Charles. Blinded as a child in an unsuccessful bid to save a brother from drowning, he was educated at a state school for the blind in St. Augustine.

Above: There are over 400 stud farms around Ocala.

Cowboys and Indians

It comes as a surprise to many Florida visitors that cowboys and rodeos are an important part of the rural scene. Cattle were introduced to Florida by the Spanish. In the 1600s, an enormous cattle ranch covered all of what is now Payne's Prairie. More than 7,200 cattle brands are officially registered with the state, and the raising of beef, dairy and breeding stock cattle accounts for a big chunk of the state's agricultural income.

The earliest wranglers, who preferred to be called cow hunters rather than cowboys, used long, cracking whips. This is thought to be one reason that southerners in general are sometimes referred to as "crackers."

Working cow hunter exhibitions are given at Lake Kissimmee State Park, 15 miles east of Lake Wales off Camp Mack Road, where, on weekends and holidays, the camp comes alive with real cow hunters who live, work and speak as though the year were 1876.

Artist and writer Frederic Remington, best known for artwork that preserved the spirit of the vanished Old West, visited Florida in 1885 and reported finding the same sort of cowboys he had immortalized in the west, complete with broad brimmed hats, six-guns slung over their hips, and long hair.

Davie, near Fort Lauderdale, has had rodeos for 40 years. Kissimmee's Silver Spurs Rodeo, the state's oldest professional rodeo, is held twice a year. A championship rodeo is held in Homestead every February. A professional rodeo takes place each September in Titusville, and Fort Myers holds a two-day championship rodeo in January.

For tourists who are interested in Indian history, Florida spreads a bountiful buffet of events and showplaces. Seminole villages are open to the public in Tampa and Fort Lauderdale. A Museum of the Sea and the Indian has extensive Indian collections in Destin. Fort Walton Beach has a museum devoted to a ceremonial mound, which was once a gathering place for tribes from miles around. Artifacts excavated here have a distinct Mayan look. Miccosukee tribes celebrate an annual festival in Miami: always held in the last week of December, it takes place in the Miccosukee village where dancing, singing and crafts of the tribe are shared with outsiders. The Miccosukee tourist "village" at Shark Valley in the Everglades has daily demonstrations of tribal cooking, sewing and alligator wrestling.

A Seminole tribal fair is held each February in Hollywood, while an Indian powwow at Fort Pierce in March features Indian foods, dancing, clothing and artifacts from tribes all over the United States. A particularly good Calusa and Seminole collection is on display at the Lawrence Will Museum in Belle Glade.

Today, Seminoles number about 1,500 and Miccosukees about 600. Most live on reservations, which are shown on state maps but which otherwise look the same as any other stretches of the Everglades and Big Cypress Swamp. Wrangles with Washington over land, hunting rights and reparations continue. In the meantime, exempt from state and local laws, some reservations are making profits by holding high-stakes bingo games and by selling cigarettes without state tax – and therefore at much lower prices. Most Indians live ordinary Florida lives; others continue placidly on ancient paths, farming, ranching and wearing the brilliantly-colored clothing that is their trademark.

Florida Horse Country

Ever since the Spanish introduced horses to North America, Florida has been a center for equestrian events.

The area around Ocala is green with pastures where thoroughbred foals frolic through the mild winters, strengthening young legs that will run at the nation's most famous tracks. Palm Beach has become so important as a polo center that Prince Charles may be seen playing here.

An Olympic-class equestrian contest goes on for three weeks each March in Tampa. The Winter Equestrian Festival in West Palm Beach, in February, attracts more than 1,500 of the world's finest horses to three grand prix events, one of them a World Cup qualifier.

Religion

Florida's religions are as diverse as its people. In dark corners of Caribbean enclaves, ancient rites of *obeah* are still practiced. It is no surprise to find stores carrying omens, symbols, chicken feet and all the paraphernalia. From special candles to magic furniture polish, these are the commonplace and arcane articles that can be used in one's personal war against evil spirits. The Church of Scientology remains a powerful presence in Clearwater, and the Mormon Church is one of the state's largest land owners.

In 1894, a group led by Chicagoan Cyrus Teed settled near Fort Myers, where they lived a celibate, communal life based on a belief that the world is hollow and they were living inside it. The group died out, but their cult newspaper, *The American Eagle*, is still published by descendants of those Teed followers who stumbled on the road to celibacy and produced offspring. The settlement has been preserved as the Koreshan State Historic Site. A group of spiritualists left New York State late in the 19th century and settled at Cassadaga near Deltona. Their community, lined with neat, narrow brick streets, is still owned by the group and contains a hotel where visitors can get a hearty, old-fashioned meal followed by a spiritual reading.

The first Christian to die for his faith in the New World is thought to have been a Spanish priest slain by the Indians he was trying to convert near Tampa Bay. Today, every world religion is represented in the state, from Buddhism to Southern Baptist. The fertile Bible-thumping soil of Florida is home to many evangelists, and their crusades have become legendary.

Florida's communities, like those anywhere in America, tend to cluster around churches and synagogues, many of them open daily to tourists. In St. Augustine, a church endowed by Henry Flagler holds the elaborate marble burial vaults of his daughter and granddaughter. Historic churches are found in Fernandina Beach, while Mount Pisgah Church outside Tallahassee is one of the state's oldest. A tiny chapel in St. Augustine marks the place where the first mass in the New World is thought to have been said.

Our Lady of Charity Shrine in Coconut Grove is a soaring 90-foot modern tower with a mural that depicts the history of Cuba. Plymouth Congregational Church in Coconut Grove has gates that were

Above: Synagogues are typical for Miami Beach. Right: Free entrance to the open-air theater in St. Petersburg.

brought here from a 17th-century monastery in the Pyrenees. In Dade County alone, four churches are on the National Register of Historic Places; Duval County and Leon County each have three. Others include St. Gabriel's Episcopal Church in Brevard County, St. Margaret's and St. Mary's in Clay County, Holy Trinity in Lake County, and First Baptist in Madison County.

It is not just the buildings alone, but their cemeteries and the eloquent stories they tell that make historic churches so important to the tourist who delves into Florida's cultural history.

The Arts

The beauty of Florida is more than skin deep. The arts are taken seriously here: the state boasts several operas and ballets, plus 24 symphony orchestras, including half-a-dozen in the Fort Lauderdale-Miami area alone. Tallahassee has two symphony orchestras; Naples, Sarasota and Venice each have one.

Miami has a monthly guide to the arts, sold at newsstands, while Jacksonville has an arts hotline – tel. (904) 353-5100 – where you can get updated information on concerts, plays and museums.

Internationally-known artists are featured at annual jazz festivals, the largest of which are held in Jacksonville, Pensacola, Tampa and Miami. Thanks to the state's diversity of peoples, its popular music ranges from gospel to salsa, from bluegrass to reggae. Every city has its hangouts for those who like rock, country and western, folk, dixieland or whatever.

Arts and crafts festivals attract artisans and artists from all over the U.S. Among the biggest and best events are those at Mount Dora, Lake Buena Vista, Winter Park, Pompano Beach, Coconut Grove, Miami and Fort Lauderdale. Unique events held in one of the state's most rural areas are the Jeanie Festival and the Florida Folk Festival, both in Stephen Foster Country on the Suwannee River at White Springs. Artists and authors who lived and worked in the state, and who

47

Above: Known to insiders only – Hemingway's favorite bar. Right: The palazzo, brought to Sarasota by Ringling.

are remembered in annual festivals or events, include Tennessee Williams, Ernest Hemingway, John James Audubon and Winslow Homer.

Mary Roberts Rinehart, the mystery writer, often visited Useppa Island, which was an aloof and plush private compound. The entire place was abandoned and fell into ruin before it was restored in the 1970s. At the neighboring island of Cabbage Key, the home built by her son is now a ramshackle inn where boaters can stop for a cold beer, a meal or an overnight stay.

Marjorie Kinnan Rawlings made an important contribution to the understanding of – and love for – the central Florida scrublands which for years had been looked upon only as a wilderness that needed taming. Best known is her Pulitzer-prize-winning book, later a movie, *The Yearling*. A more incisive look at the land and its people may be found in her book *Cross Creek*, written in 1942. Her simple home at Cross Creek near Gainesville is now a state historic site, open to the public.

Harriet Beecher Stowe's book *Uncle Tom's Cabin* fired Northern fury against slavery and helped win support for the Abolition that led to the Civil War. She had a winter home at Mandarin, near Jacksonville. The house burned down long ago, but the community is worth visiting for its art show, held each Easter weekend. Still available is Stowe's less famous but more appropriately Floridian book *Palmetto Leaves*, published in 1873 and later reprinted.

In modern times, John D. MacDonald lived and wrote in Florida. Many of the Travis McGee mysteries were written in Fort Lauderdale where MacDonald, like McGee, lived full-time on a houseboat. Later, MacDonald moved to an island near Sarasota, which was the setting for his novel *Condominium*. Few writers have so fully captured the grit and grist, sham and shame of the Sunshine State as MacDonald was able to do in his books.

Playwright Tennessee Williams spent most of his time in Key West, where the movie version of his play, *The Rose Tattoo* was filmed. His plays continue to be seen in the performing arts center that bears his name in Key West.

Annual Shakespeare and Bach Festivals are also found around the state. Orlando's Shakespeare Festival goes on for three weeks in April, and Coral Gables offers the Bard year-round at the Minorca Playhouse. The Bach Festival, in Winter Park, is one of the nation's most notable.

The British composer Frederick Delius lived for a time near Jacksonville, where he tried his hand at orange farming. The rhythms and harmonies of black Florida laborers inspired him to write works that brought him international acclaim. Today, a Delius festival is held annualy, in March, in Jacksonville. Lecturers and musicians celebrate Delius' works, including his *Florida Suite*. His home, restored and open to the public, is on the campus of Jacksonville University.

Florida's modern music idol is Jimmy Buffett, whose songs, such as *Changes in Latitudes, Changes in Attitudes*, and *Margaritaville,* capture the Florida scene perfectly. Buffet got his start singing in Key West saloons, and now owns his own bar there, called, appropriately enough, *Jimmy Buffett's Margaritaville*.

Theater thrives throughout Florida, not just imports from Broadway, but professional local productions as well. The Asolo State Theater in Sarasota is an 18th-century theater which was dismantled, imported and reassembled here. The Coconut Grove Playhouse, built as a movie palace in the 1920s, is now a state theater. Tampa's Center for the Performing Arts is one of America's great complexes, featuring state-of-the-art acoustics and backstage machinery for its theaters and concert halls. Miami's Gusman Center for the Performing Arts is

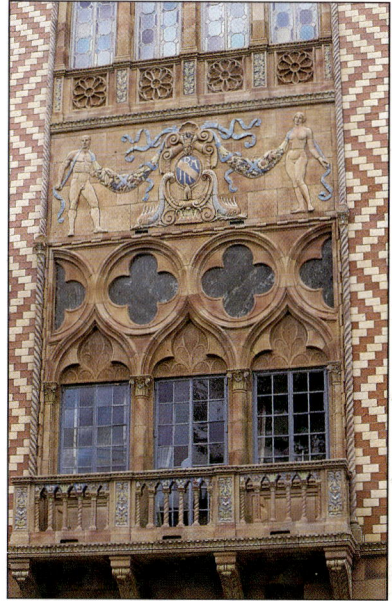

home to the Miami City Ballet, directed by Edward Villella. Miami also hosts a film festival in February.

Among the state's most important art museums are the Ringling in Sarasota, which houses one of the world's largest collections of Baroque art, and Ocala's Appleton Museum, which is amassing one of the state's largest art collections. The Cummer Gallery, in Jacksonville, has one of the largest collections of Meissen porcelain in the world, while the Lowe Art Museum, in Coral Gables, has a collection including American, primitive, Baroque and Renaissance pieces. The Norton Gallery in West Palm Beach has a French Impressionist collection, and the Jacksonville Art Museum is known for its stunning jade. The Bass Museum of Art, also worth seeing, is located in Miami.

Fort Lauderdale's Museum of Art has an important collection of CoBrA movement (Copenhagen, Brussels, Amsterdam) paintings. Impressive Boehm collections are housed in the Plant Mu-

seum at the University of Tampa, and in the Alexander Brest Museum at Jacksonville University.

The Morse Museum in Winter Park has an extensive Tiffany collection, and the Salvador Dalí Museum in St. Petersburg contains the largest Dalí collection in the world. The Universalist Church in Tarpon Springs houses an impressive collection of paintings by Florida landscape artist George Inness, Jr. Housed in the Daytona Beach Museum of Arts and Sciences is the largest collection of pre-Castro Cuban art in the United States.

For those who like architecture, there are time-warp neighborhoods of period buildings, some of them in the most unlikely places. The Art Deco district in Miami Beach is the largest, purest Art-Deco neighborhood in the nation, with block after block of fine examples of *Moderne* buildings. Between the end of

Above: Cultures meet in Ocala's Appleton Museum – the motor champ Don Garlits and an Asiatic warlord.

World War II and the mid-1950s, more hotels were built in Miami Beach than in the rest of the states combined. Some of them comprise Flabbergast Row, the extravagant high-rise hotels along Collins Avenue on Miami Beach. Street after street of Victorian homes remain intact in Fernandina Beach; a National Historic District comprising 30 blocks.

Jacksonville has entire historic neighborhoods of homes which have been caringly maintained or restored. Pensacola's North Hill Preservation District is filled with wooden gingerbread mansions built at a time when the city was exporting 200 million feet of lumber per year. Coral Gables is a sprawling neighborhood of Spanish Mediterranean homes built in the 1920s. It is anchored by the Biltmore Hotel, which stood vacant for 20 years before it was restored to its original splendor.

The world's largest concentration of buildings designed by architect Frank Lloyd Wright may be found at Florida Southern College in Lakeland.

Stop at the Administration Building to pick up a free map to a self-guided tour. On the campus of the University of South Florida's New College at Sarasota are several buildings designed by I. M. Pei. Saint Leo Abbey in Dade City is an ornate Lombardic-Romanesque design that includes a faithful reproduction of the Grotto at Lourdes.

Fun and Games in Florida

Zany happenings typify a slightly lunatic mixture that is also part of Florida. Take the nightly sunset at the Mallory Docks in Key West: tourists gather to watch the sun set into the sea, while gaggles of hucksters, peddlers and loonies sell their wares or simply show off. The city's annual Fantasy Fest is another insane and indescribable occasion. And every year Conch Republic Day is celebrated, commemorating the day in the 1980s when the Florida Keys seceded from the United States.

Other inspired silliness occurs at the King Mango Strut in Miami; the people's version of the ultra-commercial Orange Bowl parade. Every Labor Day, there are anything-goes raft races on the St. Johns River, near DeLand. The Gasparilla invasion in Tampa is preceded by the Ybor City Naval Invasion, to clear the waters. A festival in Wausau, in August, focuses on attractive features of baked opossum.

More serious events which have spread throughout the state are annual Blessings of the Fleet and nighttime Christmas Boat Parades. Both are lovely, lively pageants that celebrate all Florida's favorite place; the waterfront. When colored Christmas lights are reflected back from the water, the mirror effect is one of the season's most beautiful.

Lifestyles of the Rich and Super Rich

Even during the steamy, stultifying days before the invention of air conditioning, Florida drew its share of visitors and settlers who were rich, royal or famous – or all three.

Prince Achille Murat, a nephew of Napoleon Bonaparte, lent royal glitter to the social life of Tallahassee in the early 19th century. He and his wife, a grand-niece of George Washington, are buried in the city's Episcopal cemetery. John Ringling's palatial home in Sarasota, John Deering's Italian Renaissance estate, Vizcaya, in Miami, and Henry Flagler's echoing marble Whitehall in Palm Beach rival the world's greatest mansions.

Although Thomas Edison's home and laboratory in Fort Myers convey a simple and even austere lifestyle, experiments that were carried out here made world history. His office remains much as he left it.

Harry Truman's winter White House was in Key West. During his presidency he was a familiar figure on local streets, taking his early morning walks and stopping for breakfast at a local coffee shop. Truman Specials are still served by the restaurants he favored.

John F. Kennedy spent winter vacations in the family compound at Palm Beach. Other residents and visitors form a Who's Who of old money, new money show-biz fame or political power.

A relative newcomer to the region is billionaire Donald Trump. President Richard Nixon's home was on Biscayne Bay, and George Bush spent his first vacation after the 1988 presidential election fishing in the Florida Keys.

Less visible, but leading lives so opulent they boggle the mind, are the many oil-rich princes and sheiks who have been quietly buying up some of south Florida's most extravagant estates.

Quietly gaining its own neighborhoods of the mega-rich, most of them living low-profile lives, are other cities, including Naples, Boca Raton, Fort Lauderdale and Sarasota. Ocala has its own aristocracy of wealthy horse breeders, and Or-

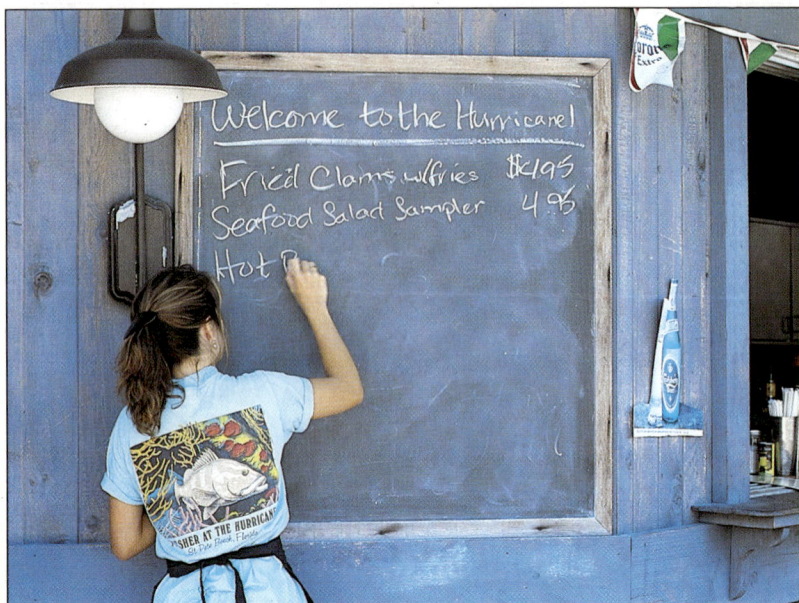

lando is attracting a growing list of movie super-stars and business moguls. It is increasingly common to see famous actors around town, taking time off from filming at Disney or Universal Studios. John Travolta, who pilots his own jet, lives in a fly-in community near Daytona Beach, while Madonna and Sylvester Stallone have homes in Miami.

The Flavors of Florida

So thoroughly is America on the move today that regional cuisines are blending one into the other until there is no single style that Florida can claim as exclusively its own. Among the influences that are most significant, unique and delicious is Cuban cuisine. America may have gone crazy for Mexican and Tex-Mex, but there are new discoveries ahead for the traveler who is encountering Cuban

Above: The Hurricane Restaurant in St. Petersburg – cooking is done by the chef himself! Right: Hard to resist!

cooking for the first time, which is subtly different from any other Latin cuisine.

At the turn of the century, the Columbia Restaurant was opened in Tampa. To this day it remains a cultural and culinary Cuban landmark, with clones in other Florida cities, too. Miami has its own "Little Havana" area, and Cuban restaurants can be found as far north in the state as Orlando and Jacksonville.

Cuban classics, some of which are sold at hole-in-the-wall restaurants for a mere pittance, include such dishes as chicken *alicante*, *paella*, black beans and rice, savory stews, Cuban coffee, and crusty Cuban bread which is still baked in the old style – creased with a palm leaf – in southern Florida bakeries.

Continental cuisine has long had adherents in Florida. The state is a major destination for business travelers, overseas tourists and jet setters. There has always been a very critical demand for the best in dining prepared by chefs trained in traditional disciplines as well as *nouvelle cuisine*.

There are only about ten five-star restaurants in the entire U.S., one of which is in Florida. One of only seven five-star hotels is here. Two of the nation's twelve five-star resorts are in Florida. Miami has two four-star restaurants, and Tampa has one. Except for the most remote rural areas, you are never more than a 30-mile drive from a good to great continental restaurant. Other ethnic cuisine, in addition to Cuban, is available in Florida restaurants; ranging from Lebanese to Thai, Italian to Chinese – and the list goes on.

Miami has a rich Jewish heritage, and has a number of popularly-priced delis with traditional corned beef and pastrami sandwiches and matzoh ball soup. Many of these are kosher restaurants.

Tarpon Springs is well known for its Greek restaurants, and Jacksonville has a group of authentic Arab eateries. In the Little Haiti section of Miami, Caribbean foods are available in restaurants, bakeries and markets.

Showcase restaurants at Walt Disney World's Epcot are operated by native Mexicans, Germans, Japanese, Chinese, Canadians, Moroccans, French, Italians and Norwegians. Ethnic flavors that may be new to you in Florida include Jamaican and Bahamian dishes.

Florida native cooking takes many forms. Among the state's most lauded, totally-homegrown restaurants are: *Chalet Suzanne*, in Lake Wales, which serves continental meals with a Florida twist; *The Colony*, on Longboat Key near Sarasota, where traditionally-trained chefs create Florida renditions of gourmet favorites; and *Bern's Steak House* in Tampa, where meltingly-tender steaks are served with organically-grown local vegetables. Key West rivals even San Francisco in the range and quality of its eateries.

Seafood anchors Florida's strongest claim to culinary greatness, in any season, shape or recipe. Fishing boats dock daily, spilling their silvery catches into seaside kitchens. The state has hundreds of seafood restaurants, all of them with lengthy menus of fish and shellfish,

which can be ordered boiled, broiled, poached, mesquite or charcoal grilled, *en papillote*, sauced or fried.

Favorites include Apalachicola oysters, stone crabs, Florida lobster, smoked mullet, all the snappers, fresh tuna, bay or sea scallops, swordfish, catfish, grouper (called scamp in some areas), shark, freshwater crab and alligator. Some restaurants also fly in fresh salmon or cod from northern waters. Menus may also list seasonal or occasional catches, such as tile fish, monk fish, bluefish or jack.

Faithful southern cooking is found only in the most rural counties. Perseverance is rewarded with consistently Deep South favorites such as perloo, "dirty" rice, country ham with red-eye gravy, greens of fresh collard, mustard or turnip served with pot liquor, corn pudding, congealed salads, okra, chicory coffee,

Above: Not a bad day's catch! Right: At Port Canaveral – doing a man's job!

and white cornbread. It is likely that your breakfast will be served with grits, unless you ask for hashed browns, even when you stay in a big city hotel.

Florida hasn't forgotten that it is a Dixie state. You can usually get good baking powder biscuits, pecan and sweet potato pie, cornbread dressing, fried chicken, pit barbecue, greens with fatback, and many other southern classics cooked to perfection. Tropical influence on Florida's citrus crops leads to a glorious colorful cornucopia of grapefruit, tangerines and varieties of different oranges making a debut at many different seasons during the year.

Juicy Key limes, mangoes, and the occasional find of less frequently cultivated citrus fruits, such as ugli fruit, kumquats, and calamondins, were introduced by the Spanish. Crown law required that each sailor departing for the New World bring 100 seeds with him. Later, they began bringing seedlings instead. Descendants of those early trees are sometimes found deep in the scrub or the Everglades.

Key lime pie is a Florida passion, resulting in equally passionate arguments over whether it should have a pastry or graham cracker crust, a whipped cream or meringue topping. Only one thing is certain: Key limes are tiny and yellow, with a faint vanilla scent; real Key lime pie is never green.

There are still secondary roads in the state where citrus can be found at roadside stands. Tune in to the seasons to discover honeybelles, which have a short, sweet harvest, or naval oranges, which appear – grapefruit-sized and zipperskinned – right after the first cold snap. Only in late summer does the citrus market slack off for a bit. The harvest is much longer and more varied than nonnatives realize. An offshoot product is orange blossom honey, which is harvested here and sold worldwide. One Volusia County producer alone ships two million pounds a year, mostly to Europe

and Japan. In addition to orange blossom honey, Florida bee-keepers gather honey from ti-ti, palmetto, sunflower, gallberry, pepper, alfalfa, sweet clover and blueberry.

Dictionary of Florida Foods

Alligator pears are an old-time Florida name for avocadoes, which grow abundantly in south Florida.

Alligator, meaning the reptile, is often seen on menus. It has a meaty taste that some people find delicious.

Black-eyed peas and *hog jowls* are a soul food classic. The dish is traditionally eaten by Floridians on New Year's Eve to bring good luck.

Blue crab is served boiled whole or in heaping, steaming dishes. All-you-can-eat blue crab specials are an excellent buy for crab devotees.

Bollos – pronounced "boy-ose" – are the spicy, deep-fried balls made from mashed peas which are sold on Key West streets.

Cactus is a sweet red "pear," eaten like fruit; marinated it can be served as salad.

Carambola, also known as star fruit, has a tart, tangy flavor, suitably served as a garnish in drinks.

Catfish served in Florida are probably farmed rather than caught in the wild. Many restaurants offer all-you-can-eat catfish specials. Fingerling catfish are served whole. Tiny and bristling with bones, they have the sweetest meat of all.

Chayote is a bland, crisp fruit sometimes served cooked as a vegetable. It's called *christophene* in the West Indies.

Conch – pronounced "konk" – is a rubbery shellfish served in chowder, fritters, or "cracked," dipped in cracker crumbs and fried. The word also refers to a person who was born in the Keys.

Coontie is wild cassava root made into a flour much like arrowroot. This is the Seminoles' basic starch. The bread baked from it is bright orange.

Cooter is a land tortoise, served in turtle soups and fricassees. *Coquina* is a tiny clam, used in broths and chowders.

Dirty rice is a soul food favorite among blacks and rural whites, made from a blend of white rice boiled with chicken gizzards, hearts and livers.

Dolphin is one of Florida's meatiest fishes, but it is not prepared from the bottle-nosed dolphin, or porpoise, which is not harvested here for food.

Flan is a caramel-trimmed custard popular in Cuban restaurants.

Florida lobsters are spiny lobsters, otherwise known as crawfish, and quite unlike the Maine lobster. Only the tail of the Florida lobster, which may weigh as much as two pounds, is eaten. Menus often list it simply as lobster. Ask which lobster is being served. Some people who eat Maine lobster are allergic to the Florida crustacean, which is generally unavailable fresh from April to July.

Grouper is called "scamp" in Florida's Panhandle. It is a name used for many types of grouper and jewfish. It is a mild, firm fish that tastes much like the most delicate breast of chicken.

Guava is a tangy fruit, sometimes available fresh at roadsides. Guava ice cream is sold in Key West.

Heart of palm is also called swamp cabbage. It may be offered cold in salad or cooked as a vegetable.

Jerk cooking is Jamaican in origin. Spicy, barbecue jerk pork, beef, chicken, fish or goat is served in Florida's increasingly popular Caribbean restaurants.

Jícama (pronounced HEE-kahm-ah) is popular in Mexican cooking. A bland and crunchy vegetable, it is found commonly in Florida markets.

Early Keys residents, who had no refrigeration and consumed canned milk, discovered that Key lime juice could be added to sweetened condensed milk to make a sweet custard. Many imitations are made, but real *Key lime pie* is made from yellow limes and canned milk.

Loquat is also called Japanese plum, a yellow plum-like fruit.

Mangoes are sweet, peach-like fruits that grow only in south Florida. The flesh is juicy and delicious. Some people are allergic to the sticky sap, so be sure to wash it off your hands.

Okra grows abundantly in Florida. A southern favorite, it is used in many ways by southern cooks who stew it up with tomatoes.

Old sour is made by mixing salt and the juice of sour oranges. The combination is then allowed to ferment and is served as a condiment.

Papaya can be grown in yards in south Florida. It is seasonally available on restaurant menus.

Purloo is probably a corruption of *pilau* or *pilaf*, a rice dish that varies according to the cook.

Soffkee is the Seminoles' everyday stew, with meat, grits and vegetables.

Snapper is a popular fish, varieties of which include red, yellowtail and mangrove snapper.

Stone crab is Florida's unique crab. It grows a hard, glassy shell, which protects a nugget of sweet, white meat. Only the claw can be legally harvested, after which the animal is thrown back into the water to grow new claws. Served hot or cold, stone crab is available fresh only from mid-October through mid-May. Frozen claws are served during other months by some restaurants.

Surinam cherries are often grown as a landscaping hedge, and they can be made into into jellies or sauces.

Persimmons are cultivated in Florida and sold at roadside stands.

Plantains look like large bananas, but don't try to eat them raw! They are not sweet, but taste fine served fried or boiled, with a bland starchy taste that only hints of banana.

Tomatillo is a vine-grown green tomato-like vegetable commonly found in Florida supermarkets.

Right: This fish head is bigger than a man's back.

SOUTHERN FLORIDA

MIAMI
MIAMI BEACH
FORT LAUDERDALE
PALM BEACH
FLORIDA KEYS
EVERGLADES

MIAMI

Differences of opinion concerning Miami are as diverse as they are extreme: some consider the city a paradise for retirees, others regard it as a steel and glass business center, while still others think of it as a sun, sand and surf paradise for young, tanned layabouts. The television series *Miami Vice* depicted Miami as a dangerous city of drug sealers, pastel-colored nightclubs and glittering architecture; of slick men in speedboats; of fast cars and fast women. Hurricanes, tourist murders and waves of immigrants keep Miami in the public eye.

First the asylum-seekers from Cuba, and then immigrants from all over Latin America and the Caribbean, arrived to turn the city into an international business center. Spanish is the majortity population's first language. Many of the Central and South American immigrants had to endure hardship and violence in their homelands, and Miami offered them a better, more hopeful world.

The once run-down Art Deco District, a seaside nighborhood with architectur-

ally-brilliant buildings from the 1920s and 30s, has been transformed into an international glamour hub for the rich and beautiful. The district is now listed in the National Register of Historic Places.

The city's international connections and wild nightlife, which is mainly concentrated along the beaches, has provided for strong growth in the number of young newcomers to Miami. They have been followed by international business people, who settle into the skyscrapers along the beach and combine business with hedonistic pleasures, which, in basically conservative Florida, gives off an aura of wickedness.

Whatever grief the city's publicized lifestyle might cause its more sober citizens, all agree that Miami, a scant hundred years old, is decidedly the best place there is south of Atlanta.

Miami is the only city in the United States with two national parks (Everglades and Biscayne) right in its "backyard." The nearby agricultural district supplies much of America's vegetable supply during the cold northern winter.

While Miami International Airport is about to surpass JFK in New York for international passenger arrivals, Miami's cruise ship port has long ranked tops.

Madonna, John Travolta, Gloria Estefan and Julio Iglesias call Miami home.

Preceding pages: Evening mood at Sandestin Beach. Fascinating day or night – Miami's skyline. Left: A typical building in the Art Deco District.

63

Culture is highly-valued in Miami: the city boasts the world-acclaimed Miami City Ballet; it has its own opera company and two symphony orchestras, and is home to four universities. Here you will find Florida's best mainstream and alternative newspapers, and America's biggest book fair, which attracts more than just bookworms to Miami.

Regardless of whether you want to enjoy the city's culture, nightlife or sun and sand, Miami is a great place to visit, no matter how long you might be planning on staying.

Miami's Origins

The discovery of Florida might put the Mayflower settlers to shame – Ponce de Leon first stepped off here seeking his fountain of youth in 1513. Miami's history, though, is considerably more recent; it was so far down the state's east coast that no civilized souls dared to venture down here. Julia Tuttle was a spirited exception.

The wife of a wealthy industrialist from Cleveland, Mrs. Tuttle arrived in Miami on a mail boat in 1875. What she found was not particularly auspicious: the ruins of a U.S. Army camp and an Indian trading post operated by the local Seminoles. Still, she thought the sunny, scenic area had possibilities, a fact she tried to impress upon Henry Flagler, the Standard Oil co-founder, railroad tycoon and developer of the east coast of the state.

At first, Flagler resisted. But the weather intervened in Mrs. Tuttle's favor: a ferocious freeze hit during the winter of 1894/95, wiping out most of Florida's citrus industry. Down south, though, in uncivilized Miami, orange blossoms were flourishing without a touch of frost. Tuttle sent Flagler a bouquet of them, and the railroad czar seemed to get the message: his railroad was extended southward, arriving in the town a year

Miramar

Hallandale Beach Rd.

858

Pembroke Park

832

Dairy Rd.

Hallandale

5

Golden Beach

Hallandale Beach

Golden Beach

Buccaneer Estates

821

County Line Rd.

441

854

Ives

Ives Estates

856

A1A

847

91

7

Gardens Dr. (NW 183rd St.)

860

Miami

Gardens

Sunny Isles

Carol City

95

EXPWY

826

Greynolds Park Spanish Monastery

NE 167th St.

826

Interama Blvd.

North Miami Beach

Bunche Park

826

9A

Haulover Beach

Opa-Locka

817

441

915

909

Biscayne Gardens 135th St.

N. Miami Recr. Facility, Florida Int'l University

9

7

NE 135th St.

916

922

Bal Harbour

Bay Harbor Islands

953

Gratigny Rd. (NW 119th St.)

924

NorthMiami (NE 125th St.)

Broad Causeway (Toll)

Surfside

1

Little River Canal (NW 103rd St.)

932

(NE 103rd St.)

5

Waterway

NORMANDY I.

North Shore Park

HIALEAH (NW 79th St.)

Miami Shores

El Portal

John F. Kennedy Causeway

934

65th St. Park

Le Jeune Rd. (NW 22nd Ave.)

Central Blvd.

Northside

934

9A

North Bay Village

Biscayne

907

A1A

Martin Luther King

9

NW 54th St.

95

1

5

Intracoastal

Ocean Front Park

Fontainebleau

Hialeah Dr.

944

Earlington Heights

Brownsville

Bay

Indian Beach Park

AIRPORT EXPWY

25 27

112 (TOLL)

NW 7th Ave.

NORTH-SOUTH

Police Mus.

JULIA TUTTLE CAUSEWAY

112

Miami Beach

Miami Internat. Airport

Palmer

Santa Clara

Civic Center

195

SUNSET I.

Alton Rd.

Collins Ave.

Collins Park

(TOLL)

EAST-WEST EXPWY

836

VENETIAN IS.

Lummus Park

968

W. Flagler St.

MIAMI

395

Overtown

Gov't Cen.

Flamingo Park

Mac Arthur Causeway

141

A1A

90

Place St. Michel

933

Tamiami Tr.

Brickell

DODGE IS.

Convention Center

CLAUGHTON I.

FISHER I.

Coral Gables

953

972

Coral Wy.

Vizcaya

Rickenbacker

VIRGINIA KEY

Miami Seaquarium

Hist. Mus. Vizcaya Mus.

Virginia Beach

Southeast Pt.

976

Douglas Road

S. Dixie Hwy.

Silver Bluff

GROVE I.

Crandon Park

University of Miami (Main Campus)

Coconut Grove

Main Hwy.

West Pt.

ATLANTIC OCEAN

South Miami

Biscayne Bay

Key Biscayne

Southwest Pt.

Crandon Blvd.

KEY BISCAYNE

Fairchild Tropical Garden

Bill Baggs Cape Florida St. Rec. Area

Matheson Hammock County Park

Cape Florida

MIAMI - MIAMI BEACH AND ENVIRONS

| 0 | 4 | 8km |
| 0 | 2 | 4 miles |

Above: Art, Business or Kitsch? Right: Hundreds of Miami Beach's Art Deco buildings were saved from dilapidation.

later. Flagler then came down himself and built a hotel. As often happened with Flagler's march down the Florida coast, wherever he went, the rich and famous soon followed, and they began to settle in Miami.

In 1912, millionaire Carl Fisher looked around Biscayne Bay, bought a vast sandbar from an avocado farmer, John Collins (after whom Collins Avenue was named), and dredged it until he hit solid ground. Here he had hotels built, and parks and golf courses laid out. And so Miami Beach, famous the world over, was born.

Fisher wasn't the last visionary in the area either. In 1921, a local boy, George Merrick, took his father's Miami farm and designed a European-inspired city within it. The result, **Coral Gables**, is still one of the city's most exclusive addresses, with its Venetian canals and

French-style houses. It may not be the most unique in appearance, however. That distinction could easily go to **Opa-Locka**, an Arabian Nights fantasy of spires, domes and parapets developed by former aviator Glenn H. Curtiss. Like his other developments, Hialeah and Miami Springs, Opa-Locka was intended as a destination for winter-weary Northerners – so-called "snowbirds" – and today, although a residential area inhabited primarily by blacks, you can see the somewhat run-down but still outstanding architecture.

The tradition of wintering in Miami was now well established. Some visitors, drawn by the warmth and the beauty, also realized that there was money to be made in real estate. Speculators jumped on the gravy train to Miami, and a population boom soon followed: in a period of only five years, the number of residents increased from 30,000 to 100,000. In addition, some 300,000 visitors came during the winter.

Not everyone was able to cash in on the deals, however. Scoundrels abounded and some developments went bust. Then Miami saw a crippling hurricane in 1926 and the beginning of the Depression in 1929. The Depression did not finish Miami off, though; in fact, some of its most enduring legacies were built during this time.

The 1930s ushered in Ocean Drive's modern, elegant Art Deco hotels. Retirees also started to stream into the area; land was cheap, there was no inheritance or income tax, and the weather was much easier on both body and soul.

After the Second World War, the area went through another real estate boom, as well as through a public relations boom, thanks to the presence of two television celebrities: Arthur Godfrey broadcast his show from Miami Beach starting in 1953, and Jackie Gleason proclaimed Miami Beach the "sun and fun capital of the world" in the 1960s. The city became

a celebrity playground. Celebrities were not the only new faces in Miami in the 1960s, though: the influx of refugees – some 265,000 fleeing Castro's Cuba – changed the sights and the sounds of the city immeasurably. Now, more than 50 percent of the city is Hispanic, as Colombians, Guatemalans, Nicaraguans and Panamanians followed the Cuban migration.

Today's ethnic mixture does not end there, however: Creole-speaking Haitians have their own neighborhood, and Brasilians, Germans, Greeks, Iranians, Italians, and even Swedes now call Miami home.

The City

The business district of Miami flaunts its success the way many American cities do; with tall steel and glass skyscrapers. These reflect the sun during the day and colored lights at night. Depending upon the time of year, the **Sun Trust Building**, 100 SE 1st Street, changes its outdoor lighting colors accordingly: red and

green for Christmas, purple and pink for Easter, orange and green for home games of the town's two football teams: the Miami Dolphins and the University of Miami Hurricanes. To take in the whole spread, drive along **Brickell Avenue** from north to south. In addition to skyscrapers there are innovative, colorful residential buildings.

Since parking downtown is very expensive, this might be a good opportunity to use **Metrorail**, the train service that started up in 1984. Once downtown, you can hop on **Metromover**, an elevated transit system that circles the commercial district. Still, it is advisable to simply walk when time and distance allow in order to get a feel for the streets of Miami.

Places of Interest

The **Dade County Courthouse**, at 73 W. Flagler Street, is one of the veteran buildings amid all this glass. It dates back to 1928 and was once the tallest building south of the nation's capital. Now the tallest building in the city – indeed, in the state – is the 55-story **Southeast Financial Center** at 200 South Biscayne Blvd.

For a little art among all this commerce, the **Metro-Dade Cultural Center**, at 101 West Flagler Street, was opened to the public in 1983 and is dedicated to art, history and scholarship. The **Center for Fine Arts** possesses no permanent collections; curators acquire temporary shows. The **Historical Museum of Southern Florida** has a collection of historical artifacts pertaining to the area. The **Main Public Library** offers three million volumes and occasional art exhibits.

For performing arts, an interesting place is the **Gusman Center for the Performing Arts** at 174 East Flagler Street, housed in a baroque former movie theater with a touch of the Orient. Inside, the Miami City Ballet performs, a company given real status by its director Edward Villella, a former star of the New York City Ballet.

For strolling and shopping, a prime stop is the **Bayside Marketplace** at 401 Biscayne Blvd. Next door is **Miamarina**, roosting place for luxury yachts and a Venetian gondola that gives rides. Another ship nearby also takes on visitors but stays at the pier: the reproduction of the **H.M.S. Bounty** that was built for the 1962 film *Mutiny on the Bounty*.

Little Havana

Southwest of downtown, in the neighborhood bordering SW 8th Street, is the section known as **Little Havana**, the area where, starting in the 1960s, Cuban immigrants settled. This is a popular area for strolling, with its brick sidewalks, tree-lined streets, food stalls and Cuban cafés. At **Domino Park**, SW 8th and 14th Avenue, you can watch residents try to outwit each other in dominoes games.

Wilder goings-on occur the first week of March every year during the **Carnivale Miami**, a nine-day festival culminating in **Calle Ocho**, a huge street party. Bicycle races, concerts, a masquerade ball in the streets, races, conga drums, live music, sambas, mambos and lots more is on offer during this festival.

Little Haiti

About 200,000 Haitian immigrants live in this 200-block section of northeast Miami. On the side-streets are elegant Mediterranean-style homes, originals from the land boom era of the 1920s, and on the main drag, NE 2nd Avenue, between 45th and 79th streets, is a panorama of brightly painted buildings, in purples, reds, pinks, greens and yellows.

In these florid buildings are shops selling foods and crafts. And in the center of Little Haiti is the **Caribbean Marketplace**, 5927 NE 2nd Avenue, worth a visit because you never know what buys you may find on art, crafts or music.

Coral Gables

George Merrick's planned community calls itself "The City Beautiful." It is not hard to see why: this wealthy section built along golf courses and canals appropriates the best of European styles and transplants them side by side. The main gates, fountains and plazas are in Spanish style, but Merrick thought residents should have a choice, so "atmospheric" neighborhoods, called *The Villages*, were created. If Spanish wasn't your style, you could choose French Country, French Provincial, French City, Dutch South African, Colonial or even Chinese.

Regardless of a person's choice of architecture, all Coral Gables residents had, and still have, one structure in common: the **Venetian Pool** at 2701 De Soto Blvd., probably the most deluxe community swimming pool in the world.

Originally the site of a coral rock quarry, it was sculpted into a lagoon in 1924. Vast and romantic – with a waterfall, caves and

■ Metrorail System with Stations
● Metromover with Stations

NW 28th St.

933

NW 29th St. NW 28th St. NE 29th St.

Fashion NW 26th St. NE 26th St.

District NW 2nd St. 5

NW 22nd St. NW 22nd St. NE 22nd St.

SANTA CLARA NW 21st St.

NW 20th St. NW 20th St.

NW 17th Ave. NW 17th St. 95 *Dorsey Park* NE 17th St. Biscayne Blvd. Bayshore Dr.

9A NW 17th St. NW 17th St. *Biscayne Park* NE 15th St. 1

Civic Center 7 Venetian Way (Toll)

(Hospitals) NE 14th St.

CIVIC CENTER NE 1st Ave. Mac Arthur

West-Expwy.-(Toll) 395 A1A Cswy.

NW 14th St. Miami Ave.

North River Dr.

East-River *Bicentennial Park*

836 Miami

CULMER 5

NW 8th Ave. NW 2nd St. OVER TOWN Biscayne Blvd.

7th Ave.

NW 7th St. NW 9th St. St.

NW 5th Ave. 9A NE 6th St. **John F. Kennedy Torch of Friendship**

NW 17th Ave. NW 14th Ave. NW 6th St. P.O. NE 5th St. 41

Orange Bowl Stadium NW 5th St. North NE 2nd St. 3rd St. **Bayside Marketplace, Miamarina, HMS Bounty Exhibit**

NW 12th Ave. *Lummus Park* Greyhound Bus Term.

NW 4th St. **Dade Country Court House** NE 1st St.

Henderson Park NW 2nd St. GOVERNMENT CENTER *Bayfront Park of the Americas*

7 **Metro Dade Cult. C.** W. Flagler St. E. Flagler St. **SE Bank Tower Financial C.**

968 West Flagler St. 968 SW 1st St. **Gusman C. Performing Arts** SE 3rd St. **Sun Trust Building**

SW 1st St. SW 3rd St. *Jose Marti Riverside Park* **Hyatt Regency Coral Gables** Miami River **Sheraton**

SW 17th Ave. SW 14th Ave. SW 3rd St. *Riverside Park* Brickell Pt. Brickell Park 1 **CLAUGHTON ISLAND**

SW 8th Ave. SW 5th Ave. SE 3rd St.

Little SW 7th St. SW 7th St. SE 7th St.

41 41 **Havana** 41 Tamiami Trail (SW 8th St.) **(Calle Ocho)** SW 8th SE 8th St. South Miami Ave. Brickell Ave.

Domino Park (Maceo Park) 933 Brickell Dr.

SW 11th St. SW 10th Ave. SW 11th St. SW 1st Ave. SE 12th St.

Cuban Mus. of Art & Culture SW 9th Ave. 95 SW BRICKELL 13th St. SE Bayshore Dr.

SW 14th St. SW 5th Ave. (Coral Way)

SW 17th Ter. 972 SW 15th Rd. *Simpson Park* 5 Pt. View

SW 12th Ave. SW 28th Rd. (Coral Way) 22nd Ave. SW 17th Rd. SE 15th Rd. *Waterway*

SW 19th St.

SW 22nd St. (Coral Way) 9A 1 North-South-Expwy. South Miami Ave. Brickell Ave. **Biscayne**

VIZCAYA 5

SW 17th Ave. 1 S. Dixie Hwy. Sam an la Dr. **Planetarium** S Miami Ave. *Alice Wainwright Park* **Bay**

Alatka St. Brickell Ave.

Villa Vizcaya (Dade Country Art Museum)

North-South-Expwy.

Wagner Cr.

NW 17th Ave. NW 12th Ave. NW South River Dr.

DOWNTOWN MIAMI

0 ——— 500m
0 ——— 0,3miles

lush foliage all around, it definitely transports you to another time and place.

So do the **Coral Gables City Hall**, at 405 Biltmore Way, a Spanish Neo-Renaissance structure built in 1928, and the showplace **Biltmore Hotel**, at 1200 Anastasia Ave. The lavish (and some say haunted) hotel, built in 1926, has a beautiful tower modeled on the Giralda Tower in Seville. The hotel did not have a successful run and was vacant for nearly twenty years before renovation started in 1986. Now it is a palace with opulent chandeliers, painted ceilings and an oversized pool.

Coconut Grove

Coconut Grove was established 20 years before Miami, so although annexed by the city in 1925, it has never quite in-

Above: At the Coconut Grove Arts Festival.
Right: Sailing – one of the great passions of Floridians.

tegrated itself. Its reputation as a Bohemian center also sets it apart: first settled by Bahamian blacks, Key Westers and transplanted New England intellectuals, it was a kind of Greenwich Village of the South, an image that still remains today, along with the lush tropical vegetation. People come here to sit in outdoor cafés and watch the well-dressed pedestrians pass by. They also come to shop, go to galleries and generally spend money.

Also worth a look on the edge of Coconut Grove is the estate we all wish we could borrow for the winter; **Vizcaya**, at 3251 South Miami Avenue. James Deering, heir to the International Harvester fortune, spent $15 million back in 1912 for this 70-room imitation Italian Renaissance palace. The ten acres of sculpted gardens add a lot to the sense of luxury and romance.

Key Biscayne

Take a drive over the Rickenbacker Causeway from Coconut Grove and you wind up on lush and tropical **Key Biscayne**. Gulls and herons were about the most famous residents here until the late 1960s, when another temporary resident began coming south for the winter – then U.S. President Richard Nixon, who died in 1994.

The **Florida White House**, as it was known, is at 485 West Matheson Drive. **Crandon Park**, **Virginia Key** and **Bill Baggs Cape Florida State Park**, with its renovated historical lighthouse, are all worth a visit. If sunbathing, looking at sailboats or watching the local fishermen casting for grouper or snapper gets to be boring, you can always rent a bike.

The **Miami Seaquarium**, at 4400 Rickenbacker Causeway, provides a day with popular deep-sea mammals. The star here is named Lolita, a killer whale who gives splashy performances along with dolphins, sharks and other creatures from the sea.

MIAMI BEACH

Miami Beach has had some tremendous ups and downs over the years. From its mangrove swamp status in 1910, it became the Riviera of the United States in the Roaring Twenties; a wild drinking and gambling playground. The big hotels from that era were supplemented in the postwar era with huge, flashy, intentionally exotic-sounding new hotels, such as the Martinique, the Barcelona and the Bombay. Motels then began to spring up on **Collins Avenue** in North Miami Beach.

Now middle-class Americans came to Miami Beach to vacation. In the 1960s and 1970s, Miami Beach as a vacation spot took a sharp downturn; older vacationers of past seasons bought houses of their own in the area, abandoning the hotels, and their hippie children, bored with Miami Beach, took off for more exotic places. Soon, some of the fancier hotels began to fall into disrepair. Lately, though, a number of hotels have come

back impressively and, with their revitalization, have made Miami Beach a lively and fashionable place once again.

Start your drive into Miami Beach by taking the **MacArthur Causeway** across the Intracoastal; on your way you will pass **Star Island**, **Hibiscus Island** and **Palm Island**, which are more notable for their residents than their location: Al Capone lived on Palm Island, author Damon Runyon lived on Hibiscus Island and *Miami Vice* star Don Johnson lived on Star Island. The Causeway will bring you into **South Beach**, the area from the southern tip to 23rd Street. You will cross on 5th Street. If you are a boxing fan you should pay attention to the corner of Washington and 5th: the 5th Street Gym has been the site of workouts by Muhammad Ali, Sonny Liston, Roberto Duran and Joe Louis, among other champions.

Fifth Street is where the **Art Deco District** begins, a little more than a mile north along the beach, but an extraordinary revival of what at the end of the 1980s was known as God's Waiting

71

Room, because of the district's elderly population.

Today it's the reverse: the district throbs with youthful round-the-clock fun. Fashion models parade for the world's glossy magazine covers, artfully shown against backdrops of Art Deco hotels, restored with new, trendy colors. The Café society rivals that of the Côte d'Azur, topless sunbathers, tattooed rollerskaters, and stars like Madonna, John Travolta and Julio Iglesias have brought fame to the district, with its fantastic food and wild nightlife. The Art Deco District has reversed the demise of Miami Beach as a family resort to re-emerge as America's reigning bastion of excess.

At 4441 Collins Avenue you will see a unique mural signaling a similarly unique hotel. The giant arch, Roman figures, waterfalls and lagoon look real but are

not – they are just covering a blank wall that shields the immense Fontainebleau (mispronounced locally as "Fountain Blue") Hotel.

This mammoth conventioneers' haven is what most people think of when they think of Miami Beach – it fronts a huge, 18-acre stretch of beach, it caters to outrageous frivolities, exemplified by the Poodle Lounge, decorated with pink poodles. It may be kitsch but it is worth a stop.

Also worth a stop is the pink and purple lobby of the **Eden Roc**, at 4525 Collins Avenue, and the elegant, glassy **Doral**, at 4833 Collins Avenue.

Somewhat farther up Collins, past **Surfside**, you come to **Bal Harbor**, an elegant, quiet stretch with shops and luxurious homes tucked away behind secure gates. The tawdry stretch of motels along **Sunny Isles** follows. Then, at the top of **North Miami Beach**, you find the quietest, most exclusive enclave of all, **Golden Beach**. Drive by for a look at the mansions.

Above: "The" event for hundreds of thousands – the Orange Bowl. Right: A touch of the Caribbean at Key West. Far right: Miami nightlife.

Nightlife

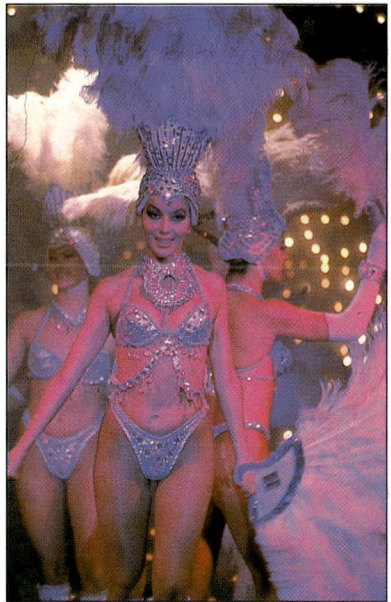

The Underworld and the Police

Sunshine is one thing almost everyone comes to Miami for; it can be an intoxicant in itself. But Miami has always had a reputation as a swinging town, and with the massive wealth pouring in from all over the world, this is even truer now. For electric nightlife the scene is South Beach in the Art Deco District, where clubs open with great panache two, three a month, ever flaunting sex, rock and roll, rap, reggae, hip hop – whatever's in vogue – and pulling crowds of jet-setters from around the world to this bastion of chic. For an elegant club with a Latin beat, Miamians have been going to **Les Violins**, at 1751 Biscayne Blvd, for over 25 years. The best blues scene is at **Tobacco Road** in downtown Miami. The **Hell Club** is the latest rave in the Art Deco District; **Baja Beach Club** the hot spot in Coconut Grove. For up-to-date information on the night scene, pick up a copy of the pop weekly *New Times* or the *Miami Herald* weekend section.

In the city one needs not look hard to encounter low-life. Crime, drugs and record-setting murder rates committed in the humid heat of the tropics makes for serious law enforcement operations, and there is no better place to house the **American Police Hall of Fame and Museum**, the nation's only memorial honoring U.S. law officers who have died in the line of duty. The museum is located in the former FBI headquarters at 3801 Biscayne Blvd.

The museum contains an interdenominational chapel and a crime prevention center. The collection includes more than 10,000 police and law enforcement exhibits, an electric chair, a guillotine, jail cells and a mock crime scene where visitors are challenged to "solve the murder." A 400-ton marble memorial stands at the center of the 1.5-acre museum. On it, the names, ranks, cities and states of officers killed in the line of duty since 1960 are inscribed.

MIAMI / MIAMI BEACH
Area Code 305

Arrival
The **Miami International Airport** is located six miles west of downtown. Metered cabs, limousines, the **Metrobus** and the **SuperShuttle**, a bus that shuttles between the airport and the hotels, can be taken into town.

Accommodation
LUXURY: **Grand Bay Hotel**, five-star elegance overlooking Biscayne Bay, 2669 S. Bayshore Dr., Coconut Grove, tel. 858-9600.

Delano, this is considered to be the hippest, hottest address in Miami Beach; actors and models can be found lounging in the ultra-chic courtyard, 1685 Collins Ave., Miami Beach, tel. 672-2000.

Mayfair House, European-style, 3000 Florida Ave., Coconut Grove, tel. 441-0000.

The Marlin, 1200 Collins Ave., Miami Beach, tel. 673-8770, this was the first in a series of brilliant transformations of Art Deco District hotels into Jamaican Deco style by Islands Records founder Chris Blackwell.

The Biltmore Hotel, 1200 Anastasia Ave., Coral Gables, tel. 445-1926, historic extravaganza, but some of the guest rooms are not up to the main rooms' decor.

Hyatt Regency Coral Gables, a tall, new building that integrates its glitziness with the old world feel of the neighborhood, 50 Alhambra Plaza, Coral Gables, tel. 441-1234.

Sonesta Beach Hotel and Tennis Club, self-contained resort on a fabulous beach, 350 Ocean Drive, Key Biscayne, tel. 361-2021.

Alexander Hotel, this charming, sophisticated, antique-filled hotel offers either ocean or bay views from every room, 5225 Collins Ave., Miami Beach, tel. 865-6500.

Turnberry Isle Resort and Club, an ideal place to stay if you want to run into tennis players – Jimmy Connors and John McEnroe have condos here – 3/19999 W. Country Club Drive, Aventura, tel. 932-6200.

The Park Central Hotel, 640 Ocean Drive, Miami Beach, tel. 538-1611.

Doral Resort and Country Club, 4400 NW 87th Ave., Miami, tel. 592-2000 or 1-800-22DORAL, 15 tennis courts, five 18-hole golf courses.

MODERATE TO BUDGET: **Hotel Place St. Michel**, small and private with antiques from all over the world, 162 Alcazar, Coral Gables, tel. 444-1666.

Park Central Hotel, this is a jewel of an Art Deco hotel, at 640 Ocean Drive, Miami Beach, tel. 538-1611.

Other choice Art Deco District hotels:

The Avalon, 700 Ocean Drive, Miami Beach, tel. 538-0133.

The Majestic, 660 Ocean Drive, Miami Beach, a companion hotel to the Avalon, also reached at tel. 538-0133.

The Leslie, 1300 Ocean Drive, Miami Beach, tel. 534-2135.

Marseilles Deco Beach Hotel, 1741 Collins Ave., Miami Beach., rooms here offer great views, free continental breakfast, tel. 538-5711 or 1-800-327- 4739.

Restaurants
Joe's Stone Crab, 227 Biscayne Street at Washington Ave., Miami Beach, tel. 673-0365, the most-famous and therefore most-crowded restaurant in town, serving the area's indigenous stone crab as it has been doing since 1913. Joe's closes when the crab is not in season, from mid-May to mid-October. Plan to wait in line for at least an hour for a table – a hassle, but worth it for a great meal. Hint: Savvy diners order stone crabs cold with Joe's mustard sauce.

Monty Trainer's Bayshore Restaurant, Lounge and Raw Bar, 2550 South Bayshore Drive, Coconut Grove, tel. 858-1431, seafood emporium with an outdoor marina-side raw bar.

Chef Allen's, 19088 NE 29th Avenue, North Miami Beach, tel. 935-2900, featuring sublime, sophisticated and expensive *Nouvelle Americaine* cuisine.

Versailles, 3555 SW 8th Street, tel. 445-7614, a lively, casual Cuban restaurant.

The Malaga, 740 SW 8th, tel. 858-4224, also serves Cuban food in a slightly more upscale environment.

Café Pavarotti, 9561 E. Bay Harbor Drive, Bay Harbor Islands, tel. 866-8779, romantic Italian restaurant.

Norman's, 21 Almeria Ave., Coral Gables, tel. 446-6767, Latin, Caribbean, Asian fusion.

Rascal House, 17190 Collins Ave., Miami Beach, tel. 947-4581. No need to call here; there is always a line of customers waiting for a table at this cavernous Jewish delicatessen. Open 24 hours a day. Huge servings, monster corned beef on rye, mountainous slabs of cherry cheesecake.

Sightseeing
Metrozoo, SW 152nd St. & SW. 124th Ave., Miami, tel. 251-0403. White Bengal tigers, gorillas, koalas and an assortment of other exotic animals wander in man-made approximations of their natural habitats in this 290-acre zoo.

Miami Seaquarium, 4400 Rickenbacker Causeway, Virgina Key, tel. 361-5705. This is home to more than 10,000 sea creatures, including sharks and dolphins.

Parrot Jungle and Gardens, 11000 SW 57th Ave., tel. 666-7834. Parrot shows, children's playground and petting zoo, ten acres of formal gardens on the bay, accessible by Metrorail.

Spanish Monastery, 16711 W. Dixie Highway, North Miami Beach, tel. 945-1462. This is a real monastery, and an authentic Spanish one at that – it was originally built in Segovia in the year 1141. Publishing tycoon William Randolph Hearst bought it and had it transported to its current location, where it was reconstructed piece by piece.

Hialeah Park, 2200 E. 4th Ave., Hialeah, tel. 885-8000. A thoroughbred racetrack with a French Mediterranean-style clubhouse on situated on 220 flowery acres. There are daily free tours when racing is not in session.

Shopping

Cocowalk, 3015 Grand Ave., Coconut Grove, this is the must-visit heart of the grove for multi-level Euro-styled shopping mixed with trendy restaurants, bars, movies, and the Improv Comedy Club.

Across the street is the more formal **Mayfair Shops**, 2911 Grand Avenue, Coconut Grove, a beautifully designed mall created for an upscale South American market.

Bayside Marketplace, 401 Biscayne Boulevard, downtown. Just about everything for for just about everybody.

Bal Harbor Shops, 9700 Collins Avenue, Bal Harbor. The place to go to do some exclusive shopping at exclusive prices.

Miami Fashion District, 5th Avenue from 29th to 25th Street. The opposite of Bal Harbor, factory outlets and discount shops.

Getting Around / Tours

The first thing any visitor needs to know is that Miami and Miami Beach are two separate entities. The city of Miami is on the mainland; Miami Beach is actually a cluster of islands linked to the mainland by a range of causeways.

Altogether, 27 separate communities comprise what is known as Greater Miami, organized on a grid quadrant system: SE, SW, NE and NW.

Before you do anything, plunk your 25 cents down to ride the **Metromover**. This is far and away the best ride for getting a quick overview of downtown Miami. You're two stories up in the air looping in and out of highrises with spectacular views over bay and river. The 1.9 mile ride operates every 90 seconds and lasts some 15 minutes.

If you want even more, connect at the Government Center Station and ride the 29-mile elevated **Metrorail**. For another $1.25 you've got yourself a glorious hour of it.

Tour companies go in and out of business all the time. The old reliable for city sightseeing is **A-1 Bus Lines**, **Mears Line of Miami**, 1642 NW 231st Terrace, Miami, tel. 1-800-826-6754 and 325-1000.

For tours that additionally offer shopping and a taste of Miami's nightlife, try **American Vision Travel & Tours**, 245 SE 1st Street, Suite 442, Miami, tel. 577-8900. Both of these tour operators offer multi-lingual guides.

If you wish the comfort and safety of a private limousine, arrangements can be made in advance through your local travel agent. A **One-Way Meet-and-Greet Service**, picking you up at the airport, should cost about $50.

The Miami Design Preservation League has a Saturday morning walking tour of the Art Deco District. The tour starts out from 1001 Ocean Drive in Miami Beach, and lasts about 90 minutes. The cost of the tour is $6 and reservations are necessary (tel. 672-2014).

Heritage of Miami is a gaffrigged wooden schooner that can accommodate about 40 passengers on daily two-hour tours of Biscayne Bay. Contact **Dinner Key Marina**, Miami, tel. 858-6264.

Sports Activities

Boating, fishing, swimming, golf, tennis – it would not be a trip to Florida without partaking in at least one of these activities.

Sailors should head for **Easy Sailing**, tel. 858-4001, in Coconut Grove for hourly or daily rentals of 19- and 22-foot sailboats. Lessons are available here.

Speed boaters may contact **Beach Boat Rentals**, Inc., 2380 Collins Ave., Miami Beach, tel. 534-4307, for 18-foot power boats.

For grander designs, **Florida Yacht Charters & Sales**, 1290 5th Street (in the Art Deco District), Miami Beach, tel. 532-7600, can provide sailboats ranging from 28 to 42 feet. Captains, if you wish, can be chartered along with the vessels.

For deep-sea fishing, the **Blue Sea II**, 1020 MacArthur Causeway, tel. 358-3416, can be chartered for half-day cruises.

Kelley Fishing Fleet, 10800 Collins Ave., Miami Beach, tel. 945-3801, offers half- or full-day deep-sea fishing trips, as well as 2-3 day jaunts to the Bahamas.

Bayside Cruises, Bayside Marketplace, 401 Biscayne Blvd., Miami, operates sightseeing cruises on the 54-foot sailing catamaran with five departures daily except Christmas.

And, for those who prefer to go solo, **Sailboards Miami** offers windsurfing boards, sailboats, kayaks and pedalboats, together with a retail store, at Hobie Beach, 3501 Rickenbacker Causeway, Key Biscayne, tel. 361-7245.

Tourist Information

The Greater Miami Convention and Visitors Bureau, Suite 2700, 701 Brickell Ave., Miami, tel. 539-3063 or 1-800-283-2707.

FORT LAUDERDALE

While Miami may walk the high wire, Fort Lauderdale has both feet planted firmly on the ground. Smaller scaled, Fort Lauderdale nevertheless has it all: beaches, downtown, shopping, nightlife, history.

In the 1980s, Fort Lauderdale was America's "spring break" capital. In March and April, misbehaving college students ran rampant here. But when the more mature visitors began to stay away, the city told the kids to find themselves another party town. The beachfront and downtown were renovated for the city's resident population.

Today's Fort Lauderdale beachfront evokes European chic: an architecturally stunning promenade, unique in Florida, with no hotels blocking the view. Pedestrians have priority over cars, and the umbrellas of sidewalk cafés can be seen

Right: Yachting – the favorite pastime in Fort Lauderdale.

everywhere. The downtown area along the New River has blossomed, too, with fine restaurants and amusing nightlife. There are also stages for performances, and the arts are well-represented here. Las Olas Boulevard remains one of Florida's best streets for shopping. The big plus of vacationing here is that Fort Lauderdale remains both as affordable and as safe as big-city Florida gets.

Fort Lauderdale's Origins

The city sounds like it should be an army camp. It is not – no military encampments remain. But it was named for an actual fort, built in 1838 by Major William Lauderdale during the Seminole Indian Wars. Years later, in 1893, a trader named Frank Stranahan, regarded as the father of modern-day Fort Lauderdale, came to the sunny area for his health. The settlement was then known as New River Camp, and he had come to run it. This was not a big job: the camp consisted only of three men and the Seminoles. He set up a trading post, buying pelts and hides from the Seminoles and reselling them. Soon, Native Americans from the Everglades were canoeing down the river to do business.

Stranahan loved the quiet life on the river, but it did not remain quiet for long. When Henry Flagler extended his railway from West Palm Beach to Miami, passing through his small settlement, people were drawn to the area, and many farming communities began to spring up.

One of these communities, **Hallandale**, was founded by Swedish settlers and named after their leader, Luther Halland. A few miles north, a group of tomato-farming Danes founded **Dania**, which, in 1904, became the first town in what is now **Broward County**. An attempt by Dania to annex Fort Lauderdale failed; it became an independent community in 1911. **Pompano Beach** soon followed suit.

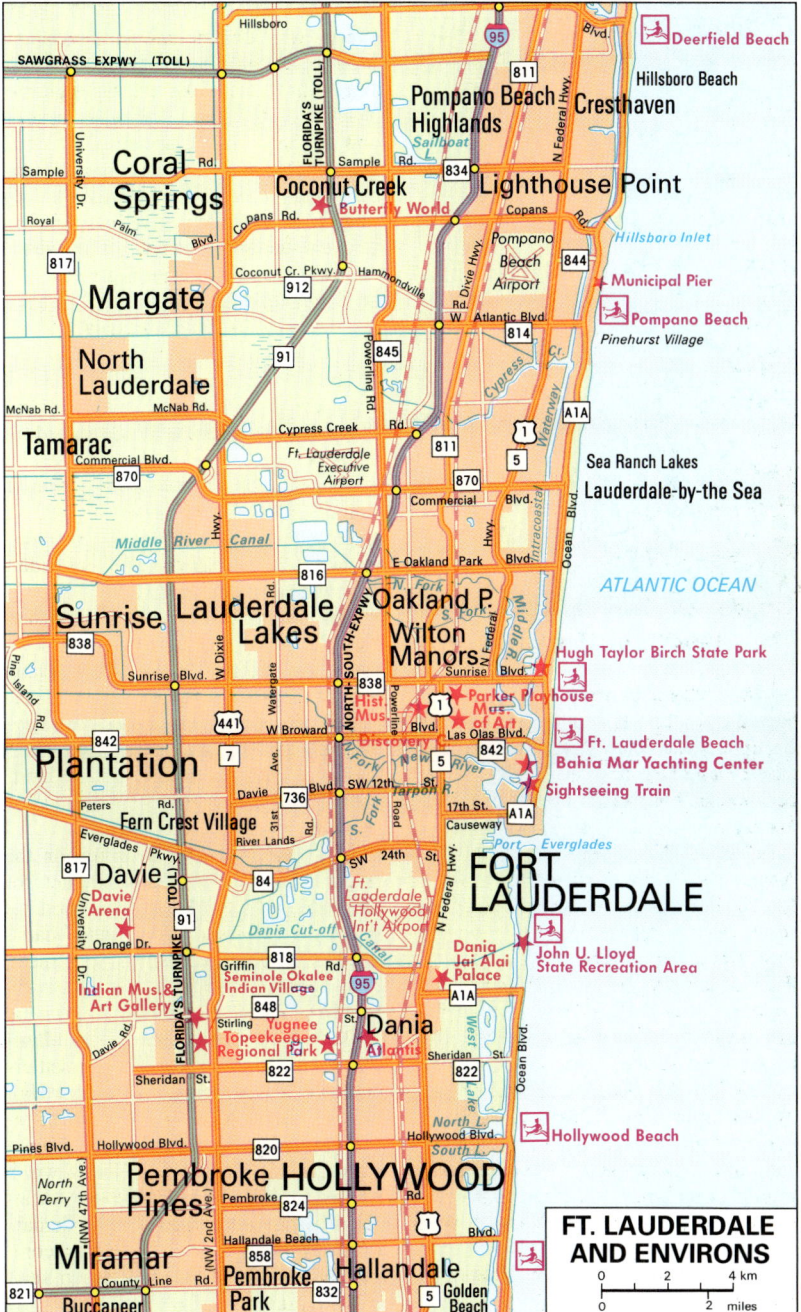

Hillsboro

🏄 Deerfield Beach

Blvd.

95

SAWGRASS EXPWY (TOLL)

811

Hillsboro Beach

Pompano Beach
Highlands

Cresthaven

University Dr.

FLORIDA'S TURNPIKE (TOLL)

Sailboat

Coral
Springs

Sample Rd.

834

Coconut Creek

Sample Rd.

Lighthouse Point

🟊 Butterfly World

Copans

Copans Rd.

817

Palm

Blvd.

Coconut Cr. Pkwy.

912

Hammondville

Pompano
Beach
Airport

844

Hillsboro Inlet

🏄 Municipal Pier

Royal

Margate

Rd.

N Dixie Hwy.

W. Atlantic Blvd.

814

🏄 Pompano Beach

Pinehurst Village

North
Lauderdale

91

845

McNab Rd.

McNab Rd.

Powerline Rd.

Cypress Ct.

Tamarac

Commercial Blvd.

870

Cypress Creek Rd.

811

1

A1A

Sea Ranch Lakes

Ft. Lauderdale
Executive Airport

870

5

Lauderdale-by-the-Sea

Commercial Blvd.

Ocean Blvd.

Intracoastal Wtrway.

Middle River Canal

816

E Oakland Park Blvd.

ATLANTIC OCEAN

Sunrise

838

Lauderdale
Lakes

N. Fork

Oakland P.
Wilton
Manors

S. Fork

Middle River

🏄 Hugh Taylor Birch State Park

817

Pine Island Rd.

Sunrise Blvd.

W Dixie Hwy.

Watergate

838

Sunrise Blvd.

🟊 Parker Playhouse

441

842

Plantation

7

Hist.
Mus.

Powerline

1

🟊 Mus.
of Art

W Broward Blvd.

Blvd.

Discovery

Las Olas Blvd.

842

🏄 Ft. Lauderdale Beach
Bahia Mar Yachting Center

N. Fork

New River

5

🟊 Sightseeing Train

Davie Blvd.

SW 12th St.

Peters Rd.

736

31st St.

S. Fork

17th St.

A1A

Fern Crest Village

River Lands Rd.

Causeway

Everglades Pkwy.

817 Davie

84

SW 24th St.

Port - Everglades

FORT
LAUDERDALE

Davie
Arena

91

University Dr.

FLORIDA'S TURNPIKE (TOLL)

Orange Dr.

Ft.
Lauderdale
Hollywood
Int'l Airport

Dania Cut-off Canal

🏄 John U. Lloyd
State Recreation Area

Griffin Rd.

818

Dania
Jai Alai
Palace

🟊 Indian Mus. &
Art Gallery

Seminole Okalee
Indian Village

95

A1A

848

Stirling

🟊 Yugnee

St.

Dania

Davie Rd.

🟊 Topeekeegee
Regional Park

🟊 Atlantis

Sheridan St.

822

Sheridan St.

822

Ocean Blvd.

West Lake

North L.

Pines Blvd.

Hollywood Blvd.

820

Hollywood Blvd.

South L.

🏄 Hollywood Beach

North
Perry

Pembroke
Pines

HOLLYWOOD

824

Pembroke

NW 47th Ave.

NW 2nd Ave.

Rd.

1

Miramar

858

Hallandale Beach

Blvd.

Pembroke
Park

832

Hallandale

5

821

County Line Rd.

Buccaneer

Golden
Beach

**FT. LAUDERDALE
AND ENVIRONS**

0   2   4 km

0   2   miles

77

Full-scale progress came about when a former gunrunner, Napoleon Bonaparte Broward, won the governorship in 1904 and embarked upon a campaign to drain the Everglades in order to create new farm land. The first settlement to be founded in the region was named Zona – though nobody knows why – then Panama, because dredgers had previously worked on the canal there. Ultimately, it was renamed, as often happens, after the area's largest landowner, a man by the name of **Davie**.

Throughout the Roaring Twenties, the boom years in the rest of south Florida, Broward County also prospered, giving rise to the vast development of **Hollywood-by-the-Sea** and to the Venice-like islands subdivision of Fort Lauderdale. In the 1950s, though, some canals were dredged and land filled for development, resulting in the new communities of

Above: A quiet beach – a good place for a leisurely walk in the evening. Right: Enthusiasm for baseball is alive and well in Florida.

Plantation, **Cooper City**, **Coral Springs**, **Sunrise** and **Tamarac**. Today, the population is still growing, with numbers hitting the 1.3 million mark in the 1990s; double what it was 20 years ago.

Many newer residents are retirees, and many businesses and services are geared specifically to them. For example, nearly every restaurant offers an "Early Bird Special," which is a bargain-priced dinner served between 5 and 7 p.m. A lot of senior citizens, who tend to go to bed rather early, certainly seem to be satisfied with this arrangement.

The American Venice

Fort Lauderdale likes to call itself "The Venice of America" because it has so many canals – 300 miles of inland waterways. Cruising on them can be the best introduction to the area.

You could take the *Jungle Queen*, an old-time steamboat that travels through the center of Fort Lauderdale. It leaves from the Bahia Mar dock on Route A1A. The *Paddlewheel Queen*, another steamboat, carries sightseers along the Intracoastal Waterway from 2950 NE 30th Street.

Another possibility is taking a water taxi; if you have a knowledgeable and talkative skipper, you will even get a guided tour into the bargain. Taxis can be hailed from the shore along A1A, picked up at hotels or phoned. And at Christmas time, Fort Lauderdale hosts a wonderful boat parade on the Intracoastal that is one of the highlights of the season.

For many, though, sightseeing is less important than sunning. The area has 23 miles of beaches, and these beaches remain the prime destination. Now that the hard-drinking kids are gone, the famous beach on the Fort Lauderdale strip, from **Las Olas Boulevard** to **Sunrise Boulevard**, is a beauty.

The shops along the strip, though, are still a nightmare: garish and junky, just

the way the student revelers liked. This is where you can stock up on T-shirts and tacky souvenirs. Still, after a period of transformation, the area is certain to be made more appealing to the more discriminating tourist.

Another popular beach is located in the middle of a state park, the **John U. Lloyd Beach State Recreation Area**, at 6503 N. Ocean Drive, Dania. Besides swimming, fishing and canoeing can also be enjoyed here in one of the more natural areas left amid the urban megalopolis that is growing, from Miami to Palm Beach and beyond, along the southeastern coast of the state.

For more serious fishing, head north to **Pompano Beach** and the rebuilt **municipal pier**; extending 1,080 feet into the Atlantic, it is said to be the longest fishing pier in Florida. If you prefer to do your fishing in even deeper seas, though, you can charter a boat in Pompano Beach at the **Hillsboro Inlet**, or at the **Bahia Mar Yachting Center** in Fort Lauderdale.

Recreational Pursuits by Day...

Snorkelers and divers find an interesting underwater world around Fort Lauderdale, where a number of sunken ships serve as housing for tropical fish and coral. The coral grows on the hulls of the ships, and where coral grows, fish soon appear, bringing new life to the depleted reef. Altogether there are 17 such underwater destinations. Perhaps the best-known of these wrecks is the **Mercedes**, a 200-foot freighter that had the bad luck to run aground near Fort Lauderdale. It is now submerged in 100 feet of water a mile off Fort Lauderdale Beach. Not far away is another sunken freighter, the **Poinciana**.

Short courses for those interested in diving, with or without hotel accomodation being arranged, can be booked though Lauderdale Diver, 1334 SE 17th Street Causeway, Fort Lauderdale, or Pro Dive, which works in conjunction with the Bahia Mar Resort and Yachting Center, on the A1A in Fort Lauderdale.

This is also a major area for golf, with many resorts, such as the **Diplomat** in Hollywood, offering ecomonimcal package deals for golfers. There are also a number of public courses available; some 50 in all in the county.

For rainy day amusements, the area has two major "beauty farms" open to the public on a daily basis: the **Sheraton Bonaventure Resort and Spa** in Fort Lauderdale, at 250 Racquet Club Drive, and the **Palm-Aire Spa Resort** in Pompano Beach, at 2501 Palm-Aire Drive North. Exercise programs, herbal wraps, massages and facials can be arranged, as can longer stays.

Other non-sun activities include a visit to the **Seminole Okalee Indian Village**, a reservation of the Seminole tribe, where crafts are sold, alligators are wrestled for the public's amusement, and a hot bingo game is held three times a day (4150 N. Route 7 in Hollywood).

Above: Retirees can be found just about anywhere in Florida.

Nearby is another preserve of the Seminole, the **Anhinga Indian Museum and Art Gallery**, at 5791 S. Route 7, where artifacts are displayed and contemporary arts and crafts are sold. And for smokers, the Seminoles sell cigarettes at prices lower than retail stores. Just drive along **Hollywood Boulevard**, north of the city of Hollywood, and watch for the signs.

If Native Americans have their home base in Hollywood, would-be cowboys ride the range in Davie. The popularity of horses around here gave rise to an all pervasive Western flavor, complete with a town hall flanked by cacti – not a native plant – and hitching posts. And swinging saloon doors serve as the entrance to the Town Council chambers. Even the local McDonald's has hitching posts and an elevated ride-through window for customers on horseback.

If you want to get into the proper attire, there are plenty of Western specialty stores in town. Then you can head out to the rodeo, held every Friday night at the domed **Davie Rodeo Arena**, at 6591 SW 45th Street in Davie.

...and by Night

Besides the rodeo, the area has another extremely popular nighttime destination: the **Dania Jai-Alai Palace**, at 301 East Dania Beach Blvd. in Dania, where you can bet on one of the fastest moving sports in the world, jai-alai, which looks somewhat like souped-up racquetball.

If your taste runs more to music than gambling, try the **Musician's Exchange Downtown Cafe**, a small club that features local bands, as well as big name jazz, rock, folk and reggae artists and groups who might be passing through (729 W. Sunrise Blvd., Fort Lauderdale).

For theater, pre- or post-Broadway productions can be seen at the **Parker Playhouse**, 707 NE 8th Street, Fort Lauderdale.

FORT LAUDERDALE / BROWARD COUNTY
Area Code 954

Arrival
Flying into Fort Lauderdale takes you to the **Fort Lauderdale Hollywood Airport**, once a sleepy little airport, now an immense ever-expanding complex. There is scant bus service to and from the airport. Many travelers prefer limousine service or taxis.

Accommodation
LUXURY: **Pier 66 Resort and Marina**, 2301 SE 17th Street, Fort Lauderdale, tel. 525-6666, circular high-rise overlooking the Intracoastal Waterway and fantasy pleasure boats; **Westin Cypress Creek**, 400 Corporate Drive, Fort Lauderdale, tel. 772-1331, flashy business hotel with a lobby inspired by an Egyptian temple; **Inverrary Hotel and Conference Center**, 3501 Inverrary Blvd. Lauderhill, tel. 485-0500, fountains, marble, crystal chandeliers; **Marriott's Harbor Beach Resort**, a deluxe tower set against 16 acres of oceanfront at 3030 Holiday Drive, Fort Lauderdale, tel. 525-4000; **Riverside Hotel**, small, European-style hotel at Fort Lauderdale's best shopping mall, 620 E. Las Olas Blvd., tel. 467-0671; **Bahia Mar Resort and Yachting Center**, 801 Seabreeze Blvd., Fort Lauderdale, tel. 764-2233, terrific views of the Intracoastal Waterway and the ocean.
MODERATE AND BUDGET: **Banyan Marina Apartments**, 111 Isle of Venice, Fort Lauderdale, tel. 524-4430, this is the best of the small hotels, canalside; **Holiday Inn Fort Lauderdale Beach**, 999 North Atlantic Blvd., Fort Lauderdale, tel. 563-5961; **Clarion Hotel**, on the Intracoastal Waterway, 4000 S. Ocean Drive, Hollywood, tel. 458-1900.

Restaurants
Cap's Place, Cap's Dock, 2765 NE 28th Ct., Lighthouse Point, tel. 941-0418, fresh seafood in an island beach shanty – the restaurant's launch takes you out. Popular with Roosevelt and Churchill during World War II, JFK after; **Burt and Jack's**, Berth 23, Port Everglades, Fort Lauderdale, tel. 522-5225, one of area resident Burt Reynolds' contributions – a Spanish villa with steaks and seafood; **Le Dome**, 333 Sunset Drive, Fort Lauderdale, tel. 463-3303, chic rooftop restaurant with *nouvelle américain* cuisine; **Café Max**, 2601 E. Atlantic Blvd., Pompano Beach, tel. 782-0606, California cuisine; **Shirttail Charlie's**, 400 SW 3rd Avenue, Fort Lauderdale, 463-3474, casual dockside cafe with fresh seafood; **Shooter's Waterfront Café U.S.A.**, 3033 NE 32nd Ave., Fort Lauderdale, tel. 566-2855, lively restaurant featuring seafood and Mexican food; **Padrino's**, 2500 E. Hallandale Beach Blvd., Hallandale, tel. 456-4550, Cuban cuisine.

Sights
Butterfly World is a 2.8-acre property which houses a screened-in tropical rain forest that is home to 150 species of butterflies. Guided tours are available, 3600 W. Sample Road, Coconut Creek, tel. 977-4400.
Two prized houses of Fort Lauderdale are now museums:
Stranahan House, on the New River (1 Stranahan Place tel. 524-4736), is the oldest residence in the city and dates from 1901, eight years after Frank Stranahan established his Indian trading post at the river. The house has been beautifully restored to its frontier character.
Bonnet House (900 N. Birch Rd., tel. 563-5393) is a 35-acre estate from the early 1920s, built by artist Frederic Clay Bartlett. Today the whimsically artistic house, the tropical grounds and the companion Birch Park (see below) are open to the public from May to November.

Shopping
This is mall country, and the spiffiest of all is the **Galleria** on Sunrise Boulevard, west of the Intracoastal. All the top shops plus upscale department stores, such as Neiman-Marcus, Lord and Taylor, and Saks Fifth Avenue are here.
For discount shopping head to **Sawgrass Mills**, located in Sunrise – one of the world's largest outlet malls.

Parks
Hugh Taylor Birch State Recreation Area, 3109 East Sunrise Boulevard, Fort Lauderdale, tel. 564-4521.
John U. Lloyd Beach State Recreation Area, 6503 North Ocean Drive, Dania, tel. 923-2833.

Tourist Information
Main tourist office: **The Greater Fort Lauderdale Convention and Visitors Bureau**, 200 E. Las Olas Blvd., Fort Lauderdale, tel.765-4466.
The Greater Fort Lauderdale Chamber of Commerce, 512 NE 3rd Ave., Fort Lauderdale, tel. 462-6000.
The Coral Springs Chamber of Commerce, 9801 W. Sample Road, 110, Coral Springs, tel. 752-4242.
The Dania Chamber of Commerce, P.O. Box 838, Dania, tel. 927-3377.
The Davie-Cooper City Chamber of Commerce, 4185 Southwest 64th Ave., Davie, tel. 581-0790.
The Greater Deerfield Beach Chamber of Commerce, 1601 East Hillsboro Blvd., Deerfield Beach, tel. 427-1050.
The Greater Fort Lauderdale Traveler's Assistance, call 527-5600 for immediate, easy-to-follow travel directions.

PALM BEACH

If ever a name was synonymous with society, it is **Palm Beach**. Elegant, expensive and exclusive – mansions, Rolls Royces and extravagant parties are pretty much ordinary sights here.

Oil millionaire and railroad magnate Henry Flagler, owner of the Florida East Coast Railway, who was so instrumental in developing Florida's coast, essentially created Palm Beach as a winter resort for his friends, and for the rich and famous of the time. He built a hotel for them, the **Royal Poinciana**, in 1894, and in 1896 built another, called **The Breakers**. It was made of wood and was destroyed in a fire early on. It was rebuilt and burned down again.

In 1926, Flagler's heirs decided to put an end to inflammable hotels and rebuilt the hotel in stone. Now as then, this hotel stands as the centerpiece of Palm Beach's grandeur.

The area is not all high end, though, which is the reason people sometimes stress the name as "Palm Beaches," not just Palm Beach. Flagler built **West Palm Beach**, a city across **Lake Worth**, to house the servants of the Palm Beach mansions; today it is the commercial center, and the place where the more down-to-earth reside.

To the south lies **Boca Raton**, an affluent city with its elegant, pink Spanish Revival-style villas, and an architectural jewel: the Boca Raton Resort, a luxury hotel built by Addison Mizner in the 1920s. To the north, **Palm Beach Gardens** is a paradise for golfers.

In exclusive Palm Beach, there is no room for wild clothing, eccentric behavior or loud rock music. In fact, this is a town that takes its noise laws very seriously: car horns are not honked here; even the tennis ball machines are only

Left: Palm trees often serve as welcome beach parasols.

allowed to operate during certain hours. Residents take pains to observe the laws, too; one woman even had her parrot's decibel level tested by the police, who set their instruments up outside her kitchen window. The bird just barely passed.

Incidentally, the Palm Beach police are headquartered in what what must be the prettiest precinct station in America: an elegant pink stucco house, surrounded by palms.

Luxury Residences in Palm Beach

To get the true sense of Palm Beach, the best place to start would probably be **The Breakers** hotel. It may remind you of a grand Italian *palazzo*, or – if you have traveled in Italy – several specific villas: the exterior is copied from the Villa Medici in Florence, the gardens and courtyard are similar to the ones at Villa Sante in Rome, and the Mediterranean Ballroom is inspired by Genoa's Palazzo Imperiale.

To learn more about the hotel, the area and Henry Flagler, guests can take the tour conducted by the hotel's "historian" every Wednesday. The tour begins in the south loggia on the ground floor, with a discussion of Flagler's development of the east coast of Florida; from his first hotel, the Ponce de Leon in St. Augustine in 1888, to his railroad, the Florida East Coast Railway. Flagler's goal for the railroad was Key West, the state's southernmost point, from where the harbor of Havana was only 90 miles away. When his trains reached it in 1912, he announced that he could now die happy. The following year, he did, in fact, die.

Moving through the rooms, the guide also points out the lavish decorations – from hand-painted ceiling frescos to 15th-century Flemish tapestries – and the hotel's brushes with historic events: a private club met during Prohibition in one room; and the hotel served briefly as a (lavish) hospital during World War II.

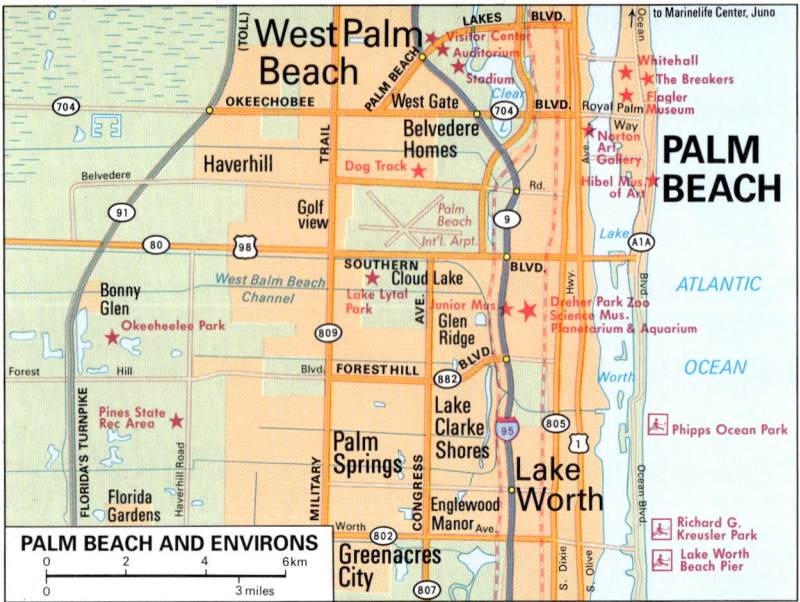

PALM BEACH AND ENVIRONS

During this time, German submarines cruised just off the beach.

To get a more in-depth look at lavishness as it applied to Henry Flagler, go over to **Whitehall** – now the Flagler Museum – on Cocoanut Row. This 55-room mansion is pure opulence, a palace built by Flagler, then 72, in 1902, at a cost of $2.5 million (it's now assessed at over $12 million) as a wedding present for his third wife, Mary Lily Kenan. He then spent another $1.5 million furnishing it with Baccarat crystal chandeliers, silk damask wallpaper, seven different types of Italian marble, and a lot of antique furniture from Europe. As you walk through it you are awed by the luxury, made even more remarkable by the fact that this was intended as a vacation house, for use only from January through March.

If Whitehall whets your appetite for mansions, there is an unending string of them on **Ocean Boulevard**; you can

Right: One of the posher hotels in the United States – The Breakers.

drive slowly by and look to your heart's content. Perhaps the most noticeable is **Mar-a-Lago**, at 1100 S. Ocean, breakfast cereal heiress Marjorie Merriweather Post's 128-room mansion built in 1927 on 16 acres of land. Tycoon Donald Trump bought the estate a few years ago, and immediately discovered that despite its extravagance, it was noisy – it is straight in the flight path to the West Palm Beach Airport. Reportedly, he tried to have the flight path moved, but scored a rare defeat.

On the north end of the street is an estate owned by the Kennedys. The estate, at 1095 N. Ocean Blvd., served as the Florida White House during John Kennedy's tenure as President, and traffic usually jammed as the curious lined up to take a look. They might also stop for a drink; JFK nieces Maria Shriver and Sydney Lawford, showing their grandfather's entrepreneurial spirit, sometimes set up a lemonade stand in front of the estate.

For a more relaxing view of different mansions, you can take a paddleboat up

the Intracoastal starting from **Phil Foster Park** on **Singer Island**, north of Palm Beach (Island Queen Riverboat Cruises, 1250 E. Blue Heron Blvd., Riviera Beach, tel. 842-0882). These mansions front Lake Worth and their famous owners are identified. One, for example, belonged to John Lennon and Yoko Ono.

Also identified is a small island of some historic note: **Peanut Island**, where a bomb shelter was built for the obviously pessimistic Kennedys during the Cuban Missile Crisis.

Also of some historic note, and definitely of shopping note, is **Worth Avenue**, extending in from Ocean Boulevard. It is hard to top such concentrated wealth: every major name in upscale retailing is represented here, from Porthault, Pratesi, Laura Ashley, Hermes and Chanel to a disproportionately large number of fine jewelers.

Of special note is Hamilton Jewelers, where the largest impulse buy on the street was recorded: a diamond necklace for $1.6 million. It is also hard to im-

agine, looking at "The Avenue," that it had very humble beginnings: at the turn of the century it was the site of **Alligator Joe's Farm**, a tourist attraction whose proprietor, "Alligator Joe" Frazier, collected 6,000 alligators, and wrestled a number of them for spectators. Towards the end of the First World War, though, "Alligator Joe" sold the land to local resident and sewing machine heir Paris Singer, who planned to build a veterans' hospital on it.

Singer hired his friend, society architect Addison Mizner, to design it, but Mizner took so long with his plans that by the time he finished, the war was over and few veterans wanted to use it. So they turned the hospital into the exclusive **Everglades Club**, and Mizner built elegant, Spanish-style shops and apartments leading up the avenue to it.

Today, those shops are filled not just with famous names, but also with one-of-a-kind items. Worth checking out: **The Summerhouse**, at 319 Worth, stocks antique porcelain, silver and accessories;

Donald Bruce, at 237 Worth, stocks an eclectic variety of indulgences, from quail eggs to gold jewelry. Bruce, whose family came to Palm Beach in 1928, is also an unofficial, irreverent historian of the area.

At **Frances Brewster**, 259 Worth, you will find outrageously opulent evening gowns, perfect for society galas and other important events. At **D. Kylene**, they stock upscale women's sportswear. You might meet Yankee, a parrot with a scandalous vocabulary who belongs to owner Kylene Barker Brandon, a former Miss America (1979). As you walk, you will notice that the names of many of the side streets are Italian – Via Parigi, Via Roma, Via de Mario, etc.

To see more of Addison Mizner's designs, a good place to stop, as well as to stay, is the **Boca Raton Resort**, in the town of the same name. This somewhat outrageous pink complex was Mizner's

dream-come-true: "the greatest resort in the world, a happy combination of Venice and heaven, Florence and Toledo, with a little Greco-Roman glory and grandeur thrown in," is how he described it.

When it opened as the Spanish-styled Cloister Inn in 1926, it was the most expensive 100-room hotel in the world. Mizner furnished it elegantly, with his own Spanish antiques, and celebrities flocked there – in part because of Mizner himself. Totally charming and eccentric, he would walk the grounds dressed in silk pajamas, leading around a few of his pets – monkeys, macaws, chows, chimpanzees. Mizner's reign ended after one season, though, when the Florida land boom went bust and he went bankrupt. His Cloister Inn re-opened under a new owner as the Boca Raton Hotel and Club.

Nightlife

If you are looking for activity after (or during) dinner, a popular spot is the **Palm**

Above: Beauty-contest – and the winner is...
Right: Ready to go body surfing.

86

Beach Kennel Club (a.k.a. The Dog Track) in West Palm Beach, near the airport, at 1111 Congress Avenue. It may sound and seem cruel, but the kennel personnel insist that the dogs really need to race. Some may have doubts. Betting is rather complicated. You can ignore the whole thing and just concentrate on dinner instead; hearty all American steaks, in their restaurant, the **Paddock**. Other possibilities for nightlife include traditional bars like **Bradley's**, on Bradley Place in Palm Beach, or **Alligator Joe**, 132 North County Road, which has live music and dancing.

Another activity is slightly more adventurous. If it is the right time of year (May through September) you can go on a nocturnal tour up on **Jupiter Beach**. Loggerhead turtles come ashore during those months to deposit their eggs in the sand, and observation trips – observing from a distance without bothering the turtles – are arranged through the Jupiter Beach Resort, at 5 A1A North in Jupiter. Consult them for times (tel. 746-2521).

Rare Sea Turtles

It probably seems at least a little strange that some 200 of the most prized residents of this bastion of the ultra-wealthy are supporters of several perilously endangered species of giant sea turtles. But guilt can do strange things to people. There is no doubt that at least part of the blame for the turtles near demise belongs to the rampant development along Florida's Atlantic coast, destroying annual breeding grounds in the march of progress.

Yet somehow, the **Jupiter Beach Resort** beachfront remains smooth and rock-free, gently sloping and well-protected by coastal vegetation, just the way these remaining loggerhead, leatherback and green sea turtles – some of them over 50 years old and weighing up to 350 pounds – like it. Swimming ashore from deeper water, some from the far distant waters of New York, South America and the Caribbean, females enter the hotel harbor-reef to dig their nests in the sand.

The slow-moving creatures chose this beach long before bipeds seeking sun and sand for recreation took it over. In fact, the seasonal appearance of the giant sea turtles lumbering out of the depths used to startle unwary guests from late-May through September, in the days before the "Turtle Watch" became a certified attraction. The hotel takes great pains to promote the environmental and conservation concerns surrounding this prehistoric ritual, at the same time aware of the obvious potential for visitors at a special time of year; a traditionally "soft" time, too, when bookings are at their lowest.

They tend not to mention what the curiosity of humans has done to upset the turtles: out of every 100 eggs produced, only a few survive. Humans, of course, poking and prying, pose one of the greatest threats to the turtles, along with predatory animals, storms, ocean currents and perhaps saddest of all, coastal pollution.

Above: These turtles are said to reach biblical ages.

Round-the-Clock Turtle Watch

The "Turtle Watch" program is one effort to help reinstate the balance of nature by protecting the sea turtle. Overseen by Florida's Department of Natural Resources, it is headed by a licensed marine researcher.

Along with endeavors to preserve and protect the turtles, programs offered to human visitors include such things as evening slide shows and lectures, providing background information on the turtles, their habits and the ongoing work to protect them, guided nocturnal tours of nesting sites along the hotel's beach, daytime patrols of egg hatcheries, where protective incubation pens have been set up, and the organized releasing of the young hatchlings into the sea, always a popular event.

In addition to the "Turtle Watch," there is the **Marinelife Center** in Juno Beach, a small marine biology museum and aquarium featuring exhibits especially designed for children.

PALM BEACH
Area Code 561

Arrival and Transportation
Flights arrive at Palm Beach Int'l Airport. Palm Beach Transportation provides taxis and limousines.

Accommodation
LUXURY: **The Breakers**, 1 S. County Road, Palm Beach, tel. 655-6611, elegant and formal.

Brazilian Court, 301 Australian Avenue, Palm Beach, tel. 655-7740, low-key, low-rise Mediterranean-style buildings with private, leafy courtyards. The management takes pride in its discretion – as a result, David – son of Robert – Kennedy's death from a drug overdose here was very unwanted publicity.

The Colony, 155 Hammon Avenue, Palm Beach, tel. 655-5430, small, elegant European-style hotel recently reopened, just off Worth Avenue.

Boca Raton Resort and Club, 501 E. Camino Real, Boca Raton, tel. 395-3000, pink palace with all sporting facilities.

PGA National Resort, 400 Avenue of the Champions, Palm Beach Gardens, tel. 627-2000, a golfer's paradise with five PGA courses.

Palm Beach Polo and Country Club, 13198 Forest Hill Blvd., West Palm Beach, tel. 798-7000, you do not have to play polo to stay in one of the luxury villas.

Jupiter Beach Resort, 5 North A1A, know for turtle watching.

MODERATE TO BUDGET: **Holiday Inn Sunspree Resort on Singer Island**, 3700 North Ocean Drive, Singer Island, tel. 848-3888.

Restaurants
Charley's Crab, 456 Ocean Blvd., tel. 659-1500, a huge waterfront seafood extravaganza; **Chuck and Harold's**, 207 Royal Poinciana Way, Palm Beach, tel. 659-1440, outdoor café in the town center, also open for breakfast and lunch; the **Dining Room** of the Brazilian Court is a sophisticated, expensive restaurant with dishes based on local ingredients, 401 Australian Avenue, Palm Beach; **The Breakers**, specifically for Sunday brunch.

Sports and Recreation
It is possible to stay in this area and only look at bastions of wealth, but it can, after a while, drive you crazy. This is where nature, the great leveler, comes in. Palm Beach is located at the tip of the Everglades, and there is a short (half-hour), interesting wildlife-spotting ride through the **Loxahatchee Wildlife Reserve** south of Palm Beach in Delray Beach. You travel in airboats, noisy things for passengers, but which do not seem to bother the animals. It is best to go early. More wildlife sightings occur during the

morning, but even if you go in late afternoon, you are bound to see at least a few alligators and birds.

For complete information contact: **Arthur R. Marshall Loxahatchee National Wildlife Refuge**, US 441 between Boynton Blvd. and Atlantic Ave., Boynton Beach, tel 734-8303.

Lion Country Safari provides a chance to see wildlife close-up. Eight miles of road through a 500-acre cageless zoo. Lions, elephants, white rhinos, giraffes and zebras. Southern Blvd. W., tel. 793-1084.

If it is polo season, January-April, you might want to take in a game at **Palm Beach Polo**, a club of such note that polo fanatic Prince Charles plays there and stays there when he is in town. 13240 Southshore Blvd., West Palm Beach, tel. 798-7000.

Croquet is also fun, although the real game is harder and more exacting than the backyard variety – it takes real muscle and strategy. Professional croquet lawns and lessons are available at the **PGA National Resort** in Palm Beach Gardens, north of Palm Beach. Players are advised to wear white. 400 Avenue of the Champions, Palm Beach Gardens, tel. 627-2000.

If fishing is your sport, you can also charter a boat for deep sea fishing north of Palm Beach at **Boomerang Tours**, 98 Lake Drive, Palm Beach Shores, tel. 844-4356, and at the **B-Love Fishing Marina**, 314 East Ocean Avenue, Lantana, tel. 588-7612.

Museums
The **Norton Gallery of Art**, 1451 South Olive Avenue, West Palm Beach, 33401, tel. 832-5194, is considered one of Floridas's major cultural attractions. Permanent exhibits are supplemented by temporary exhibits year-round. Open Tuesday-Saturday, 10 am to 5 pm, Sunday, 1 pm to 5 pm. Admission free. French- or Spanish-speaking guides are available.

The **South Florida Science Museum**, 4801 Dreher Trail North, West Palm Beach, tel. 832-1988, features permanent and temporary hands-on science exhibits for children and adults, science demonstrations, planetarium shows and the **South Florida Aquarium**. Open Tuesday-Saturday, 1 am to 5 pm, Sunday, noon to 5 pm, Friday, 6:30 pm to 10 pm. Admission free.

Shopping
The Esplanade stands near the end of glittering Worth Avenue. This small structure houses stores such as Saks Fifth Avenue, Ralph Lauren – indeed, all the right names.

Tourist Information
For more information about Palm Beach County, contact **The Palm Beach County Convention and Visitors Bureau**, 1555 Palm Beach Lakes Blvd., Suite 204, West Palm Beach, FL 33401, tel. (561) 471-3995.

THE FLORIDA KEYS

Most visitors fall in love with the Keys at first sight: for the pale turquoise of the shallows and the ink-blue Gulf Stream; for skies that make the palm fronds greener and the coral rock and sand beaches whiter. For bougainvillaea's pinks, corals and purples; for soaring eagles, man-of-war birds, pelicans flying in formation, and rows of kingfishers on telephone wires; for seafans, coral, angelfish and grouper.

They love the wooden gingerbread houses built in the Bahamas and the sense of history at Indian Key Archeological Site, Mel Fisher's Treasure Museum, and Fort Jefferson in the Dry Tortugas; the tranquility of an afternoon sail in Florida Bay or the rhythmic dip of the paddle through channels surrounded by man-

grove forests, and the excitement of the first big strike while trolling at the edge of the Gulf Stream. They look forward to the sunset celebrations in Key West, frozen margaritas and Jimmy Buffett tunes.

The Keys, from *cayo,* meaning little island in Spanish, can be divided into the Upper, Middle and Lower Keys, and Key West. Hotels, restaurants and attractions are easily located with the mile marker (MM) system. Key West, for example, is at MM 0 and Jewfish Creek at MM 108 on Key Largo. Just look for the green and white markers.

Henry Flagler's railway, laid down as far south as Key West at the beginning of the 20th century – also known as "Flagler's Folly" – was destroyed by a hurricane in 1935 and was replaced by the Overseas Highway (US 1).

As in the rest of Florida, a great deal of development has been allowed to take place along the commercial corridor of the highway, destroying much of the old-fashioned charm the Keys once held.

Preceding pages: Sunset on the Keys.
Above: The Seven Mile Bridge. Right: Being
different – a must on Key West.

Therefore, a National Marine Sanctuary was created in 1991 of virtually the entire Keys, in the hope that a sanctuary management plan will help preserve the environment. Diving and fishing are the main activities hereabouts. All along the Overseas Highway you'll find marinas where you can rent small boats by the hour, or charter a captained boat for deep-sea fishing, diving or back-country exploration.

The Upper and Middle Keys

Not counting the boat-access-only islands of **Biscayne National Park**, the **Upper Keys** begin at **Key Largo**, with its crocodile refuge at the northern end, and many small, old-fashioned lodges along the bayside.

Its main claim to fame is the **John Pennecamp Coral Reef State Park** (MM 102.5). It protects a good portion of the only living coral reef in the United States. Shipwrecks and reefs, with evocative names such as "The Elbow," "Grecian Rocks" and "Molasses," can be explored by one of the park service or private diving company charter boats. For diving, snorkeling and glass-bottom boat trips to the reef, the winds should be calm for optimal viewing conditions. Morning hours are usually best, especially in summer, when afternoon thunderstorms are common.

Farther along the road are several commercial tourist attractions, including the **Theater of the Sea** (MM 84.5), the second-oldest marine park in the world, which introduced bottle-nosed dolphins to thousands of visitors. It is a good show if you have never seen performing dolphins or if you like trained animal acts.

Upon leaving **Islamorada**, a true El Dorado for sport fishing, the highway continues from island to island towards the southwest. Many of the bridges were built recently, leaving the older ones to serve as convenient fishing piers. Hark-

ing back to earlier times are some nice, old-fashioned picnic shelters and little beaches, perfect spots for wading and swimming. If you venture out with fins and a snorkel, be sure to tow along a small bouy with a dive flag so that passing boaters will be aware of you.

Just past Islamorada, off Indian Key Fill (MM 79), are the **Indian Key State Historic Site** and the **Lignumvitae Key State Botanical Site**, which can be reached by a private rental or park service boat. Lignumvitae Key is a naturalist's paradise, with an intact tropical habitat that contains many of the local plant species, birds, butterflies and tree snails.

Long Key, the next large island after leaving Lower Matecumbe, is the site of the **Long Key State Recreation Area** (MM 67.5). Shaded by tall Australian pines, it's a fine spot for a picnic. Put on your bathing suits and enjoy splashing in the shallow waters. Bird watchers may want to take the nature trail or rent a canoe from the rangers to explore the natural riches along the marked trail.

It was here at Long Key that Henry Flagler built his famous fishing club, where Western author Zane Grey and other luminaries came to fish.

The **Middle Keys** are connected by long bridges, with **Long Key Viaduct** on one end and Seven Mile Bridge on the other.

Some 8,000 people live in the small town of **Marathon**. Here there are shopping centers and trailer parks, a yacht harbor and golf course, accommodations and the convenience of an airport offering daily flights to and from Miami. The **Museum of Natural History of the Florida Keys** interestingly documents the natural history of the Keys, and has a children's section and educational nature trail. On **Grassy Key**, the **Dolphin Research Center** can be visited. Many come to the Middle Keys for the deep-sea fishing tournaments and back-country fishing. **Sombrero Reef**, **Coffin's Patch** and **Looe Key**, with their large coral reefs and multitudes of tropical fish, attract divers from all over the world.

The Lower Keys

Leaving the Middle Keys presents a stunning sight: the **Seven Mile Bridge** swings out to sea in a high arch to accommodate the deep ships' channel, paralleling the old bridge, the world's longest fishing pier. At MM 37 you enter **Bahia Honda State Recreation Area**, with the finest ocean beach in the Keys: fine white sand beaches border turquoise-blue water and palm trees sway in the wind. There are cabins for rent here, but they are high priced and close to the road. Beach campsites are better, and as a bonus there is the high rising skeleton of the old railroad and car bridge – impressive in its way.

Big Pine Key shelters the **National Key Deer Refuge**. Off the main highway, sightings of this tiny deer are frequent in morning and evening hours, but their numbers are diminishing fast; the

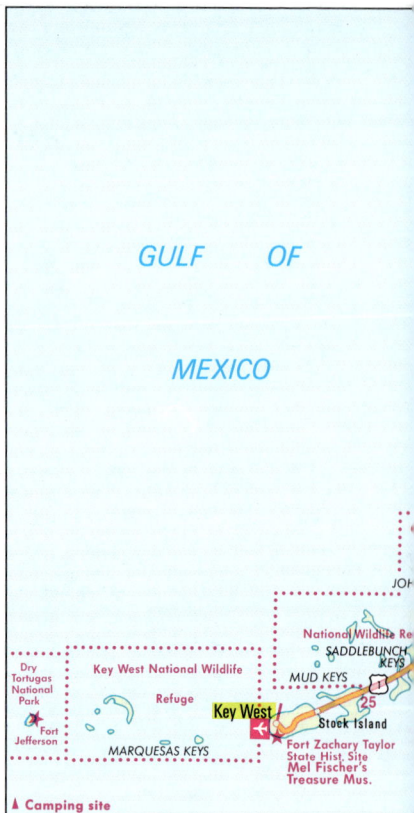

victims of road accidents and habitat depletion. **Looe Key National Marine Sanctuary**, only six miles from land and accessible by diving boat from either Marathon or **Ramrod Key** (MM 27), is, according to many divers, more beautiful than the Pennekamp Reefs.

The many islands, like **Lower Sugarloaf** and **Saddlebunch Keys**, the **Coupon Bight State Aquatic Preserve** and **Watson Hammock** on Big Pine Key can be explored by canoe or small motor boat – a respite before crowded Key West.

Key West

Key West is an ebullient haven for artists, writers, free spirits, homosexuals,

Map labels:

Pa-hay-Okee Overlook · Homestead · Naranja · ELLIOTT
Harney · Visitors Center & Park Hdqrs. · Florida City · Islandia KEY
Shark Pt. · Everglades · Long Pine Key · 905
Ponce de Leon Bay · The · National · 27 · Key Largo KEY
Whitewater Bay · Mahogany Hammock · Everglades · Barnes Sound · Turtle
Cape · Nine Mile Pond · LARGO
Northwest Cape · Park · Seven Palm Lake · Blackwater S. · Harbor · National Marine
Sable · West Lake Trail · Channel
Middle Cape · Lake Ingraham · Snake Bight · EAGLE KEY · Key Largo · John Pennekamp Coral Reef S.P.
East Cape · Flamingo · Flamingo · Sanctuary
FRANK KEY · Sunset Point · Tavernier
Florida Bay · 34 · PLANTATION KEY
Plantation · Mc Kee's Museum
Lignumvitae Key St. Botanical Site · UPPER MATECUMBE KEY · Theat. of the Sea
Islamorada
Indian Key St. Hist. Site
LONG KEY · LOWER MATECUMBE KEY
Layton · Channel Two
Heron · Great White Heron N.W.R. · GRASSY KEY · Long Key St. Rec. Area
TORCH · NO NAME KEY · 20 · Long Key Viaduct
BIG PINE KEY · Duck Key · Key Colony Beach
amrod Key · Seven Mile Bridge · Institute of Marine Science · Marathon
23 · Big Pine Key · Bahia Honda St. Rec. Area
DAF
e Key Nat'l. e Sanctuary · F L O R I D A   K E Y S

THE KEYS
0 — 20 km
0 — 10 miles

hippies and at least one million tourists a year. Like the rest of Florida, it has a violent history. Possession of the island passed back and forth between the Spanish and British several times. Incredibly lucrative salvage prizes from the many ships that grounded on the reefs and shoals, sponging and cigar-making made **Key West** the richest city per capita in the United States in the 19th century.

Yet in the 1930s, Key West went bankrupt, and its citizens suffered abject poverty from the lethal combination of hurricane destruction of the railroad, the Depression, labor troubles, sponge disease and the closing of the naval base. People were so poor that many of the old wooden tumble-down houses here that

rest in the shade of large, hundred-year-old royal poincianas, long remained uninhabited.

It wasn't until 1961 that the **Audubon House**, built orignally in 1830, with its tropical garden and wonderful Audubon bird engravings, was resored. Efforts were then made to save the old "conch" houses. A number of the early houses had been shipped piecemeal from the Bahamas, others were built from the materials of shipwrecks. They incorporate the fancies and skills of ship's carpenters, and a wide variety of architectural and environmental influences, like wide porches, steep roofs, cisterns, shuttered window and rooftop hatches. Some houses have been turned into bed and

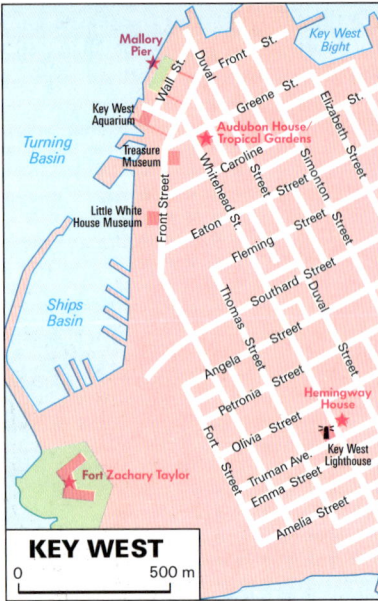

KEY WEST
0   500 m

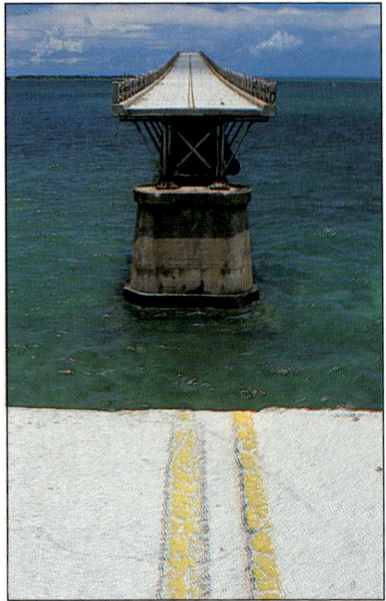

breakfast inns: the place to stay for the more modest visitor. An alternative is the renovated **Casa Marina Resort**, which is elegant and more costly.

An influx of new permanent residents, the yuppies and well-to-do individualists looking for a free and easy lifestyle, is slowly changing Key West to a city of somewhat contrived charm that is encouraging many old "conchs" (natives) who can not or will not adjust to leave.

Take in the sunset in the early evening at **Mallory Pier**. Where once ferries departed for Cuba, bagpipers, jugglers, fortune tellers and a blend of tourists and locals gather to see the day out before moving on to the many eating and drinking establishments around town.

To see the town, board the Old Town Trolley (1901 N. Roosevelt Blvd., with 14 stops), or the small-scale Conch Train. You'll visit the site of the naval base, a center of activity during the Cuban

Above: End of the road. Right: Cocktails and sunset on Key West.

Missile Crisis and the Mariel Boatlift. There is a great view from here of fishing boats and historic houses, such as President Harry S. Truman's **Little White House** (111 Front St.), the **Audubon House and Gardens** (205 Whitehead St.) and the **Hemingway House** (907 Whitehead St., with tours), and the Spanish colonial-style house where Ernest Hemingway lived with his second wife Pauline and dozens of cats.

Eighty-eight steps lead up to the viewing platform of the **Key West Lighthouse Museum** (938 Whitehead St.), an attractive white tower from the 19th century. The **Key West Aquarium** (1 Whitehead St.), which opened in 1932, features Florida's marine fauna. Highlights are the sea turtles and sharks. The **Wrecker's Museum** (322 Duval St.), built in 1839, has maritime antiques and finds from shipwrecks on display. **Mel Fisher's Treasure Museum** (200 Greene St.) exhibits treasures from the Spanish galleon *Nuestra Señora de Atocha*, discovered by Fisher: coins, in-

credible jewelry, gold- and silverware, and precious gems try to oudo each other in their sparkling beauty.

If the sight of all this wealth makes you want to splash out and spend some money, then head to the trendy boutiques, bars and restaurants on **Duval Street** downtown, where you can also get a drink at Papa Hemingway's favorite haunt, **Sloppy Joe's** (201 Duval St.).

Dining in Key West

Nowhere is the international appeal of Key West more apparent than in the wide range of dining options available.

Café Marquesa (600 Fleming Street) features spicy specialities: Delmonico steaks and *chimichuri* from Argentina; black bean and pork stew from Brazil; and Central American dishes served with red salsa. Reservations recommended. Dinners about $30-$35. **Café des Artistes** (corner of Truman Ave. and Simonton St.) features French cuisine, with local seafood served continental style. Diners can brag about having eaten in one of the city's most expensive restaurants. Reservations are necessary. Specialities include Florida lobster, grouper, yellowtail tuna, lamb, veal and filet mignon.

Louie's Backyard (700 Waddell Ave.) serves European-style cuisine with a strong French influence, spiced by the island. Reservations are necessary at this popular dining spot, where dinner for two should set you back $100 or so. **Antonia's** (615 Duval Street) specializes in pasta dishes from northern Italy, local seafood, and other Mediterranean dishes. Reservations required. Dinners about $30 per person. **Dim Sum** (Duval St.) has Indian, Thai, Burmese and Indonesian food. Reservations recommended. Dinners about $25 per person. **El Siboney** (900 Catherine Str.) is considered Key West's best Cuban restaurant and a relative bargain: dinners cost about $15. **Yer Sake** (Duval Street) serves Japanese *sushi, teriyaki* and other traditional fare. Reservations are suggested for meals that cost around $20 per person.

FLORIDA KEYS
Area Code 305

Arrival
From Miami, take the turnpike extension to US 1, south to Key West. A scenic detour is Cardsound Road, south of Florida City, to Route 905, which rejoins US 1 in the middle of Key Largo.
By Plane: Commercial service to Marathon and Key West.

Accommodation
Our choice is based on quiet, off the main road location and/or special Keys charm.
Listings are in mile marker (MM) distance from Key West.
LUXURY: **Sheraton Key Largo**, MM 97, Key Largo, tel. 852-5553, 1-800-325-3535; **Cheeca Lodge**, Box 527, Islamorada, tel. 664-4651; **Hawks Cay Resort**, MM 61, Duck Key, tel. 743-7000, 1-800-327-7775; **Hilton Key West Resort**, 245 Front St., Key West, tel. 294-4000; **Little Palm Island**, ferry at MM 28.5, Little Torch Key, tel. 872-2524, 1-800-343-8567; **Marriott's Casa Marina Resort**, 1500 Reynolds St., Key West, tel. 296-3535, 1-800-228-9290; **The Marquesa**, 600 Fleming St., Key West, tel. 292-1919; **Pier House**, One Duval St., Key West, tel. 296-4600.
MODERATE TO BUDGET: **Rock Reef Resort**, MM 98, Key Largo, tel. 852-2401; **Kona Kai**, MM 97.8, Key Largo, tel. 852-7200; **Islander**, MM 82.1, Islamorada, tel. 664-2031; **Ocean Beach Club**, near MM 54, 351 E Ocean Dr., Key Colony Beach, tel. 289-0525; **The Buccaneer**, MM 48.5, Marathon, tel. 743-9071; **Bed and Breakfast At The Barnacle**, MM 33, Long Beach Rd., Big Pine Key, tel. 872-3298; **Looe Key Reef Resort**, MM 27.5, Ramrod Key, tel. 872-2215; **Duval House**, 815 Duval St., Key West, tel. 294-1666. **The Popular House**, 415 William St., Key West, tel. 294-3630.

Restaurants
EXPENSIVE: **Marker 88**, MM 88, tel. 852-9315. **Louie's Backyard**, 700 Waddell Ave., Key West, tel. 294-1061; **Café des Artistes**, corner of Truman Ave. and Simonton St., Key West, tel. 294-7100. *MODERATE:* **Antonia's**, 615 Duval St., Key West, tel. 294-6565, Italian; **Café Marquesa**, 600 Fleming St., Key West, tel. 292-1244, South American; **Dim Sum**, Duval St., Key West, tel. 294-6239, Asian; **Italian Fisherman**, MM 104, tel. 451-4471; **Lorelei**, MM 82, tel. 664-4656; **Green Turtle Inn**, MM 81.5, tel. 664-9031; **Yosake**, Duval St., Key West, tel. 294-2288, Japanese; **A&B Lobster House**, Key West, tel. 294-2536, seafood. *BUDGET:* **Papa Joe's**, MM 80, tel. 664-8109. **El Siboney**, 900 Catherine St., Key West, tel. 296-4184, excellent Cuban food.

Parks / Museums / Attractions
John Pennekamp State Park, MM 102.5, tel. 451-1202; **Theater of the Sea**, MM 84, tel. 664-2431; **Indian Key State Historic Site and Lignumvitae Key**, MM 79, tel. 664-4815; **Long Key State Recreation Area**, MM 67.5, tel. 664-4815; **Bahia Honda State Recreation Area**, MM 37, tel. 872-2353; **Looe Key National Marine Sanctuary**, MM 27, Ramrod Key; **Audubon House**, 205 Whitehead, Key West, tel. 294-2116; **Hemingway House**, 907 Whitehead, Key West, tel. 294-1575; **Key West Aquarium**, 1 Whitehead St., tel. 296-2051; **Key West Lighthouse Museum**, 938 Whitehead St., tel. 294-0012; **Little White House Museum**, 111 Front St., Key west, tel. 294-9911; **Mel Fisher Maritime Heritage Society Museum**, 200 Green, Key West, tel. 294-2633; **Wrecker's Museum**, 322 Duval St., Key West, tel. 294-9502.

Shopping
Fastbuck Freddy's for kitsch, costumes and gifts; **Haitian Art Co.**, the best Haitian gallery in Florida.

Sightseeing
Conch Train, Key West, tel. 294-5161; **Old Town Trolley Tours**, Key West, tel. 296-6688. **Key West Sea Plane Service**, tel. 294-6978.

Water Sports / Boat Rentals and Charters
Moon Dancer Sunset Dance Cruise, Key West, tel. 294-0990; **Atlantis Dive Center**, MM 106.5, tel. 451-3020; **Divers World**, MM 99.5, tel. 451-3200; **Whale Habor Marina**, MM 83.5, tel. 664-4511; **Bud 'n' Mary's Fishing Marina**, MM 79.5, tel. 664-2461; **The Diving Site**, MM 53.5, tel. 289-1021; **Faro Blanco Resort**, MM 48, tel. 743-9018; **Looe Key Dive Center**, MM 27.5, tel. 872-2215; **Key West Pro Dive Shop**, Garrison Bight Marina, tel. 296-3823, 1-800-426-0707; **Princess Fleet**, A & B Lobster, House Docks, Key West, tel. 294-2536, glass bottom boats; **Yankee Fleet**, 31 Boca Chica Rd., tel. 294-7009, fishing in Tortuga Banks.

Festivals
January-March: *Old Island Days*, Key West. April: *Indian Key Festival*, Indian Key. October: *Fantasy Fest*, Key West.

Tourist Information
Florida Keys Information, tel. 1-800-FLA-KEYS; **Chamber of Commerce Key Largo**, MM 106, Key Largo, tel. 451-1414; **Islamorada**, MM 82.5, Islamorada, tel. 664-4503; **Marathon**, MM 48.5, 3330 Overseas Highway, Marathon, tel. 743-5417; **Lower Keys**, MM 31.9, Big Pine Key, tel. 872-2411; **Key West**, 402 Wall Street, Key West, tel. 294-2587.

THE EVERGLADES

One of the most fascinating and wildest landscapes in south Florida is the **Everglades** – an immense swamp region, 60 miles wide and about 120 miles long, of slow-flowing, grass-covered surface water stretching from **Lake Okeechobee** in the north to the **Ten Thousand Islands** and **Florida Bay** in the south and southwest.

At least, that's the way it was until the beginning of the century. It took nature thousands of years since the last Ice Age to build the sawgrass prairies, the hardwood hammocks, pine-lands, mangrove islands and estuaries, cypress swamps and freshwater sloughs, but in less than a hundred years human beings have come close to destroying this entire, unique ecosystem.

Today, approximately half of the living Everglades are gone. What we have left are a million and a half acres in **Everglades National Park**. For these precious wetlands we owe thanks to a few visionaries from early in the century, who acquired **Paradise Key** and **Royal Palm Hammock** for the public in order to save at least a small section of the region from the loggers and plume hunters who had decimated the wading bird population to a perilous degree.

Not until 1947 were land purchases completed, and the National Park, as it exists now, dedicated. Your travels through south Florida will reveal what happened to the rest of the Everglades if you look for the signs. Sugarcane fields around the lower crescent of Lake Okeechobee pollute the waters downstream. Two major highways, **Alligator Alley** (Interstate 75) and the **Tamiami Trail** (US 41) cut through and alter the natural

flow of water on which the life of the Everglades, Florida's drinking water, and the state's climate depend.

Florida cities have grown to the very edge of the wetlands and beyond. In efforts at flood control, the water supply to the park has been severely compromised, with potentially lethal consequences to life cycles in the Everglades which depend on natural dry spells and flooding at the proper times.

Fortunately, the idea that the Everglades are for birds, alligators and a few crank bird watchers is disappearing. No one denies that this is the eleventh hour for the fragile Everglades, and the challenge to preserve this truly unique wilderness remains. The number of voices heard in defense of conservation is growing, along with the number of people who love and appreciate the stillness and immensity of the grassy waters.

The park service rangers take great pains to introduce first-time visitors to the park. Their advice: Don't expect imposing vistas, go into slow gear, watch

Preceding page: Ice cream anyone? Left: Nature is the dominant factor in the Everglades. Above: Forest-fires in the Everglades are not uncommon.

101

EVERGLADES
NATIONAL PARK

0   20 km

0   10 miles

and listen, let the quietude and the tranquility surround you. There is only one road for you to travel on, 38 miles long, from the main visitors' center southwest of **Homestead**.

Intelligently written explanations with pictures can be found along the road, pointing to views of a particular habitat or community. You can look and become more aware of what you are seeing. You will soon be differentiating between the sawgrass prairie and the dwarf cypress forest, or know the red from the black mangroves and the buttonwoods. It takes practice to recognize the telltale bumps sticking out of the water at **Nine-Mile Pond** as an alligator, even though you may have seen his little brother on the **Anhinga Trail** earlier.

You will see birds, anhingas, of course, along the Anhinga Trail boardwalk, together with several varieties of egret: the stately American, the tri-

colored, great and little, blue, reddish, green. Less common is the Great White Heron. Farther down, towards Flamingo, on the wide flats of **Snake Bight**, you might, with luck, see a few flamingos that have flown in from the Bahamas or Hialeah Race Track. The sandbars just in front of the visitors' center and restaurant in Flamingo are especially fertile birdwatching grounds for sandpipers, black skimmers, the ubiquitous brown pelican squatting on pilings at the marina, or a flock of white pelicans doing their communal fish herding.

To give you an idea why the Everglades are so dear to bird watchers: nearly 300 species of birds have been recorded here, made up of winter and yearround residents, as well as those who only stop by on their way north or south during spring and fall migration.

The big wading birds are the easiest to identify, and the rangers, who lead regular nature walks in the cooler months, will be happy to point them out to you. A good field guide, which you can pick up

Right: A peaceful encounter with an alligator in an Everglades swamp.

at the visitors' center book store, will be of assistance. If you also have a pair of binoculars with you, you will be perfectly equipped and ready to go.

Flamingo is the southernmost outpost on the mainland and the starting point for a full range of outdoor activities, including fishing, bird watching, canoeing and hiking. At the marina store you can pick up the bare necessities for a picnic or full day's outing, things such as beverages, packaged sandwiches, cans of beef stew, matches and sterno, and mosquito repellent, which is necessary almost year-round, especially when the wind dies down at night.

In Flamingo you can camp right on Florida Bay or stay in the modest motel or in wooden cabins. In the winter months, however, you have to call ahead for a reservation.

Ride the train or paddle your rental canoe to **Snake Bight** for incomparable wading-bird sightings, or else head up **Buttonwood Canal**, the starting point for the seven-to-ten-day canoe trip through bays, sloughs and mangrove channels to the park's western gateway in **Everglades City**.

This is an excursion that should not be undertaken lightly: with strenuous paddling, possible adverse weather conditions, primitive camping on platforms or in the mangroves, and absolutely no facilities – but what rewards! An easier alternative is a houseboat rental. If you can drive a car, after a one-hour lesson you will be able to maneuver in protected waters. For a few days you can lose yourself in the channels and wide open stretches of **Coot** or **Whitewater Bay**. Chances of seeing eagles are excellent.

Canoeing in the Everglades

There is something utterly relaxing about the gentle "glurp-glurp" sound of a paddle pressing through calm waters, and in many ways that peacefulness makes canoeing in the Everglades an especially intimate way to explore this natural wonderland of the world. Flat-water

canoeists flock to many of south Florida's waterways, and nowhere more so than within this national park – so do not expect perfect solitude.

In winter, when the temperatures are cooler and the mosquito population dwindles, you will find many other paddlers out there. The seasons of April to May and October to November are recommended. You probably would not want to canoe here in summertime, due to the heat, the rain and the insects, but if you do, you will experience the park and wetlands in as close to their pristine natural state as it is possible to encounter in this day and age. Just do not forget the strongest insect repellent you can find, along with the best sun-block. Bring plenty of water. Wear a hat. Forget about a tan; stay covered up.

Now that you are sufficiently prepared to tackle Mother Nature, obtain a free permit for overnight camping at Flam-

ingo or Everglades City. Although a permit is not required for day-trips, it is wise to leave word of your plans in case you do not return at the specified time. It is flat water, but it is very easy to get lost in the labyrinth of waterways. A word to a friend staying behind, a park ranger, or even a note left behind in your car can prevent a disaster.

Everglades National Park contains five marked canoe trails in the Flamingo area, as well as the southern end of the 100-mile-long **Wilderness Waterway**, which stretches to Everglades City. Maps, as well as pertinent information on weather predictions and other canoeing conditions, are available at park ranger stations.

As for guided canoeing, North American Canoe Tours at **Glades Haven** offers canoe excursions from November 1 to March 31 with an experienced and knowledgeable guide. Children under eight years are not accepted, but for those old enough to qualify these trips are approved by the National Park Service.

Above: Another happy family enjoying life in the Everglades.

EVERGLADES NATIONAL PARK

Getting There

Take the Florida turnpike extension south to US 1. Turn west on Palm Drive and follow Route 9336 for eleven miles to the park's Headquarters and Visitors' Center.

Visitors' Center / Admission

The Visitors Center is located southwest of Florida City. Park services and information are administered daily from 8 am to 5 pm. Free services include natural history displays, a short film about the park and advice. Maps and books are available for sale. Tel. (305) 242-7700.

The National Park charges a $5 per car entry fee, but the receipt is good for as many as 14 days.

There is a second Visitors Center at Flamingo.

Accommodation

There is no expensive or luxury accommodation in the Everglades. Moderate priced **Flamingo Lodge Marina and Outpost Resort** is the only place to stay, other than camping. The complex is made up of 102 bay view rooms and individual housekeeping cottages. Screened pool, laundry, restaurant. Fifty-slip marina. Reservations are essential in high season from November to May. For information contact: P.O. Box 428, Flamingo, FL 33030, tel. (941) 695-3101.

Camping

There is a campsite at **Flamingo**, located directly at Florida Bay. Information: P.O. Box 428, Flamingo, FL 33030, tel. (941) 695-3101. The **Nine Mile Pond Camp Ground** is halfway between Flamingo and the park's headquarters. **Long Pine Key Camp Ground** near the park's headquarters also offers hook-ups and sites for tents or mobile homes, located near main park entrance. Primitive tent sites are situated in back country areas. Permits are required. These are available for free at ranger stations or the Visitors Centers. Canoe, motorized skiff or house boat rentals are available at Flamingo.

Restaurants

Flamingo Restaurant, located at the Visitors' Center, Flamingo, is the only restaurant in this part of the park, and it is closed from May to October, tel. (941) 695-3101 for information.

Outdoor Activities

Flamingo park rangers lead back-country hikes, canoe trips, bird walks and campfire programs. A train tour is available to Snake Bight. Whitewater and Florida Bay boat trips are offered, as well as sunset cruises under power or sail, skiff or canoe rentals. Then there is Florida Bay, immensely rich spawning and feeding grounds for fish, playpen for bottle-nosed dolphins, full of sandbanks, turtle grass, deep channels, mangrove islands and the shell-strewn beaches of Cape Sable.

Sign up for an evening sail, watch the roosting flight of herons and ibis, or arrange with a nature/fishing guide to take you well out into the bay, through Lake Ingraham, and around Cape Sable, where mangrove islands dot the horizon and dolphins gambol. Experiencing this unspoiled, primitive wilderness we hope that the words, uttered so optimistically by President Truman in his dedication speech in 1947, will hold true: "We have permanently safe-guarded an irreplaceable primitive area."

EVERGLADES CITY

Area Code 941

Arrival

Follow Route 29 south from US 41.

Accommodation

Moderately priced at the **Rod and Gun Club**, Everglades City, tel. 695-2101; **Barron River Marina**, Everglades City, tel. 695-3331, offers villas, cabins, trailer rentals, trailer sites, marina.

Outdoor Activities

Everglades National Park Boat Tours are available for $10 per half day. The tour boats are kept near the Gulf Coast Ranger Station in Everglades City, tel. 695-2591 or 1-800-455-2400; **North American Canoe Tours** at Glades Haven offers canoe rentals as well as guided Everglades tours, 800 South East Copeland Ave., Everglades City, tel. 695-2746.

Privately-operated activities: Contact Capt. Dave Pricket, tel./695-2286, expert fishing and nature guide, island charters, full and half day.

Tourist Information

Gulf Coast Ranger Station: Tel. 695-2591 for park information, details on boat tours, canoe rentals, natural history displays and maps.

SHARK VALLEY

Area Code 305

Arrival

Driving, take the Tamiami Trail, US 41, for 30 miles west of Miami, tel. 221-8776 for information.

Admission

$3 per car, good for seven days entry, or the fee can be applied towards main park admission.

Activities

Train tours are offered year-round, tel. 221- 8455 for information, also details on bicycle rentals, hiking, natural history displays and book store.

Accommodation / Restaurants

No accommodation or restaurants inside the park.

For moderate dining just outside park boundaries try the **Miccosukee Restaurant**, Tamiami Trail, near Shark Valley entrance, tel. 223-8389; **Coopertown Restaurant**, 22700 SW 8th St., on the way to Shark Valley, is also located outside the park, on the Tamiami Trail, tel. 226-6048.

WEST COAST

TAMPA BAY
ST. PETERSBURG
CLEARWATER AND LARGO
NAPLES
FORT MYERS
SARASOTA

The **Tampa Bay** area is Florida's fastest growing area and one of the fastest growing regions in the United States. Many people are lured by the 28 miles of beaches stretching along the gentle coast of the Gulf of Mexico, while others come for the booming job market that accompanies the unprecedented growth. Many of the 2.1 million residents came first to vacation and then decided to stay.

What this means for the typical visitor is that real life goes on here, not simply tourism, and thus many travelers find prices of accommodation, dining and attractions to be more reasonable than in other parts of Florida.

The first outsiders to move in were Spanish *conquistadors* in the 16th century, pressing on the traditional homeland of early Timucuan Indians. These were followed by Catholic missionaries, Cubans who were drawn to the bountiful fishing grounds or who came to make cigars, and the colorful Greek sponge divers who found the gulf waters reminiscent of their Mediterranean homeland.

Henry Plant's railroad reached **Tampa** in 1884, and this was followed by the construction of the luxurious **Tampa**

Preceding pages: The skyline of highrise buildings in Tampa. Left: A modern-day beachcomber.

Bay Hotel, modeled on the Moorish Alhambra castle in Granada, Spain, complete with 13 silver minarets. Guests were transported around the grounds in rickshaws. The hotel is now part of the University of Tampa, but you can still see Plant's handiwork, as it also houses the Henry B. Plant Museum.

The development of **St. Petersburg** followed, also in the 1880s. A Russian named Peter Demens built his Orange Belt Railroad and produced a master plan for the backwater community that he named after his home town. Then came Cubans seeking a deep-water port for large ships. They established **Ybor City**, which is today classified as a historic district. Here you can still see Cuban cigar-makers at work, hand-rolling and wrapping the golden tobacco leaves exactly the way their ancestors did more than 100 years ago.

Cities on both sides of Tampa Bay – Tampa, Clearwater and St. Petersburg – offer tremendous opportunities for the tourist in west Florida. Here you will find cutlure and entertainment, moderately-priced accommodation and luxury resorts that are virtual Florida landmarks. The **Don Cesar Hotel** on St. Petersburg Beach, for example, is an enormous pink stucco presence, and is one of the top hotels on the Gulf Coast.

Honeymoon I. State Rec. Area Island

Tarpon Springs

Ozona

Palm Harbor

584

19

Curlew Creek

Cswy.

586

Oldsmar

Rd.

589

Gunn

Rd.

Track

Tampa Bay Downs Race Track

Linebaugh

CALADESI ISLAND

Caladesi State Park

ALT 19

STREET

Rd.

580

Memorial Hwy.

Sheldon Rd.

Hanley Rd.

Waters Rd.

584

Main

580

593

590

Hillsbo

Dunedin

Clearwater Harbor

55

Safety Harbor

Tampa Airp

Clearwater Beach

GARDEN MEM. CSWY.

590

Drew St.

Mc Mullen

COURTNEY CAMPBELL CAUSEWAY

60

Rocky Pt.

Clearwater Pass

Old Tampa Bay

Clearwater

HOWARD FRANKLAND BRIDGE

93

Belleair Beach

Belleair

Marine Science Center

Belleview Mido

Largo

693

BAY BLVD.

686

DR. ROOSEVELT

Boatyard Village

St. Petersburg-Clearwater Int'l. Airport

St. N.

275

Ben T. Davis Mun. Beach

Belleair Shore

Belleair Bluffs

697

ULMERTON

688

RD.

BLVD.

1st St.

GANDY BRIDGE

Indian Rocks Beach

Heritage Park

694

Lake Seminole

19

686

92

600

Derby Lane Greyhound Track

Indian Shores

699

Tiki Gardens

595

695

Bot. Gardens

Starkey

Belcher

Pinellas Park

GANDY

687

Sawgrass Lake Park

Weedon Island State Pres.

Suncoast Seabird Sanct.

GULF

PARK

Seminole

BLVD. N.

595

589

ST. PETERSBURG

Redington Shores

Sand Key

Oakhurst

Bay Pines

Kenneth City

54th Ave. N.

N. Redington Beach

BAY PIN S BLVD.

ALT 19

38th Ave. N.

Sunken Gardens

Redington Beach

66TH ST.

Park St.

TYRONE

Tampa

Madeira Beach

Boca Ciego Bay

Junior College

691

49th St.

22nd Ave. N.

34TH ST.

92

Mus. of Fine Arts

Auditorium

BLVD.

5th Ave. N.

Hist. Museum

The Pier

Central Ave.

Bayfront Center Theatre Arena

Treasure Island

Blind Pass

Pasadena

Gulfport

9th 4th

Salvador Dali Museum

699

Scenic Mus.

22nd

Ave. S.

Lakeview Blvd.

Coquina Key

Wax Mus.

34TH ST. S.

Lake Maggiore Park

6th St. S.

St. Petersburg Beach

Treasure Long Key

Pinellas Island Blvd.

Pinellas Bayway

54th Ave. S.

682

Point Pinellas

GULF

OF

MEXICO

Pass-a-Grille Beach

Tierra Verde

275

Pinellas Natl. Wildlife Refuge

19

679

Fort DeSoto Park

Mullet Key

Ft. DeSoto

SUNSHINE SKYWAY BRIDGE

Fletcher Ave.
Ave.
I-275
FOWLER
BR 41
Lake Carrol
582
30th St.
Mus. of Science & Industry
Adventure Is.
Busch Gardens
Temple Terrace
Ave.
AVE.
582
Lake Thonotosassa
580
Thonotosassa
579
580
to Orlando
587
Ave.
Busch
580
Lowry Park
Hillsborough Co. Mus.
River
583
Blvd.
I-75
4
41
56TH
93A
92
4
580
Hillsborough
ST.
Ave.
EXPWY.
Fla. St. Fairgrounds
Mango
Dover
574
Buffalo
574
Nebraska
22nd
YBOR CITY
ST.
574
Broadway
Seffner
Sydney
TAMPA
Florida
7th
Ave.
Ave.
Brandon
Mus. of Art
Ybor City Mus.
FRANK ADAMO
Limona
DRIVE
60
nnedy
Blvd.
618
BR 41
McKay Bay
599
EXPWY.
618
Valrico
T.H. CROSSTOWN
Davis Island
50TH
Cause Way Blvd.
676
Lithia
Durant
TAMPA
TRAIL
640
i-Alai Fronton
Hillsborough Bay
45
Riverview
Alafia
River
Catfish Point
East Tampa
ill
Force Base
Gibsonton
Rd.
Rd.
Gadsden Point
Riverview
Boyette
Adamsville
301
Rd.
Boyette
TAMIAMI
672
Balm- Picnic
672
Rd.
Apollo Beach
Wimauma
Rd.
Rd.
41
Carlton Lake
Ruskin
Ruskin
Wimauma
Sun City Center
Rd.
Wimauma
Balm
674
Gulf City
674
Keene
Rd.
Sun City
Little
Manatee
River
Valroy
I-75
93A

ST. PETERSBURG - TAMPA AND ENVIRONS

| 0 | 5 | 10 | 15 km |
| 0 | 4,5 | | 9 miles |

DOWNTOWN TAMPA

0   500m
0   0,3 miles

North of there, in Clearwater, the **Belleview Mido** is a rambling structure, it is, in fact, the largest occupied wooden building in the world. And for golfers and sports-lovers, **Innisbrook Resort**, sitting amidst acres of lush landscaped grounds, provides the perfect environment for those seeking peace and quiet in the midst of a burgeoning urban landscape, as well as some of the nation's top golfing on highly-rated courses.

The cities on Tampa Bay offer a rich cutlural program. Starting in **Ybor City**, you can visit Ybor Square downtown. This is the name given to the **Historic District**, where, among other things, you can find an old-time cigar factory that has been transformed into a modern tourist complex that is worth a visit.

The **Ybor City State Museum** was once the Ferlita Bakery. Today it houses exhibits and artifacts of the cigar industry and the Hispanic community. The **Cigar-**

Right: The Don Cesar Hotel – a top address in St. Petersburg.

Workers House Museum and **Tampa Rico Cigars** offer, respectively, a glimpse of a restored 1895 house and one of the last commercial bastions of hand-made cigars, where you can watch the cigar-making process and purchase stogies made the old-fashioned way.

Tampa's **Busch Gardens** theme park combines a recreated African veldt, where animals such as lions, tigers, hippopotami and elephants roam freely, with an amusement park, featuring waterslides and three hair-raising roller coasters. The 300-acre property containing several different theme areas also offers live entertainment, monorail tours of the park, a large number of shops and more. You can easily spend a day here observing the alligators and monkeys, watching belly-dancers and listening to brass bands. The admission price includes all rides, shows and attractions.

A less expensive stop for seeing exotic animals is **Noell's Ark Chimp Farm**, across the Bay in **Tarpon Springs**. The Noell Family once had a touring chimp

show, including a gorilla that would box with all comers. In retirement, the family moved here and opened their doors to a variety of ex-performing primates who were past their prime. All are allowed to live out their days in the Florida sunshine, like so many other retirees. The Chimp Farm charges only $3.25 for admission and is open every day of the year.

After a stop at the Chimp Farm, wander the nearby sponge docks and stop in at **Pappas Restaurant** for some *ouzo* and *baklava*. The enormous restaurant is a sight worth seeing in itself, and features the best of Greek foods.

In Tarpon Springs visitors can find a bustling Greek community that still makes a living off the gulf sponge beds. In the **Spongeorama Museum**, many kinds of sponge are on display. This may well be where you can find more varieties of sponge than you ever knew existed, and there are also the local pastry shops and markets where authentic Greek culture thrives within the context of modern-day Florida.

A visit to the **St. Nicholas Greek Orthodox Church** on a Sunday morning, when traditionally-clothed women in long dark dresses amble down the narrow streets, can be quite interesting. The church is a replica of the Hagia Sophia in Istanbul. It is one of the best American examples of Neo-Byzantine architecture, with an interior of sculpted Grecian marble, wonderful icons and stained-glass windows.

Beaches around Tampa Bay

The seaways and ports of the Tampa Bay area are the life blood of the community. Deep-water ports are now home to a number of cruise ships, including the *Sea Escape* and the *Ocean Spirit* – a modern 457-foot mobile scuba diving complex that carries passengers to the Bay Islands of **Roatan** and **Guanaja**, located south of the Belize reef in Central America, one of the world's top diving sites. The weather here is most conducive to water sports, with an average of 361

113

days of sunshine a year, and an average temperature of 75° F.

St. Petersburg Beach is one of Florida's broadest and best-maintained. It stretches for 7.5 miles from **Blind Pass** to **Pass-a-Grille Beach**, the oldest settlement in the area. Theories suggest that the name came from the French *Passe aux Grilleurs* (Grillers Pass) or the Spanish *Paso de Grillo* (Cricket Pass), though no one knows for certain. Along with sunny urban areas, nature lovers can enjoy the pristine beauty of **Fort De Soto National Park** on Mullet Key, south of St. Petersburg, where there is a fort that was built in 1898.

Caladesi State Park, on the island of **Caladesi**, has the best natural beach in Florida. Reached by ferry from Dunedin, Caledesi offers a quiet escape from the hustle and bustle of the cities. The park contains nature trails and boardwalks winding through sand dunes flecked by sea oats. Activities include swimming, sailing, windsurfing and hiking, or simply picnicking at one of the many shaded picnic tables scattered throughout the preserve.

For those seeking more action, **Clearwater Beach**, on a spit of land in the heart of the city, packs in young people who fill the air with frisbees, the sound of boom-box radios and the youthful buzz of fun-in-the-sun punctuated by the lapping tides.

Surfing, though not especially common in calm Florida waters, is said to be best along a sand bar that runs the length of **Indian Rocks Beach**, **Indian Shores** and **Redington Beach**. These are not the Big Kahuna waves of Hawaii, however, making this a particularly good spot for novices seeking to test their surfing prowess. Surfboards are also available for rental.

Windsurfing, too, is increasing in popularity. Beginners can try the bay side of **Sand Key**, north of the **Belleair Causeway Bridge**. Experienced windsurfers are more likely to be found in the open gulf waters beyond the sandbar near the Don Cesar Hotel. The two- to three-foot swells are the largest in the area.

And families can usually be found congregating at several area beaches noted for especially calm waters. Indian Rocks Beach is protected by a sandbar that keeps waves small and also warms the water. Another beach that is well suited to children's activities is the **Ben T. Davis Municipal Beach**, situated between Tampa and Clearwater on State Road 60 on the Courtney Campbell Causeway. Shallow water reaches far into the bay before it tops little ones' heads.

Florida contains over 650 miles of beaches full of shells, but the very best place for collecting them is on the beach at Caladesi Island. Most serious seekers come out at the morning's low tide. Winter is considered best, and collecting shells after a full moon is recommended by experts.

ST. PETERSBURG

St. Petersburg was one of Florida's first recreational centers. The Pier is a focal point for downtown visitors. At the end of the structure jutting out into the bay is a five-story building, like an inverted pyramid, housing a number of inexpensive restaurants, retail shops, a farmer's market, an observation deck and an aquarium.

The city's **Historical Museum** is also downtown, within walking distance of the Pier. It features artifacts and documents, as well as exhibits including china, glassware, coins, dolls, shells and pictures of early community life.

One of the cultural highlights of St. Petersburg is the **Salvador Dalí Museum** (103 3rd Street South), containing the largest collection of the late artist's works of surrealism in the world. The **Museum of Fine Arts** (255 Beach Drive NE) is also located in St. Petersburg, and ex-

DOWNTOWN
ST. PETERSBURG

hibits a collection of European and American masterpieces.

A tremendously popular museum for children is called **Great Explorations** (1120 4th Street South), in which a number of exhibits can be experienced in hands-on fashion.

Visitors to St. Petersburg can also find the **Shuffleboard Hall of Fame**, located at the St. Petersburg Shuffleboard Club. Here, mostly elderly residents and visitors partake of the sport that epitomizes the lure of Florida: easy days, no hassles, just one endless game of shuffleboard (a game in which discs are shoved down a narrow 39-foot-long court using a special stick – called a cue – onto a target area at the other end; famous for not being a particularly strenuous activity).

A **Planetarium** located at St. Petersburg Junior College runs shows during the school year, from September through May, in a "sky theater" beneath a 24-foot domed ceiling projection screen.

Sawgrass Lake Park, within the city limits, is a 360-acre learning center for schools and community groups. A mile of elevated boardwalks run through a maple swamp, while an observation tower provides a panoramic view of Sawgrass Lake. An **Environmental Education Center** houses a laboratory, classroom and displays.

St. Petersburg's **Sunken Gardens** (1825 4th Street North) offers an exotic collection of 50,000 tropical plants and flowers – including orchids, azaleas, gardenias and camelias – which bloom year-round in this benign, if not sublime, climate. Palm and jacaranda trees sway in the breeze, and in the aviary, you can see an incredibly assorted collection of tropical birds. There is also a show featuring trained parrots, as well as a huge souvenir shop.

South of St. Petersburg, spanning Tampa Bay and connecting the city with neighboring Manatee County, is the impressive, high-altitude, four-mile-long **Sunshine Skyway** bridge. It was modeled after the Brotonne Bridge over the Seine, in France, and built to replace

the previous bridge, which was was rammed and severely damaged by a tanker in 1980. The roadway towers a dizzying 183 feet over Tampa Bay.

CLEARWATER AND LARGO

Heading back down the Gulf Coast, in Clearwater, visit the **Boatyard Village**, a recreated 1890s fishing village nestling in a cove on Tampa Bay, not far from the airport. Included are restaurants, shops, galleries and a theater.

Also in Clearwater, the **Marine Science Center** features live and model displays of indigenous marine life. This is a working research and rehabilitation center, which includes tanks containing numerous varieties of fish, as well as popular baby sea turtles.

Yesterday's Air Force, located adjacent to the St. Petersburg-Clearwater International Airport, features a display

Above: The Columbian Restaurant in Ybor City is a colorful architectural gem.

of post-World War II aircraft and aviation artifacts.

In **Largo**, the **Heritage Park and Museum** is another interesting collection of restored homes and buildings situated on 21 wooded acres. A historical museum here depicts pioneer life with exhibitions of frontier arts such as spinning and weaving.

Nearby, also in Largo, is the **Suncoast Botanical Gardens**, a 60-acre property wonderfully landscaped in suncoast cactus, 85-foot tall eucalyptus trees, palms, crepe myrtle and hundreds of flowering plants.

The **Suncoast Seabird Sanctuary** in **Indian Shores**, southwest of Largo, is the largest sanctuary and rehabilitation center for waterfowl in the world. A non-profit organization tends to more than 500 injured and crippled birds, who are brought here from all over the state with injuries such as broken wings or swallowed fishing hooks and are nursed back to health.

Many of the birds are released back into the wild upon recovery; those that have little or no chance of survival on their own remain. The sanctuary is home to brown pelicans, cormorans, white herons, and various birds of prey and songbirds. Admission is free, though a small donation is always welcome.

Madeira Beach is the home of **John's Pass Village**, a shopping area overlooking the fertile fishing grounds of John's Pass. John's Pass Village is also home to a large commercial and charter fishing fleet. From the looks of the seafood pouring onto the docks, this seems like a good place for those interested in sport fishing to make arrangements for seagoing excursions.

Out of the village, *The Southern Belle*, a 100-foot paddlewheeler, offers luncheon and sightseeing cruises of the Intracoastal Waterway, and the *Europa Sun* leaves here for six-hour lunch or dinner cruises into the Gulf of Mexico.

TAMPA / ST. PETERSBURG / CLEARWATER
Area Code 813

Arrival and Transportation
Tampa International Airport is served by Continental, British Airways, Pan Am, Transworld, Northwest and many other airlines. Car rentals, taxis and limousine services are available, many hotels provide gratis airport transfers.
Amtrak trains service Tampa, information tel. 1-800-872-7245.
Greyhound Lines/Trailways, tel. 1-800-231-2222, provide bus service between Tampa Bay communities and other areas of the state and country.
Hillsborough Area Regional Transit provides local service in Tampa.

Accommodation
LUXURY: **Westin Innisbrook Resort**, 36750 US 19 North, Palm Harbor, tel. 942-2000, deluxe resort on 1,000 wooded acres.
Saddlebrook Resort, 5700 Saddlebrook Way, Wesley Chapel, tel. 973-1111, 15 miles north of Tampa, golf, tennis.
Don Cesar Beach Resort, 3400 Gulf Blvd., St. Petersburg Beach, tel. 360-1881.
Belleview Mido Hotel & Spa, 25 Belleview Blvd., Clearwater, tel. 442-6171.
Guest Quarters, 555 N. Westshore Blvd., Tampa, tel. 875-1555, all suites.
Tradewinds, 5500 Gulf Blvd., St. Petersburg Beach, tel. 367-6461, canal-laced property with a wide beachfront.
Sheraton Sand Key Resort, 1160 Gulf Blvd., Clearwater Beach, tel. 595-1611, overlooks the gulf.
MODERATE TO BUDGET: **Holiday Inn Busch Gardens**, 2701 E. Fowler Ave., Tampa, tel. 971-4710;
Best Western Sirata Beach Resort, 5390 Gulf Blvd., St. Petersburg Beach, tel. 367-2771.

Restaurants
EXPENSIVE: **King Charles Room**, at the Don Cesar Hotel, tel. 360-1881, continental dining with harp music. Reservations are suggested; **Bern's Steak House**, 1208 S. Howard Ave., Tampa, tel. 251-2421, steaks, wine and organically-grown vegetables. Reservations suggested; **Palm Court**, Tradewinds Resort, tel. 367-6461. Nouveau Américain menu: veal, shrimp, lamb, duck.
MODERATE: **Julie's**, 351 S. Gulfview Blvd, Clearwater Beach, tel. 441-2548, seafood, casual; **Hurricane Seafood Restaurant**, 807 Gulf Way, St. Petersburg Beach, tel. 360-9558, live jazz; **Leverock's Seafood House**, 10 Corey Ave., St. Petersburg Beach, tel. 367-4588; **Pappas Riverside**, 10 W. Dodecanese

Blvd., Tarpon Springs, tel. 937-5101, the Greek salad is a must – and so are reservations.
BUDGET: **Harp and Thistle Pub**, 650 Corey Ave., St. Petersburg Beach, tel.360-4104, Scottish/Irish/English-style pub food and numerous beers on tap; the **Pelican Diner**, 7501 Gulf Blvd., St. Petersburg Beach, tel. 363-9873, open 24 hours a day.

Events
The *Hall of Fame Bowl*, football championship played in Tampa Stadium, January; *Epiphany*, Tarpon Springs, a day-long Greek Orthodox celebration including diving for a cross in Spring Bayou, January; the *Florida State Fair*, Tampa, February; *SPIFFS International Folk Fair*, St. Petersburg Beach, March; the *Highland Games*, Dunedin, April; *Fun'n' Sun Festival*, Clearwater, April; *La Fiesta de la Riba*, St. Petersburg's annual Spanish Festival held at the Dalí Museum, May; *Pirate Days Invasion*, Treasure Island, July; *Clearwater Jazz Holiday*, October; *John's Pass Seafood Festival*, one of the biggest seafood feeds in the state, October.

Parks
Caladesi Island State Park, 1 Causeway Blvd., Dunedin, tel. 469-5918; **Hillsborough River State Park**, 15402 US 301 North, Thonotosassa, tel. 987-6771; **Honeymoon Island State Recreation Area**, 1 Causeway Boulevard, Dunedin, tel. 734-5263; **Little Manatee River State Recreation Area**, 215 Lightfoot Road, Wimauma, tel. 671-5005; **Weedon Island State Preserve**, 1500 Weedon Island Drive NE, St. Petersburg, tel. 579-8360.

Tourist Information
The Greater Tampa Area Chamber of Commerce, 801 E. Kennedy Boulevard, tel. 228-7777; **Ybor City Chamber**, 1800 East 9th Avenue, Tampa, tel. 248-3712; **The Tampa-Hillsborough Convention and Visitors Association**, 111 Madison Street, Suite 1010, tel. 223-1111, or toll-free 1-800-826-8358; **The Greater Clearwater Chamber of Commerce**, 128 N. Osceola Avenue, tel. 461-0011; **The St. Petersburg Beach Chamber of Commerce**, 6990 Gulf Boulevard, tel. 360-6957; **The St. Petersburg Area Chamber of Commerce**, 100 Second Avenue, 33701, tel. 821-4069; **The Tarpon Springs Chamber of Commerce**, 210 South Pinellas Avenue, tel. 937-6109; **The Tampa Bay Visitor Information Center**, 3601 East Busch Boulevard, Tampa, tel. 985-3601; **The Greater Pinellas Park Chamber of Commerce**, 5851 Park Boulevard, Pinellas Park, tel. 544-4777; **The Greater Dunedin Chamber of Commerce**, 301 Main Street, Dunedin, tel. 736-5066; **The Gulf Beaches Chamber of Commerce**, P.O. Box 273, Indian Rocks Beach, FL 34635, tel. 595-4575.

117

NAPLES, FORT MYERS
AND SARASOTA

The far southwest coast of Florida, starting at the northern boundary of the Everglades and stretching past Fort Myers to Sarasota, is a popular area with urban Floridians seeking respite from big city ills. And now, with the enlargement of the Southwest Florida International Airport in Lee County, the area is more accessible than ever before.

Naples

This small, but very proper community has been a retirement haven for years, and only recently has it begun to enjoy a major tourism influx. With zoning restrictions galore, designed to preserve the city's long-cherished exclusivity, **Naples** is something of a haven of tranquility amidst the booming growth and congestion that characterizes so much of modern-day Florida.

In past years, Naples has been a sort of Palm Beach west, a semi-exclusive preserve of the rich and powerful, dating back to its founding by a Civil War general from Kentucky named John S. Williams, and his friend Walter N. Haldeman, owner and publisher of the *Louisville Journal*. The two men visited the area, and Williams is credited with naming the city in honor of his friend, the king of Naples, Italy.

In the early part of the 20th century, the city and surrounding wilderness areas became known as a rich man's hunting and fishing grounds, even though a visit here required a strenuous 40-mile boat trip from Fort Myers. Today, although hunting opportunities are not what they once were – except when alligators are in season – the fishing is still outstanding along 41 miles of public beaches.

Left: Relaxing in Naples. Above: There's an ideal breeze most of the time.

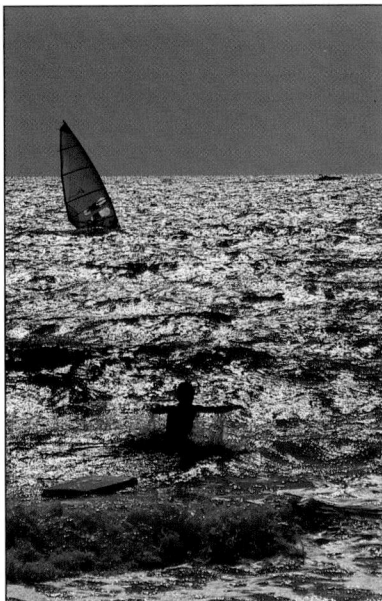

The city is sandwiched between the **Big Cypress National Preserve**, a swamp that extends out of the Everglades, and the Gulf of Mexico. The National Audubon Society runs the **Corkscrew Swamp Sanctuary**, an 11,000 acre wildlife habitat 35 miles west of Naples. It is the site of the world's largest remaining stand of virgin bald cypress trees. Many of the trees are more than 500 years old and over 100 feet tall.

Along with flora, one can find endangered species of woodstorks nesting in the tall trees, as well as alligators lolling in the swampy lowlands. These sights are most readily visible from an almost two-mile-long boardwalk.

In the same area, in the city of **Palmdale**, is one of Florida's more curious attractions: the **Cypress Knee Museum**. Run by the late Tom Gaskins, Sr. until well into his 80s (he died in May 1998), the museum and adjacent cypress swamp (served by a three-quarter-mile-long boardwalk) were until recently touted along rural Route 27 with crude

119

roadside signs saying: "Lady, if he won't stop, hit him over the head with a shoe."

The focus here is on cypress knees, which are gnarled stumps and shoots growing out of cypress trees. Gaskins not only gave names to these natural creations, such as "Lady with a Baby," or "Lady Hippo Wearing a Carmen Miranda Hat," he created his own living art by shaping the growth of certain trees around empty bottles or other items. This strange place, now run by his son, Tom Jr., is somehow representative of the spirit of Florida (tel. 941-675-2951).

For a commercial view of wildlife, **Caribbean Gardens Zoo** features wildlife shows, animals and birds from all over the world, including a "tiglon," which is a rather rare cross-breed between a tiger and a lion.

In Naples, when not partaking of golf, tennis, swimming, sailing or other sports,

shoppers flock to Fifth Avenue South or Third Street South shops, and boutiques featuring pricey goods. The **Old Marine Market Place** at **Tin City** is a cluster of art galleries, artist's studios and more trendy shops enclosed in old-time fisherman's shacks.

Fort Myers and Lee County

The Lee Island Coast is comprised of the communities of Sanibel/Captiva, Fort Myers Beach, Fort Myers, Cape Coral, Bonita Springs, North Fort Myers, Pine Island and Lehigh Acres.

Inland communities are residential or commercial enclaves, while coastal areas tend to house resorts. The region boasts the greatest number of golf courses per capita of any place in America, and there are a great many tennis courts, many of them open to the public for free.

Fort Myers is nicknamed the City of Palms for the thousands of towering royal palms that were planted along Mac-Gregor Boulevard by an early winter

Above: A good place to roost – the Naples pier. Right: Over a thousand patents were registered by Thomas Alva Edison.

resident, Thomas Alva Edison. Edison's 14-acre riverfront property, including his Florida home, experimental gardens and laboratory, is now a tourist attraction. The gardens are well-maintained, and include a banyan tree presented as a seedling to Edison as a gift by Harvey Firestone, a friend who made tires.

Today, the tree's circumference is more than 30 feet. And the lab is left just the way it was in Edison's time. The royal palms Edison planted have become something of a local trademark. They can be seen, with their thick trunks and towering height, standing like sentinels along the boulevard.

The **Lee Island Coast** is also known for tarpon fishing and sea shells. Tarpon, a prized game fish known for its size and aerobatic abilities, come to spawn in the Gulf of Mexico from as far away as Nova Scotia and South America. Their season here, in the calm, warm waters of the gulf, is summer. Among anglers in the know, **Boca Grande Pass** is considered the tarpon capital of the world.

As for shells, this is the home of the "Sanibel Stoop," that oddly crooked ritual step affected when scouring the coastal sands and tide pools for more than 400 varieties of seashells. Hundreds of prowling shell-seekers come out to Sanibel and Captiva beaches in the hazy hours before dawn. Many carry flashlights, but aficionados wear miners helmets with lights to scour for scallops, clams and coquinas, conchs, fluted tulips and speckled junonia.

There are more varieties of shells found here than in any other North American beach area. But for those who would like to see a rare shell on the mantel without getting sand between their toes, the **Shell Factory**, in North Fort Myers, is an enormous retail store that resembles a museum.

The **Caloosahatchee River** passes alongside downtown Fort Myers, serving as a starting point for scenic day cruises or dining cruises which explore regions of the Everglades, as well as secluded gulf-side inlets and bays. The **City Yacht**

Basin is the home port for many of the tour boats.

A popular travel mode based at the **Port Sanibel Yacht Club** is flotilla sailing: a string of sailboats captained by tourists follow the lead of a real captain who knows where he is going and what he is doing. Sailing instructions are available for beginners, then, after proficiency is established, the boats sail the gulf waters for as long as a week, docking at a different gulf port nightly.

Thoroughfares through Sanibel and Captiva are chock-a-block with resorts, and only recently have efforts been made to limit future construction.

On the north side of Sanibel Island, the **J.N. "Ding" Darling National Wildlife Refuge** is another effort to preserve elements of natural Florida against development. The refuge, administered by the U.S. Forest Service, covers more than

5,000 acres that may be explored by car, on foot, by bicycle or in a canoe. A five-mile dirt road leads visitors past 290 species of birds and numerous varieties of reptiles. Bird watchers favor an observation tower off the side of the road.

Some call **Captiva Island**, connected to Sanibel via a causeway, "Florida's Tahiti." Like it's South Seas role model, the barrier island is noted for its white sand beaches bordered by thick mangrove swamps. It is said that pirate José Gaspar kept prisoners on Captiva in the 18th century. Lime and coconuts have been commercially grown here, and these barrier islands were later a fishing retreat for winter tourists from up north.

Cayo Costa State Island Preserve is another site worth seeing for shell collecting and naturalist-led tours. Across Pine Island Sound, on **Pine Island**, you can find an old-time-style Florida fishing village, and you can also see rare mango groves in one of the few places in North America where the tropical fruits are able to grow.

Above: A popular souvenir. Right: Besides the Ringling Circus Museum there is also a Circus School.

Cabbage Key is accessible by boat only. It is the site of an ancient Calusa Indian shell mound and burial site, as well as an evocative country inn and restaurant built by American novelist Mary Roberts Rinehart in 1938.

Sarasota, Venice and Bradenton

The **Sarasota** area has been something of a cultural center in Florida ever since the circus came to town. The circus that came to spend winters in nearby **Venice** was run by a man named John Ringling. It was "The Greatest Show on Earth," the Ringling Brothers, Barnum and Bailey Circus. You can still see winter dress rehearsals here.

Ringling had been a long-time winter resident of Sarasota, and his home, which he shared with his wife, Mabel, is now a tourist attraction as part of the **Ringling Museum of Art**, Florida's state art museum. Called Ca'd'Zan, the house is a 30-room Venetian-style palace which is filled with tapestries and works of art.

More of Ringling's fabulous art collection is on view at the two adjacent buildings, the **Art Gallery** and the **Circus Gallery**. Situated on 38 acres of manicured grounds, the Art Gallery contains one of the world's top collections of Rubens paintings, and the Circus Gallery houses one of the largest collections of circus memorabilia and artifacts. Also on the grounds is the **Asolo State Theater**. The building was once a Scottish opera house. It was dismantled, then carefully reconstructed here in 1950. The much loved speciality of the theater is 18th-century Italian plays.

Another wonderful museum for the general public is **Bellm Cars and Music of Yesterday**, which boasts a collection of 200 restored antique cars, including a few Rolls-Royces. The adjacent Great Music Hall has an exhibition of 1,200 music boxes, calliopes and a 30-foot-tall Belgian organ.

Sarasota Jungle Gardens is home to more indigenous Florida wildlife and flora. The jungle trails pass through 15

acres of fern and hibiscus gardens bordered by a banana grove, and a number of animal and reptile shows are performed daily. The **Kiddie Jungle Playground** is a must for young ones.

Another garden spot is the **Marie Selby Botanical Gardens**, where you can stroll through 14 acres of gardens with an incredible variety of orchids. Located near the **Island Park Yacht Basin**, the site stretches along Sarasota Bay.

Marine scientists display many species of ocean life at the **Mote Marine Aquarium**. Sharks and manta rays are included in the sealife brought here for study out of local waters.

And on the south shore of the **Manatee River**, west of Bradenton, stands **Fort De Soto National Memorial**. The exact site where Hernando De Soto and his band of conquistadors landed in 1539 is in fact unknown, though it was between Fort Myers and St. Petersburg. A film

Above: You can buy antiques in this out-of-service train.

shown in the visitors' center describes De Soto's explorations, costumed guides give demonstrations of the workings of period weapons, and a number of nature trails have been laid out in the area for your own exploring.

In **Ellenton**, across the Manatee River from Bradenton, you can visit the only surviving antebellum mansion still standing in south Florida. It was built in 1850 by Major Robert Gamble, and was the headquarters of a 3,500-acre sugar-cane plantation. This handsome mansion is one of the best extant examples of the peculiar Florida construction material called "tabby," which was a mortar compound consisting of crushed shells mixed together with molasses produced from the sugar works.

Sarasota County also contains ten beaches offering swimming, fishing, volleyball, playgrounds, horseshoe pits, nature trails and picnic grounds. Several beaches include boat ramps and tennis courts. And the shell collecting is nearly as good as farther south.

NAPLES / FORT MYERS / SARASOTA
Area Code 941

Access / Transportation
Southwest Florida International Airport, tel. 1-800-282-2781 or locally 695-2781, serves the Ft. Myers Naples area. Connections on Continental, American, Delta, Northwest, United. Sun Lines airport limousine service is the least costly to hotels and resorts. Rental cars are available. **Sarasota County Transit**, tel. (813) 316-1007, and **Lee County Transit System**, tel. 275-8726, provide local bus service.

Accommodation
LUXURY: **Ritz-Carlton Hotel**, 280 Vanderbilt Beach Rd., Naples, tel. 598-3300, Mediterranean-style gulf-front resort; **Sundial Beach & Tennis Resort**, 1451 Middle Gulf Dr., Sanibel, tel. 472-0554, golf, tennis, watersports, condos and villas on the gulf; **South Seas Plantation**, South Seas Plantation Rd., Captiva, tel. 472-5111, cottages and villas on 330 secluded acres at the tip of the island; **Sonesta Sanibel Harbor**, 17260 Harbor Point, Ft. Myers, tel. 466-2150, located on San Carlos Bay; **The Meadows Golf & Tennis Resort**, 3101 Longmeadow Dr., Sarasota, tel. 371-6000, all suites, golf courses with 54 holes, 16 tennis courts.
MODERATE: **Robert E. Lee Motor Inn**, 13021 Cleveland Ave., tel. 997-5511, balconies on the Caloosahatchee River; **Sandpiper Gulf Resort**, 5550 Estero Blvd., Ft. Myers Beach, tel. 463-5721. Apartment motel on the beach: **Days Inn Sarasota-Siesta Key**, 6600 S. Tamiani Trail South, Sarasota, tel. 924-4900. Save money by staying a mile from the beach.

Restaurants
EXPENSIVE: **The Chef's Garden**, 1300 3rd St., Naples, tel. 262-5500, award-winning continental cuisine, dress jackets are required in winter; **LaTiers**, Sheraton Harbor Place Hotel, 2500 Edwards Dr., Ft. Myers, tel. 337-0300, continental cuisine; **The Bubble Room**, Captiva Rd., Captiva, tel. 472-5558, 1940s music, Art Deco decor; **Café L'Europe**, 431 St. Armand's Circle, Sarasota, tel. 388-4415, featuring continental and New Zealand cuisine.
MODERATE: **Truffles**, 1300 3rd St. S., Naples, tel. 262-5500, informal dining upstairs from the Chef's Garden; **The Prawnbroker**, 13451-16 McGregor Blvd., Ft. Myers, tel. 489-2226, seafood; **The Mucky Duck**, 2500 Estero Blvd., Ft. Myers Beach, tel. 462-5519; **McT's Shrimphouse and Tavern**, 1523 Periwinkle Way, Sanibel, tel. 472-3161, shrimp and crab; **Truffles at Casa Ybel**, Casa Ybel Resort, 2255 W. Gulf Dr., Sanibel, tel. 472-9200, Cajun, Creole and continental cuisine; **Nick's on the Water**, 230 Sarasota Quay, Sarasota, tel. 954-3839, classic Italian, seafood; **Café of the Arts**, 5230 N. Tamiani Trail, Sarasota, tel. 351-4304, international cuisine.
BUDGET: **Miami Connection**, 11506 S. Cleveland Ave., or 2112 2nd St. S., Fort Myers, tel. 936-3811, Kosher delicatessen; **Woody's Bar-B-Q North**, 13101 N. Cleveland Ave., Ft. Myers, tel. 997-1424.

Events
Edison Pageant of Light, Ft. Myers, February.
Pine Island Seafood Festival, Pine Island, March.
Bonita Springs Tomato Snook Festival, Bonita Springs, March.
Cracker Festival, N. Ft. Myers, April.
Safe Boating Festival, Ft. Myers, June.
Jazz on the Green, Sanibel, October.
Munich in Cape Coral, Cape Coral, October.
Sand Sculpture Competition, Ft. Myers Beach, November.

Guided Tours
Florida Adventure Tours and Charters, tel. 394-8870, bus and mini-bus tours to greyhound races, the Everglades, the Edison home.
Le Barge, tel. 366-6116, 65-foot boat tours of Sarasota Bay.
Everglades Jungle Cruise, tel. 334-7474, river trips of from three hours to two days.
Wooten's Everglades, US 41, tel. 394-8080, hovercraft and swamp buggy trips.

Parks
Cayo Costa State Preserve, P.O. Box 150, Boca Grande, FL 33291 tel. 964-0375.
Collier-Seminole State Park, Rte 4, Box 848, Naples, tel. 394-3397.
Delnor Wiggins Pass State Recreation Area, 11100 Gulf Shore Dr., Naples, tel. 597-6196.
Gasparilla Island State Recreation Area, P.O. Box 1150, Boca Grande, FL 33291, tel. 964-0375.
Koreshan State Historic Site, P.O. Box 7, Estero, FL 33928, tel. 992-0311.
Big Cypress National Preserve, S.R. Box 110, Ochopee, FL 33943, tel. 262-1066.
Corkscrew Swamp Sanctuary, Route 6, 1875 A., Naples, tel. 657-3771.
J.N. "Ding" Darling National Wildlife Refuge, 1 Wildlife Drive, Sanibel, tel. 472-1100.

Tourist Information
Lee County Visitor and Convention Bureau, 2180 W. 1st St., Ft. Myers, tel. 335-2631.
Naples Area Chamber of Commerce, 3620 N. Tamiami Trail, Naples, tel. 262-6141.
Sanibel-Captiva Islands Chamber of Commerce, Causeway Rd., Sanibel, tel. 472-1080.

CENTRAL FLORIDA

WALT DISNEY WORLD
ORLANDO
CAPE CANAVERAL
DAYTONA
GAINESVILLE

WALT DISNEY WORLD

Orlando was originally called Jernigan, after a man named Aaron Jernigan who came to Florida from Georgia and settled here in 1843. The town grew slowly around an army post from the Seminole Wars that had been abandoned in 1849, Fort Gatlin.

The town's name was changed to Orlando in 1857. While a number of different versions of the origin of the name are told, the official account is that the name came from one Orlando Reeves, a soldier killed in 1835 by an Indian's arrow. The city was officially incorporated on July 21, 1875.

More than 1.1 million people now reside in the Greater Orlando area, which consists of three counties – Orlando, Osceola and Seminole. The airport services over 1,000 flights daily. There are more than 84,000 hotel rooms, 100 golf courses, 800 tennis courts and hundreds of special events year-round. The area has more shopping space – 32 million square feet – than any other U.S. city of comparable size.

Preceding pages: The wonderful world of Mickey Mouse – a modern-day fairy tale land. Left: Children still get a thrill from Walt Disney's creations.

But it is the area's unforgettable attractions that keep visitors coming back. Walt Disney World, Sea World, Universal Studios and Church Street Station are the top draws, but offbeat exhibits like Gatorland, Wet 'n' Wild Water Park or Jungleland Safari Zoo give visitors a boundless array of things to do. With so many choices of activities, it is best to plan your itinerary well in advance.

The top draw in central Florida is without a doubt **Walt Disney World**. Located 20 miles southwest of Orlando off Interstate 4, Disney can be overwhelming to first-time visitors. It's twice the size of Manhattan and includes four theme parks, three water parks, the Pleasure Island nightclub theme park, 27 resorts, five championship golf courses and the Discovery Island zoological park. There are pools and lakes for swimming, boating, parasailing, waterskiing and fishing, as well as jogging paths and horseback riding.

Downtown Disney is a shopping, dining and entertainment complex with more than two dozen shops and restaurants. There's even a Wedding Pavilion, where more than 1,000 couples tie the knot each year, and **Disney's Wide World of Sports**, an ultra-modern complex where more than 30 types of sports are on offer.

Disney's new town of **Celebration**, with accommodations for 8,000 people, and plenty of educational and recreational activities, as well as shops and fitness centers, recently welcomed its first visitors.

Whoever thinks that all this in itself is overwhelming, there is even more: Disney opened its newest theme park, **Disney's Animal Kingdom**, in April 1998, and the first ship of their new cruise line was christened three months later.

All of Walt Disney World is connected with an efficient transportation system that operates for free. You can stay anywhere on Disney property and not need your own car, and the trip from one sight to the next takes no more than 20 minutes.

Disney World is not an especially inexpensive vacation destination, with one-day tickets costing around $40. Check with your travel agent for special rates or package deals. If you plan to spend several days there, purchase a multi-day "Disney Passport," which allows unlimited entrance to the theme parks and water parks. Allow some flexibility in your schedule, though; Disney recommends that guests start their days early in the theme parks, take a break for lunch, a swim or even a nap, then return to the parks later for evening fireworks and entertainment.

For a more relaxed and enjoyable visit, it pays to be aware of Disney World "rush hours," information about which can be obtained from your hotel's reception desk.

A weekly schedule of events is available in the Magic Kingdom's City Hall, as well as in the visitors' centers in Epcot and Disney-MGM Studios. Times of shows (with waiting times!) are posted at the entrances to the theme parks, which should help to avoid unpleasantly-long waits in line.

For reservations for lunch or dinner, phone: (407) 939-3463.

Toronto Rd.
Maitland
Lake Howell
eggs Rd.
Pembrook Rd.
Keller Rd.
441
Lockhart
Forest City
Lake Minnehaha
Long Lake
Eatonville
400
 RD.
436
Maitland Lake
Goldenrod AVE.
426
rcona Rd.
Ben White Raceway
LEE
Edgewater
ORLANDO
Lake Osceola
ALOMA
Goldenrod
Aloma
5
Pine Hills
423
424 A
426
Rollins College
527
Winter Park
Aloma University
L. Irma
438
Fairvilla
Orange
Mead Bot. Gardens
Lake Virginia
SEMORAN
Goldenrod
DRIVE
551
Pine Hills
431
424
MILLS
Hist. Mus.
Leu Bot. Gardens
COLONIAL
408
WEST COLONIAL
DR. EAST
Science Center
50
HOLLAND
Lawne Lake
Lake Fairview
JOHN YOUNG PKWY.
Tampa Ave.
Church Street Station
Lake Eola Park
Orlando Executive Airport
Azalea Park
408
EAST
WEST
St.
EXPWY.
552
Orlovista
Columbia
Ave.
ORLANDO
BLVD.
Curry Ford
Rd.
435
Lake Mann
Clear Lake
15
Conway
L. Frederica
400
4
Rlo Orange
L. Holden
Bumby
Pershing
Pershing Ave.
15A
Universal Studios
Honour
Holden Ave.
Gatlin Ave.
436
ke Cain Hills
Americana Blvd.
Edgewood
Little Lake Conway
Hoffner
15
Ave.
Mystery Fun House
Dag Ridge Rd.
506
Rd.
Hoffner
Lake Conway
Ave.
Narcoossee
91
KIRGMAN
Tangelo Park
LAKE
482
RD.
Sky Lake
Belle Isle
Judge
506
SEMORAN
528
SAND
Morningside Park
(TOLL)
BEE LINE
EXPW.
423
Visitor Information Center
Taft
15
BEE LINE
EXPWY.
91
FLORIDA'S
527
Orlando Int. Airport
528
Sea World
92
Lake Nona
Buck Lake
441
17
Flamingo
TURNPIKE
Mud Lake
Gatorland Zoo
Shingle Creek
Tupperware Int'l. Hdqrs. & Mus.
Old Dixie
527
(TOLL)
Jungleland Safari Zoo

ORLANDO AND ENVIRONS

0   2   4   6 km

0   3 miles

131

Magic Kingdom

Usually the starting point for every Disney vacation, the Magic Kingdom has 41 major attractions in seven "lands" – Adventureland, Liberty Square, Frontierland, Main Street U.S.A., Fantasyland, Tomorrowland and Mickey's Toontown Fair.

Main Street U.S.A. is your first experience; a turn-of-the-century gateway to the other six lands. There are lots of shops and snack bars, and Cinderella's Castle beckons you from the far end of the street. The lure of souvenirs is strong, but plan your shopping as you exit the park so that you won't have to carry packages around all day.

At this point you may well want to start your day with a ride on the **Walt Disney World Railroad**. This is a 20-minute journey that skirts the Magic Kingdom

Above: In Cypress Gardens there is always time for a chat. Right: In Epcot you are transported into the 21st century.

with stops in Frontierland and Mickey's Toontown. It's a good way to gauge the size of the park and the lay of the land. Or, if you prefer, you can take a ride in one of the old-fashioned cars or horse-drawn trolleys that drop you off in front of **Cinderella's Castle**.

This castle, a copy of Neuschwanstein Castle in Bavaria, is undoubtedly the most-famous and most-photographed site at Walt Disney World, with fabulous murals on the inside walls created from millions of tiny pieces of Italian glass in hundreds of brilliant colors, and silver and 14-karat gold trim.

The castle is the gateway to **Fantasyland**, popular with children of all ages. Long-time favorites, like **Peter Pan's Flight**, **Mr. Toad's Wild Ride**, **Dumbo**, **The Mad Tea Party**, **Cinderella's Carrousel** and **It's a Small World** continue to enchant visitors. **Snow White's Adventures** has a new look, with Snow White appearing in the attraction in five new scenes. **Legend of the Lion King** brings the characters of the animated film to life with gigantic puppets.

A fun way to reach **Tomorrowland** is via the **Skyway**, a ten-minute ride from Fantasyland. Tomorrowland has a "retro" space-age look in the style of 1930s and 1940s science-fiction, and it's here you'll find the newest "out-of-this-world" experience, **Alien Encounter**, an attraction that "beams" a very nasty alien being into the pitch-black room – an experience that may be too intense for young children.

Nearby **Space Mountain** is still among Disney's most popular attractions. Other new Tomorrowland favorites include **Timekeeper**, which features a wacky robot and a fabulous 360-degree film that transports riders around the world. **Carousel of Progress**, best remembered from the 1964-65 New York World's Fair, has been updated with 21st century scenes.

Mickey's Toontown Fair is the newest version of Mickey's Starland and in-

cludes a new childrens' roller coaster. This is the place to find Disney's most-popular characters strolling about for photos – Mickey Mouse is still the favoirite, of course. Many famous figures from Disney cartoons appear in a show. Other must-see Magic Kingdom attractions are **Pirates of the Caribbean** and the **Jungle Cruise** in Adventureland, **Splash Mountain** and **Big Thunder Mountain Railroad** in Frontierland, and **The Hall of Presidents** and **The Haunted Mansion** in Liberty Square.

Epcot

There's something new around every corner at **Epcot**, Disney's "discovery" park. Divided into **Future World** and **World Showcase**, this is Disney's largest park, twice the size of the Magic Kingdom. An important note: Future World and World Showcase have differ-

Above: High-tech surroundings. Right: Italian theater at Epcot Center.

ent operating hours. Future World opens in the morning and closes early in the evening; World Showcase opens in the afternoon and stays open until **IllumiNations** – the not-to-be missed nightly fireworks, light and laser show – ends.

In Future World, the giant **Spaceship Earth** has a show about life in the 21st century's "global neighborhood," while the adjacent buildings house **Innoventions**, a showcase for gadgets and gizmos of the near future. And one of the best new attractions at Disney, **Honey, I Shrunk the Audience**, is in Future World's **Imagination** pavilion. **The Land** has been renovated with the motion picture "Circle of Life," starring characters from "The Lion King," and the **Living With the Land** boat ride takes guests through the greenhouses of the future, where plants have been thriving since the park opened in 1982.

In **Universe of Energy** you encounter frightening dinosaurs. **The Living Seas**, home to thousands of fish, now allows guests who are certified divers to take a

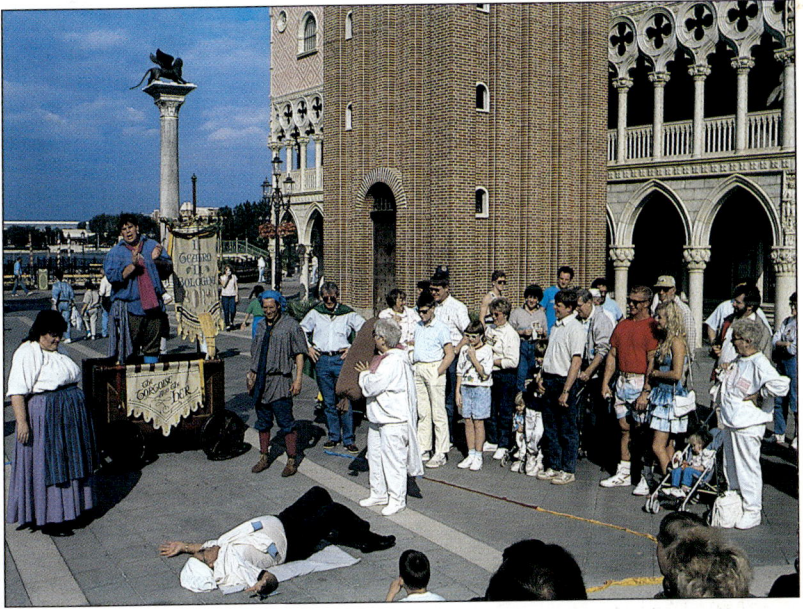

dip in one of the world's largest aquariums. **Body Wars** in the **Wonders of Life** pavilion, takes riders on a hair-raising trip through the human body. The **Test Track** lets drivers push their automotive skills – and their nerves – to the limit on a "test drive," the longest and fastest ride at Walt Disney World.

Cross the bridge into **World Showcase**, and you are in an entirely different environment, with eleven countries from around the globe harmoniously arranged side by side around a mile-long promenade. Students from each of the eleven countries spend a year working in the pavilion representing their country, interacting with guests and sharing their cultures through shows, attractions, restaurants and shops. This is the place to spend a leisurely afternoon, dining, shopping and strolling the wide promenade with entertainment from around the world.

The following attractions – moving clockwise around the promenade – are not to be missed: the authentic cuisine in the **Mexico** pavilions' San Angel Inn; the Viking ship voyage in the **Norway** pavilion; **China's** Circle-Vision 360 film; **Germany's** all-you-can-eat buffet and the garden with an elaborate miniature railway; **Italy's** hilarious street theater; **American Adventure's** imaginative show; the cuisine and belly dancers of **Morocco**; **Great Britain's** lovely flower gardens and **Canada's** Circle-Vision 360 film. Afterwards you can do some shopping in each of the nations. A real feast for the eyes is the **Epcot International Flower and Garden Festival** (April-June), when 30 million blossoms fill every corner of the park.

Disney-MGM Studios

Disney's third theme park, **Disney-MGM Studios**, combines motion picture and television production with a theme park featuring attractions and shows based on the glamour of Hollywood movie-making. It's smaller than the other three parks, making it an easy day's visit.

135

WALT DISNEY WORLD

Magic Kingdom
Reams Rd.
Cast Dr.
Bay Lake
DISCOVERY ISLAND
River Country
Ft. Wilderness Res. & Campground
Floridian Way
Vista
Winter Garden - Vineland Rd.
Blvd.
Bonnet Creek Rd.
Epcot Center Dr.
Main Entrance to Resorts & Magic Kingdom
World Drive
Disney Institute
Epcot Center Main Entrance
Epcot Center
Community Disney
Downtown Disney
Buena N. Dr.
Typhoon Lagoon
Epcot Center Dr.
Animal Kingdom
Disney-MGM Studios
Blizzard Beach
World Drive
I-4
192

1 Polynesian Resort
2 Grand Floridian Beach Res.
3 Transportation & Ticket Center
4 Contemporary Res.
5 Wilderness Lodge
6 Kinder Care
7 Village Resort
8 Reception Center
9 Pleasure Island
10 Boardwalk
11 Carribean Beach
12 WDW Dolphin, Swan Hotel
13 Yacht & Beach Club Resorts
14 Port Orleans Res.
15 Dixie Landings
16 Disney's Old Key West Resort
17 All-Star Sport & Music

VICINITY

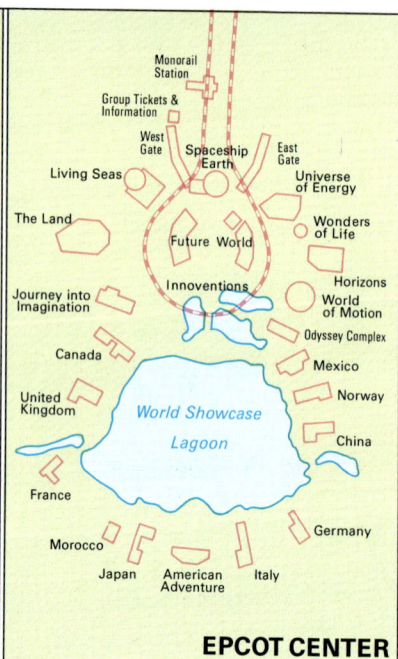

Monorail Station
Group Tickets & Information
West Gate
East Gate
Spaceship Earth
Living Seas
Universe of Energy
The Land
Future World
Wonders of Life
Journey into Imagination
Innoventions
Horizons
World of Motion
Canada
Odyssey Complex
Mexico
United Kingdom
World Showcase Lagoon
Norway
China
France
Germany
Morocco
Japan
American Adventure
Italy

EPCOT CENTER

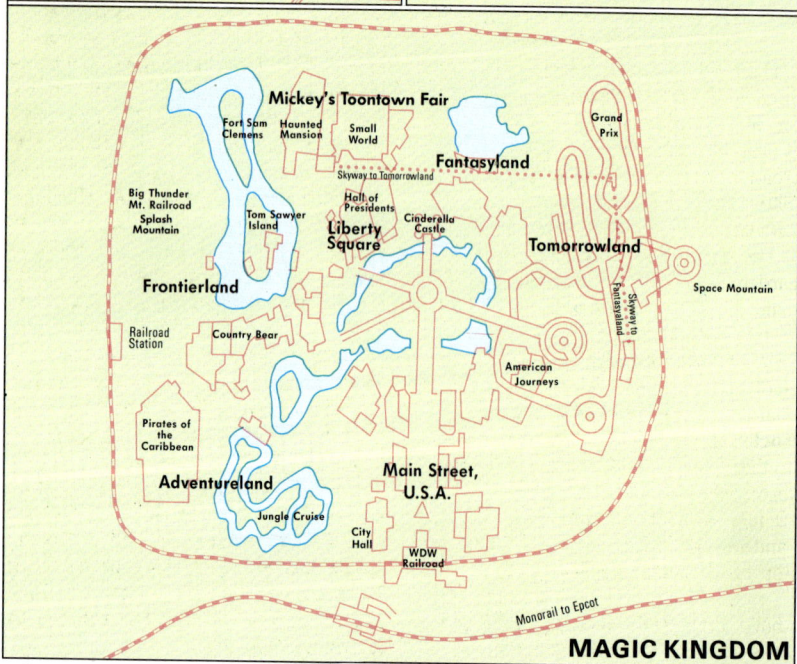

Mickey's Toontown Fair
Fort Sam Clemens
Haunted Mansion
Small World
Grand Prix
Fantasyland
Skyway to Tomorrowland
Big Thunder Mt. Railroad
Splash Mountain
Tom Sawyer Island
Hall of Presidents
Cinderella Castle
Liberty Square
Tomorrowland
Skyway to Fantasyland
Frontierland
Space Mountain
Railroad Station
Country Bear
American Journeys
Pirates of the Caribbean
Adventureland
Jungle Cruise
Main Street, U.S.A.
City Hall
WDW Railroad
Monorail to Epcot

MAGIC KINGDOM

The latest, greatest attraction is the **Twilight Zone Tower of Terror**, a thrilling experience that culminates in a 13-story plummet in a "runaway elevator."

The Studios park is home to the elaborate stage versions of Disney's blockbuster animated films: **Hercules, Beauty and the Beast, The Hunchback of Notre Dame** and **The Little Mermaid** are currently playing.

The most popular attractions include the **Star Tours** flight simulator adventure; the **Magic of Disney Animation** tour; **SuperStar Television**, capsulizing 40 years of TV history in an interactive show; **Monster Sound Show**, with guests demonstrating how sound effects are used; **The Great Movie Ride**, a journey into the movies; **Indiana Jones Epic Stunt Spectacular**, with daring stunt artists, and **Jim Henson's Muppet Vision 3D** film spectacular.

Disney's Animal Kingdom

Disney's Animal Kingdom, which opened in April 1998, covers 500 acres on the western edge of Walt Disney World and is home to thousands of wild creatures. It combines thrilling rides, dramatic landscapes and close encounters with exotic animals.

The entrance is at **The Oasis,** a lush garden with colorful and unusual animals, and the first stop is **Safari Village,** an island of tropical greenery and equatorial architecture. Safari Village is encircled by **Discovery River**, where you board launches to such places as **Dragon Rocks**, passing by quirky geysers and mythical monsters. Towering 14 stories above Safari Village is the **Tree of Life**, 50 feet wide at its base and intricately hand-carved by Disney artists. You can step inside and see a 3-D exhibition on

various insects. The main attraction is **Africa**, beginning in Harambe, a modern-day town on the edge of a wildlife reserve. You board **Kilimanjaro Safaris** to explore more than 100 acres of savanna, forest, rivers and rocky hills. Herds of giraffes, zebras, hippos and other animals roam about freely. The journey ends at **Gorilla Falls Exploration Trail**, where visitors are invited to walk through the domain of two troops of lowland gorillas, observe hippos from an underwater viewing area, and get close to exotic birds. Nearby Conservation Station is the veterinary and administrative headquarters. The area can be reached aboard the **Wildlife Express** train.

In the **Boneyard** playground at **Dino-Land U.S.A.**, kids can slide, bounce and slither through the bones of a tyrannosaurus rex, a triceratops and a 50-foot-tall brachiosaurus. The giants come roaring to life as guests are whisked back 65 million years to witness the fiery end of the age of the dinosaurs in **Countdown to Extinction**.

Above: Even in Epcot one wants to looks one's best.

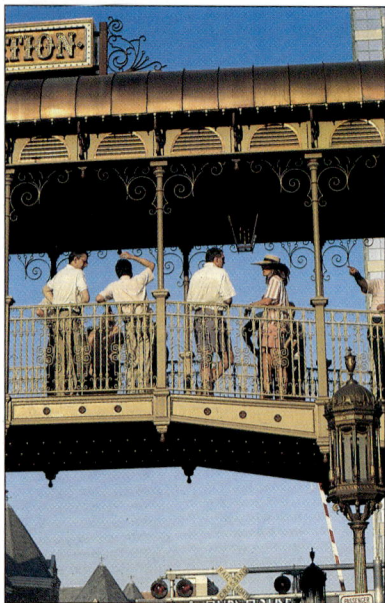

Of course, Disney's animated characters have their place in this park as well, namely in **Character Grove**, where you can meet Mickey, Minnie and may other popular Disney creations. A large theater stages a show starring characters from *The Lion King*.

Disney Water Parks

There are now three water parks at Walt Disney World, each of which is devoted to a specific theme: River Country, Typhoon Lagoon and Blizzard Beach. All three of the parks are elaborately designed and offer a variety of breathtaking slides and other aquatic attractions.

River Country is the old-fashioned original, created in a corner of Bay Lake at Fort Wilderness campground. You can swim with passive sharks – well fed and

Above: Orlando's entertainment center, Church Street Station. Right: A must at Epcot are the dolphin shows.

therefore not dangerous to humans, or catch an impressive four-foot wave at **Typhoon Lagoon**. **Blizzard Beach** boasts the world's tallest and fastest slide: starting out from 350 feet in the air, riders sometimes reach speeds of 55 miles per hour or more.

All three parks fill up quickly on hot summer days, Blizzard Beach generally closes earliest, sometimes around noon. All have fast-food restaurants, merchandise shops and dressing rooms. Lockers are available, but it's best to leave valuables in your hotel room.

Downtown Disney

This shopping, dining and entertainment complex recently expanded, with three distinct areas: Pleasure Island, the West Side and the Marketplace.

Pleasure Island is nightlife Disney style, with seven nightclubs plus shops and restaurants on a six-acre island. Admission is free to enter the island, and you pay a single admission (around $16) if you choose to enter the nightclubs. The drinking age is 21. The street itself is one big party, with live music, dancing and a nightly fireworks show. There's a club for every taste; even **Planet Hollywood** is part of the line-up.

Pleasure Island and the adjacent Marketplace and West Side for shopping and dining have nearly doubled in size. There are two new celebrity nightclubs, **Bongo's**, featuring the flavors and rhythms of Cuba, and **The House of Blues**, with a 1,500-seat music hall and restaurant; **Rainforest Café**, simulating a tropical environment with cascading waterfalls and tropical birds; **Wolfgang Puck's Café**, the first in Florida for the world-famous Austrian chef; **Fulton's Crabhouse** aboard the old Empress Lilly riverboat; the **World of Disney**, the world's largest character merchandise shop, and 14 new movie screens at the **AMC Theater Complex**.

Disney Institute

This is a new concept in "smart fun" vacationing as only Disney can do it. Picture yourself as a television star, a gourmet chef or a Disney animator. The **Disney Institute** offers a holiday of discovery with more than 40 programs available each day in six areas: Animation, Culinary Arts, Disney Discoveries, Communication Arts and Entertainment, Home, Gardens and the Great Outdoors, and Sports and Fitness.

There are special programs for guests age ten to 17, and seven-to-nine-year-olds can participate in Disney Day Camp, a half-day adventure, while parents learn how to bake an apple pie or take to the fitness center. Disney has created a lakeside "campus" with bungalows, tennis courts, golf and all the amenities.

Disney Resorts

Disney has more than two dozen resorts on its property in all price ranges, and divides its resorts into four geographic locations: the Magic Kingdom Resort Area, Epcot Center Resorts, the Downtown Disney Resort Area and Disney's All-Star Resort Area. Resorts are further divided into deluxe, moderate and value-priced. When booking a room, be sure to tell your travel agent or the Disney reservationist if your family has any special needs – grandparents or small children, for example. Every hotel is served by the efficient Disney shuttles or the monorail, and all are handicapped-accessible. The value-priced resorts only have self-service restuarants.

Disney's newest resort is **Coronado Springs**, a southwestern-inspired hotel. The **Boardwalk**, adjacent to Epcot, offers villas and hotel rooms surrounding an old-fashioned boardwalk lined with shopping and dining experiences. It joins the **Walt Disney World Dolphin** and **Swan** hotels and **Disney's Yacht and Beach Club Resorts** to form the Epcot Resort Area. These hotels are walking distance from Epcot, and a short boat ride

139

from Disney-MGM Studios. The Yacht and Beach Club has one of the best hotel pools at Disney World.

Disney's Caribbean Beach, though not as close to the parks, is also part of the Epcot Resort Area. This was Disney's first value-priced resort, and is extremely popular with budget-minded travelers. **Wilderness Lodge** is the newest addition to the Magic Kingdom Resort Area, nestled in the pine trees. Artist Point restaurant is one of the finest on the property.

Other Magic Kingdom hotels include the **Contemporary**, Disney's first hotel, recently refurbished; the **Grand Floridian Beach Resort**, the *non plus ultra* in luxury; the **Polynesian** and **Fort Wilderness**, with economy-priced campsites and trailer parks. The Polynesian, Contemporary and Grand Floridian are the only three Disney hotels served by the efficient monorail system.

Above: Journey to Atlantis – one of Sea World's popular attractions. Right: Marilyn Monroe at Church Street Station.

The Village resort area includes the moderately-priced **Port Orleans** and **Dixie Landings**; the villas at **Disney Institute**; **Disney's Old Key West Resort**, part of the Disney Vacation Club resort ownership system, and seven non-Disney hotels: **Buena Vista Palace, Grosvenor Resort, Doubletree Guest Suites, the Hilton, Courtyard by Marriott, Hotel Royal Plaza** and **Travelodge**.

Finally, the All-Star Resort area has two hotels: **All-Star Sports** and **All-Star Music**, the best hotel value at Walt Disney World. They are farther from the parks, but are served by the shuttles and are close to Blizzard Beach Water Park.

Other Theme Parks

Central Florida's other theme parks offer completely different experiences. **Sea World** is the world's most popular marine-life park, with more than 20 shows, including Shamu, the famous killer whale. You can walk through a shark habitat, feed the dolphins or take a simulated voyage to the North Pole to view frolicking polar bears. Penguins, manatees, sea lions – if it lives in the sea, chances are you'll find it at the park. The newest exhibit is **Key West at Sea World**, a salute to the Florida Keys, with three habitats for bottle-nosed dolphins, stingrays and sea turtles.

Located ten miles southwest of Orlando, **Universal Studios** recreates the glamour of Hollywood, complete with a real working studio containing more than 40 sets. Not-to-be-missed attractions include "Back to the Future... The Ride," "Earthquake: The Big One," "E.T. Adventure," "Jaws" and "Kongfrontation." The latest thriller is "Terminator 2: 3-D," billed as the world's first cyber-optic adventure. In addition, there are nine shows, the most popular of which are *The Animal Actors Show*, *Ghostbusters* and *The Wild, Wild West Stunt Show*.

Universal has its own animated characters to compete with Disney's: Woody Woodpecker, Rocky and Bullwinkle, George Jetson, Fred Flintstone, Scooby Doo and Yogi Bear greet visitors to the park. **City Walk** is Universal's new entertainment complex, featuring restaurants, clubs and shopping.

Cypress Gardens, in nearby Winter Haven, is the oldest theme park in central Florida, with acres of splendid gardens and a butterfly conservatory. Another old-timer is **Gatorland**, with nearly 5,000 alligators and crocodiles in their natural habitat. The newest theme park is **Florida's Splendid China**, featuring 60 exhibits from this mystery-enshrouded land, including the Great Wall, the Leshan Buddha, the Forbidden City and the Stone Forest.

Two water parks – **Wet 'n' Wild** and **Water Mania** – offer plenty of ways to cool down after all the heated sightseeing. Both have surfing pools and water rides for all ages. Wet 'n' Wild has more daredevil slides than any other central Florida water park: the *Black Hole*, in which you race through a tunnel with outer space effects, the *Fuji Flyer*, a breathtaking aquatic roller coaster and *Der Stuka*, the fastest water-slide in the world.

ORLANDO

"The City Beautiful" had its own identity long before the theme parks arrived on the scene. Orlando offers an array of cultural and special-interest attractions, as well as the beauty and serenity of parks and gardens.

In the heart of historic downtown is **Church Street Station**, a lively, block-long entertainment complex with restaurants, shops and live music for dancing. **Terror on Church Street** takes visitors on a frightening adventure through a maze of darkened rooms.

For peace and quiet, **Lake Eola Park** in downtown Orlando is perfect for an afternoon or evening stroll, with huge swan paddle boats for rent. Springtime brings the Shakespeare Festival to the park's

amphitheater. Nearby **Harry P. Leu Gardens** boasts the largest camelia collection and the largest rose garden in the South. The original Leu home from the 1920s-30s period has been restored and today houses a museum.

The **Orlando Museum of Art** has doubled its gallery space, with a growing permanent collection of 19th- and 20th-century American art, pre-Columbian artifacts and African objects, plus traveling exhibits.

For a bit of local history, the nearby **Orange County Historical Museum** traces Orange County's past with exhibits of a country store, pioneer kitchen, picture gallery, 1800s parlor and antiques. In the renovated **Firehouse No. 3** (built in 1926) antique fire trucks can be seen.

The impressive new **Orlando Science Center** is filled with hands-on exhibits

Above: In some parts of the world luxury is an everyday thing. Right: Architectural accent – the Kress store at Orlando.

and activities, and has an ultra-modern state-of-the-art planetarium.

Ripley's Believe It or Not on International Drive is a unique museum of the peculiar. This entertainment experience presents curiousities, optical illusions and weird inventions. More of old Florida can be found at **Wekiva Springs State Park**, where canoeing, boating, camping, fishing, swimming, hiking and picnicking can be enjoyed.

For visitors who like to get their adrenaline rush from discount shopping, Orlando offers a number of large shopping malls. At the **Belz Factory Outlet Mall & International Designer Outlets** on International Drive, you will find more than 160 discount stores selling name-brand items.

Winter Park

This lovely city just north of Orlando is home to one of the best shopping streets in central Florida, **Park Avenue**. Small boutiques and specialty shops sit

next to retail giants like The Gap, Ann Taylor, The Limited and Laura Ashley. Upscale restaurants provide lovely outdoor dining spots along the avenue.

Park Avenue is home to the **Morse Museum of Art**, with the world's largest collection of Tiffany glass. When the Tiffany home on Long Island burned down, much of the surviving glasswork found its way here. The museum also features paintings and furniture of the late 19th and early 20th centuries. Nearby is **Rollins College**, with a beautiful campus, and the **Cornell Fine Arts Museum**, with more than 6,000 works; one of the largest collections in Florida.

Albin Polasek Galleries is another Winter Park site, showing the work of Polasek, a Czech-American sculptor. You can stroll through his lakeside home, studio and peaceful garden dotted with unusual sculptures.

For the best view of Winter Park's multi-million-dollar homes, take the **Scenic Boat Tour**, a Winter Park tradition for more than 50 years. The one-hour cruise through beautiful lakes and canals takes in many magnificent mansions.

Kissimmee

Most visitors know this area for US Highway 192, the long, crowded strip of hotels, motels and eateries closest to Disney World. Far removed from all this is the town of Kissimmee, with its brick-paved streets, lovely shops and restaurants in the old town. The **Flying Tigers Warbird Air Museum** in Kissimmee has one of the finest collections of old planes in the United States. At **Green Meadows Farm** you can see more than 300 farm animals, and learn how to milk a cow. **Jungleland** is home to 2,000 alligators and other reptiles.

Cowboys are kings of the Kissimmee Countey Stadium in February and July, when the legendary **Silver Spurs Rodeo**, the largest in the eastern United States, comes to town. Local cowboys and bull riders join the world's top rodeo athletes for this professional event.

143

ORLANDO AND
WALT DISNEY WORLD
Area Code 407

Accommodation

LUXURY: **Disney Grand Floridian Beach Resort**, in Walt Disney World, tel. 824-3000, 900 rooms and suites in the grandest of Victorian style; **Hyatt Regency Grand Cypress**, I Grand Cypress Blvd, Orlando, tel. 239-1234, 675 rooms and suites and 146 villas, pool with waterfalls, all part of an enormous hotel/resort complex; **Disney's Old Key West Resort**, Walt Disney World, tel. WDISNEY or 934-7639, one- and two-bedroom apartments with recreation area, golf; **Buena Vista Palace, WDW Hotel Plaza**, Lake Buena Vista, tel. 827-3333, 1-800-432-2920 (FL); 1-800-327-2990 (US), 841 units; **The Peabody**, 980I International Dr. Orlando, tel. 648-8459, 1-800-221-0496 (FL); **Radisson Plaza**, 60 S. Ivanhoe Blvd., Orlando, tel. 425-4455, efficient, courteous businessperson's hotel downtown; **Renaissance Orlando Resort**, 6677 Sea Harbor Dr., Orlando, tel. 1-800-HOTELS-I, 35I-5555 (local), world's largest atrium encloses a magnificent aviary; **Disney's Vero Beach Resort**, tel. WDISNEY, theme park with beach.

MODERATE: **Harley Hotel**, 151 E. Washington St., Orlando, tel. 841-3220; **Sonesta Village Resort**, I0000 Turkey Lake Rd., Orlando, tel. 352-8051; **Holiday Inn Main Gate East**, 5678 US I92, Kissimmee, tel. 396-4488, 1-800-523-2309; **Disney's Port Orleans and Dixie Landings**, tel. WDISNEY or 934-7639.

BUDGET: **Comfort Inn Maingate**, 757I Irlo Bronson Hwy., US 192, Kissimmee, tel. 396-7500; **Economy Inns of America**, 8222 Jamaican Ct., Orlando, tel. 345-1172; **Disney's All Star Music** and **All Star Sports Resort**, Walt Disney World, tel. WDISNEY or 934-7639.

BED & BREAKFAST: **Courtyard At Lake Lucerne**, 211 N. Lucerne Circle E., Orlando, tel. 648-5188, 1-800-444-5289, beautiful compound of historic buildings including oldest house in Orlando.

Restaurants

EXPENSIVE: **Fulton's Crab House** at Disney's Pleasure Island, tel. 934-2628, open seven days a week for lunch and dinner; **Arthur's 27**, Buena Vista Palace, Reservations necessary, tel. 827-3450, dinner until I0:30 pm, men's jacket and tie required; **Atlantis**, Stouffer Orlando Resort, reservation recommended, tel. 35I-5555; **Enzo's**, 1130 S. Hwy. 17-92, tel. 834-9872, lakeside Italian dining, Tue-Sat noon-2:30 pm and 6-11 pm, closed Sun and Mon; **Christini's**, 7600 Dr. Phillips Blvd., tel. 345-8770, Mon-Sat 6 pm-midnight; **Manuel's**, 28th, 390 N. Orange Ave., tel. 246-6580, reservation required, open for dinner Tue-Sat;

Maison et Jardin, 430 Wymore Rd., Altamonte Springs, tel. 862-4410, reservation required.

MODERATE: **Bubble Room**, I35I S. Orlando Ave., Maitland, tel. 628-333I; **Café Tu Tu Tango**, 8625 International Dr., tel. 248-2222, open daily for lunch and dinner; **La Cantina**, 4721 E. Colonial Dr., tel. 894-449I, open for dinner, except Sun and Mon; **Hard Rock Café**, Universal Studios, 5800 S. Kirkman Rd. (park admission not required). tel. 351-7625, burgers, sandwiches, rock 'n' roll memorabilia and loud music, open daily for lunch and dinner; **Maison des Crêpes**, 348 Park Ave., N. Winter Park, tel. 647-4469, crêperie, specializing in seafood, lunch, Mon-Sat, dinner Tue-Sat; **Planet Hollywood**, Disney's Pleasure Island (admission not required). tel. 827-7827, burgers, salads, sandwiches, giant video screens show movie clips, open daily for lunch and dinner.

BUDGET: **The Black-Eyed Pea**, two locations: 5305 W. Irlo Bronson Hwy., Kissimmee, tel. 397-1500; 3150 University Blvd., Winter Park, tel. 679-7576, daily 11 am-10 pm, Fri and Sat till 11 pm; **Old Munich**, 5731 S. Orange Blossom Trail, tel. 438-8997, lunch and dinner daily; **PRs**, 499 W. Fairbanks Ave., Winter Park, tel. 645-2225, south-of-the-border atmosphere with great Mexican food, open daily for lunch and dinner; **Numero Uno**, 2499 S. Orange Ave., Orlando, tel. 84I-3840, small setting for authentic Cuban cuisine, daily except Wed 11:30 am-9:30 pm; **Ming Court**, 9188 International Dr., tel. 363-0338, Hunan, Szechuan, Cantonese, Mandarin menu, lunch buffet, daily from 11 am; **Cock of the Walk**, Wekiva Marina, 1000 Miami Springs Drive, Longwood, tel. 862-9640, a taste of real Florida seafood – fried catfish served on the back porch of a "down home" restaurant, open only for dinner Tue-Thur, lunch and dinner Fri-Sun, closed Mon; **Cedar River Seafood**, 7101 S. Orange Blossom Trail, Orlando, tel. 858-0525, lunch and dinner daily; **Little Saigon**, 1106 E. Colonial Drive, Orlando, tel. 423-8539, Vietnamese specialties, open for lunch and dinner daily; **Bahama Breeze**, 8849 International Drive, Orlando, tel. 248-2499, Caribbean cuisine; opens daily at 4 pm; **Italianni's**, 8148 International Drive, Orlando, tel. 345-8884, open daily for lunch and dinner.

Dinner Theater

Aloha! Polynesian Luau at Sea World, tel. 363-2200, two hours of authentic island entertainment; **Arabian Nights**, tel. 239-9223, 25 acts with horses and trick riders; **Hoop-Dee-Doo Revue** at Walt Disney World's Fort Wilderness Resort, tel. 824-4321, Disney characters, Country & Western show; **Medieval Times Dinner & Tournament**, tel. 239-8666, back to the days of knights in armor and regal feasts; **Wild Bill's Wild West Dinner Extravanganza**, tel. 351-5151, can-can girls, square dancing, archery and lots more action.

Jazz Clubs

Pinkie Lee's Jazz and Southern Cuisine, Orlando; **Pleasure Island Jazz Company**, Disney's Pleasure Island; **Rosie O'Grady's Goodtime Emporium**, Church Street Station, Orlando.

Live Music and Dancing

Backstage, Clarion Plaza Hotel, International Dr., Orlando; **Calico Jack's**, Kissimmee; **International Reggae Club**, Orlando; **Kimonos**, Walt Disney World Swan; **Laughing Kookaburra Good Time Bar**, Buena Vista Palace, Lake Buena Vista; **Orchid Garden Ballroom**, Church Street Station, Orlando; **Rock 'n' Roll Beach Club**, 8Trax, Pleasure Island.

Museums and Galleries

Orlando Museum of Art, 810 E. Rollins St., Loch Haven Park, Orlando, 19th- and 20th-century American art, pre-Columbian artifacts, African objects, tel. 896-4231; **Orange County Historical Museum**, 812 E. Rollins St., Loch Haven Park, Orlando, includes **Orlando Firehouse No. 3**, built in 1926, tel. 897-6350; **Orlando Science Center**, 811 E. Rollins St., Loch Haven Park, Orlando, tel. 896-7151; **Charles Hosmer Morse Museum of American Art**, 445 Park Ave. N., Winter Park, world's largest collection of Tiffany glass, tel. 645-5311; **Cornell Fine Arts Museum**, Rollins College, Winter Park, 6,000 works, one of the largest art museums in in the entire state, tel. 646-2526; **Albin Polasek Galleries**, 633 Osceola Ave., Winter Park, work of Czech-American sculptor with large garden, home, tel. 647-6294; **Flying Tigers Warbird Air Museum**, Kissimmee Airport, 231 N. Hoagland Ave., Kissimmee, displays, guided tours. tel. 933-1942.

Walt Disney World

General information about **Walt Disney World**: P.O. Box 10040, Lake Buena Vista FL 32830, tel. 824-4321.

All **Walt Disney World hotels**: P.O. Box I0000, Lake Buena Vista, FL 32830, tel. 824-4321. Independent hotels in Walt Disney World Village have their own addresses.

WDW packages are available through travel agents or **Walt Disney Travel Co.**, P.O. Box 22094, Lake Buena Vista, FL 32820.

Internet surfers can find all the latest information on the world's No. 1 tourist destination on the World Wide Web. The address is www. goflorida.com/ orlando

Walt Disney World has its own separate address on the World Wide Web: www.disneyworld.com

Major Sporting Events

The *Orlando Magic* play professional basketball, the *Orlando Predators* play arena football, and the *Orlando Solar Bears* play ice hockey.

The *Citrus Bowl Football Classic* is a yearly Orlando event, every January l.

Golf events include October's *Walt Disney World Oldsmobile Golf Classic*, and the *Bay Hill Invitational PGA* tournament in March.

Silver Spurs Rodeo in Kissimmee is the largest in the Eastern U.S., held every February and July.

Events

Scottish Highland Games, January.
Central Florida Fair, February.
Mt. Dora Arts Festival, February.
Bluegrass Festival, Kissimmee, March.
Winter Park Sidewalk Arts Festival, March.
Bach Festival, Winter Park, March.
Orlando Shakespeare Festival, April.
Epcot International Flower Gardens Festival, April-June.
Florida State Air Fair, late Fall, Kissimmee.

Zoos, Parks and Attractions

Jungleland Safari Zoo, 4580 W. Hwy. 192, Kissimmee, 396-1012, one acre, but home to 2,000 alligators and other animals, admission; **Central Florida Zoological Park**, 3755 NW Hwy. 17-92, Sanford, tel. 323-4450, more than 500 creatures including monkeys, lions, elephants, tigers, birds, snakes, open daily, admission. East of St. Cloud on US 192 is **Reptile World Serpentarium**, 5705 E. Irlo Bronson Hwy, tel. 892-6905, which offers half-hour programs at 11 am, 2 or 5 pm. Experts "milk" snakes for venoms used in treatment and research, more than 60 species can be seen, daily except Mon, 9 am-5:30 pm, admission; **Gatorland**, 1450l S. Orange Blossom Trail, Orlando, tel. 855-5496; **Cypress Gardens**, State Road 540, Winter Haven, tel. (941) 324-211; **Florida's Splendid China**, Theme Park, US 192 (exit 25B), tel. 396-7111; **Sea World**, 7007 Sea World Dr., tel. 351-3600 or 1-800-432-1178 (FL), 1-800-327-2424 (US); **Universal Studios Florida**, 1000 Universal Studios Plaza, Orlando, tel. 363-8000; **Terror on Church Street**, 135 S. Orange Ave., Orlando, tel.649-3327; **Ripley's Believe It or Not!**, 8201 International Dr., Orlando, tel. 363-4418.

Emergencies

Dial 911 for fire department, ambulance, or police.

Tourist Information

Convention & Visitors Bureau, 7208 Sand Lake Road, Orlando, FL 32819.

Visitor Information Line, tel. 363-5871. Most economical accommodations in the area are in Kissimmee.
Convention & Visitors Bureau, 1925 E. Irlo Bronson Hwy., Kissimmee, FL 32741, tel. 847-5000, 423-6070, 1-800-327-9159 (FL), 1- 800-432-9199 (US).

CAPE CANAVERAL

Cape Canaveral is located at the midpoint of Florida's east coast between Miami and Jacksonville. The distinctive shape of the cape makes it easy to identify on a map or from the air.

Some evidence exists of migratory Indians having visited the area from time to time, and the Spanish explored this general vicinity about 450 years ago, but the cape's history was not worthy of much mention until July 8, 1947, when the U.S. government picked this isolated spot as the launch site for its Atlantic Missile Test Range. It was from here that American and German rocket pioneers tested and perfected the forerunners of today's rockets. However, the Cape still received little notice until the U.S.S.R. launched its *Sputnik* spacecraft. Once the race to explore space got underway, national attention focused on Cape Canaveral, and it grew rapidly until too little space remained at the site for the moon mission facilities.

In 1964, the Space Center was relocated to adjacent **Merritt Island**, and the current NASA **Kennedy Space Center** was opened, from which the Apollo missions were staged and the Space Shuttle is launched. The early launch facilities and some military installations remain at Cape Canaveral, however, public access is only allowed on special bus tours from the Kennedy Space Center Visitor Complex.

Space Travel and Environmental Protection

The Kennedy Space Center encompasses 84,000 acres of land including over 25 miles of beach area. Much of this land is open to the public as a National Wildlife Refuge. In 1975, 16,600 acres

Left: The perfect illusion of meeting a real-life astronaut.

were designated as part of the **Canaveral National Seashore**. The resulting dichotomy of space-age technology and wildlife refuge may seem strange at first, but it appears to work very well.

The Space Center includes the launch facilities for the Saturn V moon missions, the two Space Shuttle launch pads, the **Vehicle Assembly Building**, the **Shuttle Landing Facility** and the **Kennedy Space Center Visitor Complex**.

Kennedy Space Center Visitor Complex

Access to the **Kennedy Space Center** is strictly controlled. All visitors must enter through the public access at the **Visitor Complex**. This facility offers free parking, a multilingual staff and guide books, a number of free displays, ticketing for bus tours of the Space Center and a large theater and museum facility. Bus tours are available for both the older Cape Canaveral Air Force Station and the Kennedy Space Center. As a rule, tours are conducted in English; for pre-scheduled groups of 53 or more people, though, foreign language tours can be arranged. The exact tour schedule and what can be seen on any particular day are governed by flight operations.

All visitors to the Kennedy Space Center start at the Visitor Complex. Bus tours can be taken from here to the old facilities at Cape Canaveral or the new ones at the Kennedy Space Center. In addition to the bus tours, the Visitor Complex offers a number of free and pay attractions. The free attractions include a simulated space station which focuses on the many types of satellites, and an outdoor display of rockets, lunar vehicles, capsules and other large space hardware. For children there is an **Exploration Station**, where they are shown demonstrations and hands-on displays related to space (advance arrangements are necessary for large groups).

405
402 Parrish Park
406
Titusville
95
405
1
South Titusville

Beach
Canaveral Nat'l. Cape Seashore
Gates closed to public
Gate 4
Wildlife Refuge Hdqrs.
Merritt Island Nat'l. Wildlife Refuge
Green Bush Pt.
Kennedy Pkwy.
Banana River
Brock Flats
Indian River

Canaveral Nat'l. Cape Seashore
Playalinda Beach
Gate 5
Launch Complex
Shuttle Landing Facility
False Cape
Shoal
Cape Shoal Rd.

Vehicle Assembly Building
John F. Kennedy Space Center (N.A.S.A)

WEST
NASA CAUSEWAY
Gate 3
407
405
NASA PARKWAY WEST
405
East Nasa Rd.
ICBM
Rd.

Complex 37
Complex 34
Complex 19
Complex 14
Complex 13
Complex 12
Complex 36

Kennedy Space Center Visitor Complex
Kennedy Space Center Hdqrs.
Bellwood
PKWY. S.
Gate 2
Courtenay
Delespine
3
KENNEDY

Causeway Rd.
Space Flight Control
Cape Canaveral

Port St. John
Hall Rd.
Sharpes
Kars Park
Home Pt.
Cape Canaveral Air Force Base Station
Gate 1 closed to public
Cape Rd.
Space Mus.
Cape Canaveral Bight
Pier
Complex 5,6

528
BENNETT
Canaveral Acres
524
CAUSEWAY
401
Port Canaveral
Mus. of Sunken Treasure
Jetty Park
528
Cape Canaveral

520
501
OLD DIXIE HWY.
Merritt Island
Sykes Cr.
Banana River
520

Canaveral Pier
Sheppard Park
ATLANTIC

Cocoa
Rockledge
Thousand Islands
Newfound Harbor
Sidney Fischer Park
Cocoa Beach

Lake Poinsett
West Rockledge
502
Buck Pt.
Georgiana
OCEAN

Bona-venture
1
Banana River Aquatic Presurve
Lotus
Patrick A.F.B. Missle Test Center

Pineda
509
PINEDA CSWY.
404
A1A

95
9
Palm Shores
Satellite Beach
Pelican Beach Park

511
West Eau Gallie
Eau Gallie
Melbourne
518
Indian Harbor Beach
Paradise Beach Park

CAPE CANAVERAL
0   6km
0   3 miles

The **NASA Art Gallery and Space Shuttle Exhibits** include over 250 paintings by some of America's greatest artists. A series of short (15-30 minute) films are shown almost continuously in various theaters. Three IMAX movies, which are histories of the space program, are shown on a giant screen (admission fee). From the Visitor Complex there are buses to the old Cape Canaveral Air Force Base, and to the new installations of the Space Center. There is a charge for these tours.

The **Kennedy Space Center** tour normally begins at the Vehicle Assembly Building (tourists are not allowed inside), where the Space Shuttle's various parts are checked out and assembled, then heads to the Headquarters Building and the Operations and Checkout Building, where the payloads are assembled and checked out prior to launch.

If your visit coincides with a launch date, you may get a chance, about three weeks ahead of time, to see the launch-ready Space Shuttle being transported from the Assembly Building aboard the Crawler Transporter. This gigantic vehicle is the size of a baseball diamond and weighs over 2,722 metric tons. It is designed to move at a sedate one mph and attain a top speed of two mph when not carrying cargo. The Crawler can transport a fully assembled Space Shuttle with mobile launch platform – a weight of over 6,500 tons.

The Space Shuttle is a truly multinational undertaking. While the United States developed the Shuttle itself, ten nations of the European Space Agency designed, funded and built "Spacelab," which is a versatile and reusable flight unit carried in the Shuttle's cargo bay. Austria, Belgium, Denmark, France, Germany, Italy, Holland, Spain, Switzerland and the United Kingdom all share in the operations of Spacelab.

Above: One of the more important harbors on the East Coast – Port Canaveral.

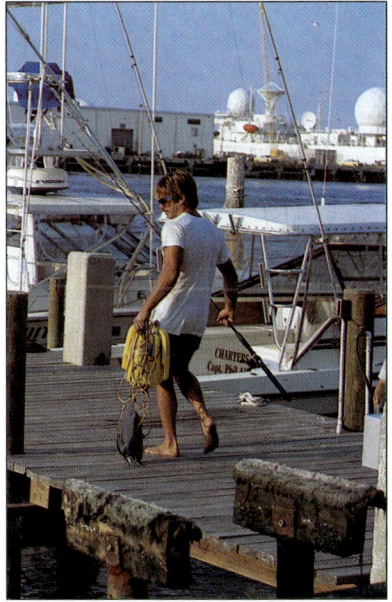

The Spaceport facilities are open from 9:00 a.m. to dusk daily except on Christmas Day. The smallest crowds are encountered on weekends, and it is strongly suggested that visitors arrive early and purchase tickets for the bus tours and movies immediately upon arrival. The various tour departures are announced throughout the facility shortly before they are ready to load.

Canaveral National Seashore

In 1963, NASA turned over to the U.S. Fish and Wildlife Service the management of all non-operational areas outside the Space Center. More endangered and threatened species reside at this immense area of the Canaveral National Seashore than at any other wildlife refuge in the continental United States.

Merritt Island Wildlife Refuge

On the seven-mile Blackpoint Wildlife Drive through the **Merritt Island** Wild-

149

life Refuge, visitors can observe many endangered species of animals. The best times for viewing are early morning or late afternoon between October and March.

Birds you can see here include wood storks, bald eagles, hawks, owls, brown pelicans, herons, spoonbills, ibis, cormorants and egrets. Land animals include deer, wild boars, bobcats, foxes, armadillos, and a variety of reptiles including the Eastern Diamondback Rattlesnake. Otters and turtles also abound in the refuge, as do alligators and manatees.

The Space Coast

The three largest towns in the area of the Space Center are **Titusville**, **Melbourne** and **Cocoa Beach**. Titusville and Melbourne are inland and have have no access to the sea. Cocoa Beach offers traditional beach activities, sailing and a

Above: Pride and public relations instead of secrecy in the Kennedy Space Center.

wealth of restaurants and hotels. Historically, Cocoa Beach is where the astronauts lived and played during the heyday of the space program. Today, they are housed at the Space Center during training and pre-launch.

While nowhere in central Florida is inexpensive, you can expect to find better room and food buys in the Space Coast area than in Orlando.

Port Canaveral is completely independent of the Space Center. It is the home port for the *Premier* and *Sea Escape* cruise lines, and is the second largest passenger cruise terminal in Florida. From here, Sea Escape Cruise Lines offers daily trips out to open sea that allow the passenger to experience the luxury and relaxation of a cruise ship. Passengers can indulge in a large number of activities, and upon reaching international waters, they are even free to gamble. After three typically enormous meals, the ship heads back to port. Premier Cruise Lines offers three- and four-day cruises to the Bahamas.

CAPE CANAVERAL
Area Code 407

Arrival / Transportation
BY AIR: Melbourne Regional Airport is serviced by American, Continental, Delta, Eastern, U.S. Air and United Express.

BY SEA: Via Port Canaveral for ocean-going vessels and a number of private marinas on the Inland Waterway for smaller vessels.

BY LAND: There are two primary entrances to the Kennedy Space Center, State Route 405 runs east from the mainland and State Route 3 runs north along Merritt Island. Follow the signs for Kennedy Space Center, not those for Cape Canaveral.

For visitors staying in Orlando, follow the Beeline East from Orlando to State Route 407. Proceed north on State Route 407 to State Route 405 and take State Route 405 east to the Space Center. Tour bus service is available from most of Orlando's larger hotels but not from Titusville or Cocoa Beach.

Accommodation
No accommodation exists at the Space Center itself. However, over 8,000 rooms are available in surrounding communities, and many visitors stay in Orlando, taking a bus from their hotel directly to the center.

Titusville is ten miles west of the Space Center. There you can find comfortable, moderately-priced accommodation at the Ramada Inn, Best Western, Rodeway and Quality Inn, all chain motels with toll-free 800 phone numbers listed in the *Guidelines* at the back of the book.

Cocoa Beach is 25 miles south of the Space Center on US Highway A1A. There you can select from among a Holiday Inn, Hilton and Howard Johnson's Lodge on the beach, also with 800 numbers listed in the *Guidelines*.

The Space Coast has no truly luxury properties. Economy accommodation can be found at any number of camp grounds, trailer parks or economy chain hotels such as Motel Six or Econo Lodge.

Restaurants
EXPENSIVE: **Mango Tree Restaurant**, 118 N. Atlantic Ave., Cocoa Beach, tel. 799-0513; **Bernard's Surf**, 25 Atlantic Ave., Cocoa Beach, tel. 783-2401, the seafood here is particularly good.

BUDGET: **Herbie K's**, 2080 N. Atlantic Ave., Cocoa Beach, tel. 783-6740, burgers in a 1950s-style diner. The Space Center also has two snack bars, the **Snack Port** and **North Food**.

Museums / Art Galleries
The Gallery of Space Flight, NASA Art Exhibit, **Rocket Garden** and the **Galaxy Theater** are all located at the Space Center. The surrounding communities enjoy a wealth of theaters, art galleries and museums.

For cultural activities in Titusville you will find the **Titusville Playhouse**, and, in Melbourne, the **Maxwell C. King Center for the Performing Arts**, the **Space Coast Science Center**, the **Melbourne Civic Theater**, the **Ensemble Theater** and the **Brevard Art Center and Museum**.

Cocoa and Cocoa Beach are home to the **Porcher House**, the **Astronaut Memorial Space Science Center**, the **Brevard Museum of History and Natural Science**, the **Cocoa Village Playhouse** and the **Surfside Playhouse**.

Hospitals
A nurse is on duty at all times at the Space Center. The **Jess Parish Memorial Hospital** is in Titusville, ten miles from the facility, at 951 N. Washington Ave., tel. 268-6111.

Post Office
The space port has its own post office, where letters can be postmarked Kennedy Space Center.

Shopping
The **Gift Gantry** at the Space Center sells space-related gift items, film, batteries and an absolutely mind-boggling variety of other souvenir items.

Parks
The Canaveral National Seashore and Merritt Island National Wildlife Refuge, Titusville, tel. 267-1110.

Fort Pierce Inlet State Park, 2200 Atlantic Beach Avenue, Fort Pierce, tel. 468-3985.

St. Lucie Inlet State Park, 16450 SE federal Highway, Hobe Sound, tel. 744-7603.

Sebastian Inlet State Recreation Area, 9700 South AIA, Melbourne Beach, tel. 984-4852.

Tourist Information
The Brevard County Tourist Development Council, 2235 North Courtenay Parkway, Merritt Island, tel. 453-2211 or 1-800-USA-1969.

The Brevard Cultural Alliance, tel. 636-ARTS.

Visitor Complex, Kennedy Space Center, tel. 452-2121, admission free, open daily from 9 am to dusk except Christmas.

The Titusville Area Chamber of Commerce, 2000 South Washington Ave., Titusville, tel. 267-3036.

The Cocoa Beach Area Chamber of Commerce, 400 Fortenberry Road, Merritt Island, tel. 459-2200.

The Greater South Brevard Area Chamber of Commerce, 1005 E. Strawbridge Ave., Melbourne, tel. 724-5400.

DAYTONA BEACH

The "World's Most Famous Beach," as **Daytona** likes to bill itself, enjoys fame for its surf and clean sands and its many fine resorts. The area also draws unwanted notoriety for its high crime rate, as well as for the crowds of college students who flock here during spring break to party.

Ever since the days when speed records were beginning to be set on the hard-packed sands of Daytona Beach by the automotive greats of the early 20th century, Daytona's image has been tied to automotive speed. It was here that Arthur McDonald roared to a 34.04 mph record in l905, and Sir Malcolm Campbell set a land speed record of 276.82 mph in l935, breaking his own existing record for the fifth time.

Above: Killing time. Right: Parking is allowed on these huge beaches. Far right: View of the race track from a Daytona racer's cockpit.

In l959, races were moved from the beach to an inland 2.5-mile oval known to racing fans around the world: the **Daytona International Speedway**. The best-known races include the Daytona 500, the Sun Trust 24 for sports cars, and the Daytona 200 for motorcycles.

The track is busiest during Speed Weeks in February, when Formula One and stock cars races are held, but equally exciting are major motorcycle races in March and October, stock car races in July, and go-kart races just after Christmas. Call (904) 253-6711 for information on all of these.

As a Mecca for motorcyclists, Daytona Beach attracts thousands of passionate bikers from all over the world; especially tatooed Harley owners and their "motorcycle mamas."

Daytona Beach has one irrefutable claim to fame: you can drive on the beaches. This is a boon to some, but a bane to others. The line seems to be drawn between those who do not mind having to watch for traffic while they

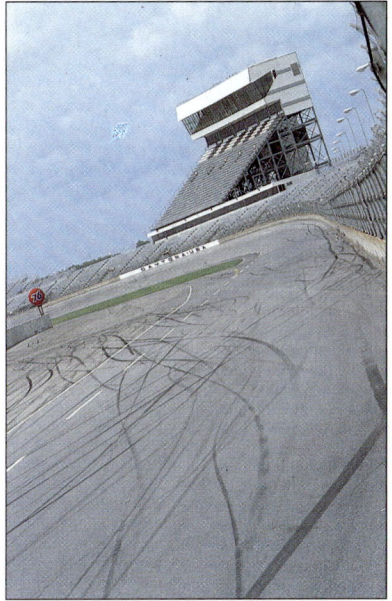

sunbathe, and those who prefer beaches free of internal combustion engines.

The 500-foot-wide sand beaches themselves stretch for 23 miles; 18 miles are open to cars during daylight hours and until an hour after sunset. The speed limit is 10 mph; the beach toll is $4. In 1990, the racing movie *Days of Thunder*, starring Tom Cruise, was filmed here. A special permit was issued, allowing racing scenes to be filmed on the beach.

Families with children love to come here, as the wide sandy beach, with its array of recreational activities, is located not far from Orlando, Walt Disney World and the Kennedy Space Center.

Although there are long, quiet stretches of beach, attention focuses on the **Boardwalk**, with its band shell, fishing pier, amusements, hot dog vendors, and rides – including a Ferris wheel. For years this was a sort of Coney Island South, alight with daily sunshine and nighttime neon, but the honky tonk is giving way to a bright, new, family-oriented image as part of a city-wide ren-

ovation project. Inexorably, the rising price of irreplaceable beachfront land is forcing out the smaller hotels and the occasional lone, single-family dwelling, and with it goes the cozy, personal atmosphere. Taking their place are tall luxurious hotels now offering more than 16,000 rooms, and relatively affordable apartment blocks.

The late 1980s saw the opening of **Ocean Center**, a 225,000-square-foot convention center that is often the scene of blockbuster attractions, from boat shows to ice shows, from rock concerts to circuses. Nearby **Peabody Auditorium** hosts concerts, operas and dance performances. New in the 1990s, in the bandshell area across from Ocean Center and Peabody Auditorium, is the soaring **Adam's Mark** hotel complex with 402 rooms.

Daytona has a very lively atmosphere, to say the least. The city's colorful **Halifax Harbor Marina** bristles with 400 new yacht slips, in the center of what will become a waterfront complex rivaling

153

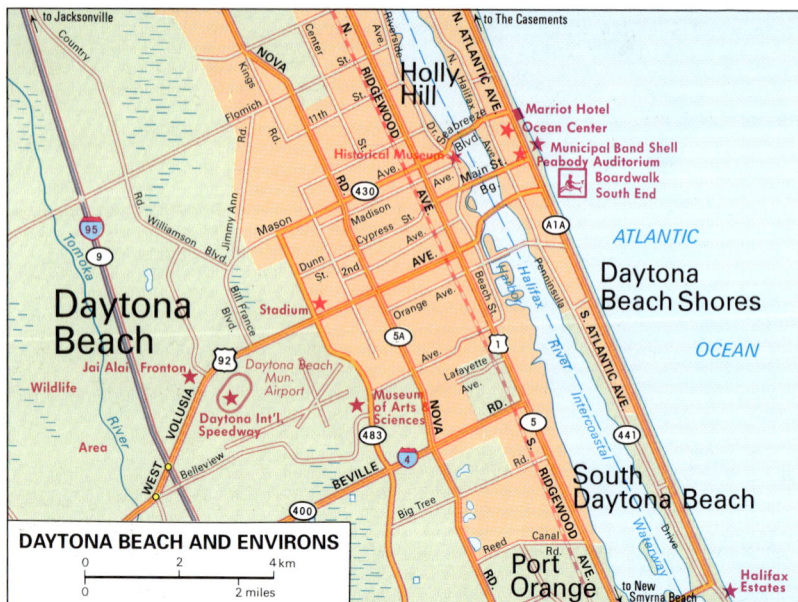

DAYTONA BEACH AND ENVIRONS

0 — 2 — 4 km
0 — 2 miles

Jacksonville's Riverwalk and Miami's Bayside Marketplace. About 100,000 square feet of speciality shops, restaurants and offices will set off a ten-acre park and river garden.

In 1918, multi-millionaire John D. Rockefeller built a winter home, **The Casements**, in Ormond Beach, where he hosted some of the great names of U.S. automotive history: Henry Ford, Harvey Firestone and Sir Malcolm Campbell. For years Rockefeller was known here as Neighbor John. Today, his former home is the **Ormond Beach Cultural and Civic Center**. Art exhibitions, ballets and concerts are now held here. Inside the building there is a display of Rockefeller memorabilia, as well as a small **Boy Scouts Museum**.

Also located in Ormond Beach is the **Birthplace of Speed Museum**, popular with racing fans of all ages. Here, the races of Daytona Beach and the development of the automotive industry are well and interestingly documented. Not only automotive history and historical photographs, but many very old artifacts of Native Americans and Spaniards can be found in the **Halifax Historical Museum**. The **Museum of Arts and Sciences** is a true bonanza: besides a dinosaur skeleton and fossils in the prehistory section, there is Cuban and American artwork on display, as well as traveling exhibitions.

The **flea market** held west of town Friday through Sunday is enormous, so give it an entire day. At the Volusia County Fairgrounds, the **Farmer's Market**, held every Wednesday, is a folk event not to be missed, with everything from food to flea market items on sale.

Daytona is thrice blessed with watersports venues: the ocean, the **Intracoastal Waterway**, and a wealth of fresh water, including the **St. Johns River** system. Fishing in all its forms is superb. To fish the famous bass waters of the St. Johns, call guide Bob Stonewater at (904) 736-7120. For deep-sea of freshwater fishing, a number of boat rental companies and guides are available.

DAYTONA BEACH
Area Code 904

Transportation
Daytona Beach Airport is served by American, Continental and Delta. The city is served by **Greyhound** buses. **Amtrak** stops at DeLand, 30 miles west. Airport shuttle vans also serve Daytona from Orlando International.

Accommodation
LUXURY: **Hilton Daytona Beach**, 2637 S. Atlantic Ave., tel. 767-7350; **Adam's Mark Daytona Beach Resort**, 100 N. Atlantic Ave., tel. 254-8200 or 1-800-282-9269; **Inn at Indigo**, 2620 Volusia Ave., tel. 258-6333.
MODERATE: **Best Western Aku Tiki Inn**, 2225 S. Atlantic, DAB Shores, tel. 252-9631 or 1-800-528-1234, motel, ocean beach, heated pool, kiddie pool; **Captain's Quarters**, 3711 S. Atlantic Ave. DAB Shores, tel. 767-3119, family-operated, all-suites, on beach, rates include newspaper and breakfast for two, other plans available, balconies with rockers, rooms sleep four and six, pool; **DeLand Hilton**, 350 International Speedway Blvd., DeLand, tel. 738-5200, inland on east edge of quaint college town, rooms, suites, nightclub, restaurant, pool.
BUDGET: **Super 8 Speedway**, 2992 W International Speedway Blvd., tel. 253-0643; **Esquire Beach Motel**, 422 N. Atlantic Ave., tel. 255-360I; **Ramada Inn Speedway**, I798 Volusia Ave., tel. 255-2422 or 1-800-352-2722; **Sun and Surf**, 726. N. Atlantic Ave., tel. 252-8412; **DeLand Country Inn**, 228 W. Howry Ave., DeLand, tel. 736-4244.

Restaurants
EXPENSIVE: **Karling's Inn**, 4640 N. US Hwy. 17, tel./985-5535, German cuisine, reservations recommended, closed Sun, Mon; **La Crêpe en Haute**, 142 E. Granada, Ormond Beach, tel. 673-1999, open Tue-Fri for lunch, Tue-Sun for dinner, reservations recommended; **Pondo's**, 1915 West Old New York Ave., DeLand, tel. 734-I995, a hideaway on a lonely road, reservations.
MODERATE: **Anchorage**, 607 Dunlawton, Port Orange, tel. 756-8102, dinner Mon-Fri, lunch weekends; **Aunt Catfish's**, 4900 Halifax Dr., Port Orange Bridge. tel. 767-4768, locals flock here, Sunday brunch, bar, open daily.
BUDGET: **Asian Inn**, 25I6 S. Atlantic Ave., DAB Shores, tel. 788-6269, Cantonese, Japanese, Szechuan, Mongolian, dinner daily except Tue until 2 am; **Blackbeard's Inn**, 4200 S. Atlantic Ave., tel. 788-9640 and N. Dixie Highway, New Smyrna Beach, fried fresh fish with chowder, salad bar, raw bar, lounge, children's menu. Hours vary.

Nightlife
J. J.'s Hideaway, 288 N. Nova Rd. Mon-Sat 11 am-2 am, dining, drinking, dancing, tropical setting; **Boulevard Station**, 542 Seabreeze Blvd., tel. 259-3827, disco, two dance floors, bars, three levels, special events, 7:30 pm to 3 am.

Museums
Birthplace of Speed Museum, 160 E. Granada, Ormond Beach, tel. 676-3346, Stanley Steamer, Model T, Model A, Glenn Curtiss memorabilia.
DeLand Museum, 449 E. New York Ave., DeLand, tel. 734-437I, local history and Southeastern artists, Native American collection.
Museum of Arts and Sciences, 1040 Museum Blvd, tel. 255-0285, a giant ground sloth, which roamed the earth I5,000 years ago, is on display, the largest skeleton ever found in North America. Cuban art from the pre-Castro period is featured.

Annual Events
Daytona Speedway events for cars and motorcycles attract an international audience. Contact the Speedway at P.O. Drawer S, Daytona Beach, FL 32015 for a yearly schedule.
An *Azalea Festival* is held in Palatka in March.
A Central *Florida Balloon Classic* is held in DeLand in May.
An *Antique Car Meet* is held in Ormond Beach on Thanksgiving weekend.

Parks
Blue Springs State Park, 2700 W. French Ave., Orange City, tel. 775-3663; **Bulow Plantation Ruins State Historic Site**, P.O. Box 655, Bunnell, FL 32010, tel. 517-2084; **De Leon Springs State Recreation Area**, P.O. Box 1338, De Leon Springs, FL 32028, tel. 985-4212; **Flagler Beach State Recreation Area**, 3100 South A1A, Flagler Beach, tel. 517-2086; **New Smyrna Sugar Mills Ruins State Historic Site**, P.O. Box 861, New Smyrna Beach, FL 32069, tel. 427-2284; **Tomoka State Park**, 2099 North Beach Streat, Ormond, tel. 676-4050.

Tourist Information
Destination Daytona, 126 E. Orange Ave., Daytona Beach, tel. 255-0415 or 1-800-854-1234.
Daytona Beach/Halifax Area Chamber of Commerce, P.O. Box 32115, Daytona Beach, FL 32115, tel. 761-7163.
Daytona Beach Shores Chamber of Commerce, 3048 South Atlantic Ave., Daytona Beach, tel. 761-7163.
DeLand Area Chamber of Commerce, 336 N. Woodland Boulevard, DeLand, tel. 734-4331 or 1-800-7494350.

GAINESVILLE

Gainesville is located in **Alachua County**, one of Florida's oldest regions. Some say the name is an Indian word for "jug," describing the deep chasm south of town which is so uncharacteristic of otherwise flat Florida. The city's original land grant goes back to the year 1817, when the King of Spain gave 289,000 acres to Don Fernando de la Maza Arredondo and his sons. Even today, thousands of Florida homeowners find that their deeds go back to the original Arredondo Grant.

Tourism has touched the little town of Gainesville – population about 100,000 – less than almost any other Florida city, yet in spite of this the area has some surprising bonuses to offer the motivated traveler.

Most people come to Gainesville on **University of Florida** business, which could mean anything from Gators football games to treatment at the university's famed teaching hospital, Shands. In all respects it is a college town, with the typical American college amenities, like fast food and inexpensive motels, all geared to a college student's budget.

It is well worth taking a stroll through the **Gainesville Northeast Historic District**, where almost 300 historic buildings, erected in the years between 1890 and 1910, show real Americana – a time of spacious wooden homes and sprawling green spaces.

The **Florida Museum of Natural History** is the southeast's largest natural science museum. Of special interest are a faithful replica of a Mayan palace and a Timucuan Indian household typical of those found here when the first Spanish explorers arrived. The **Fred Bear Museum** on Archer Road documents the history of archery.

Left: Like an abstract painting – a diver.
Above: A school bus.

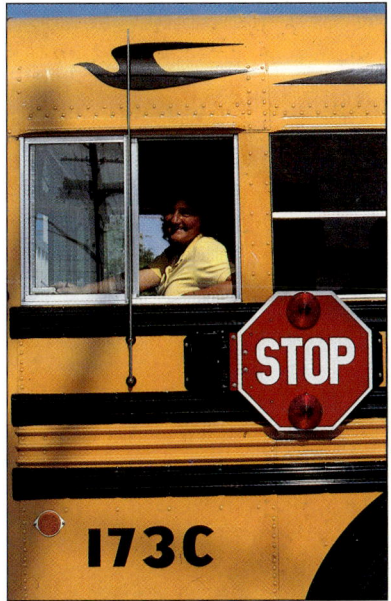

Amble through the **Kanapaha Botanical Gardens** at 4625 SW 63rd Blvd. Its collections include lovely butterfly, bamboo and palm gardens. Also in the city, off SW 13th St., is the **Lake Alice Wildlife Preserve**, a quiet place for picnicking and birdwatching.

At the edge of town is the **Devil's Millhopper State Geological Site** (4732 NW 53rd Ave.); an enormous sinkhole, so deep (574 feet) and wide (138 feet) that it has its own cool, damp, unique ecosystem which allows hundreds of plant species – some of them rare in Florida – to flourish here. The **Living History Farm** at **Morningside Nature Center**, where familiar farm animals roam pleasant pastures, is a good place to take children. It provides an inside look at timeless picturebook farm scenes.

Marjorie Kinnan Rawlings, whose book *The Yearling* won a Pulitzer prize, fled the city of New York to find inspiration in country life and a simple home at **Cross Creek**, 21 miles southeast of Gainesville, and her tough, earthy

presence can still be felt when visiting her house. Her typewriter sits on a table on the ramshackle porch, some of her home-canned foods remain timelessy in the kitchen, and park rangers continue to tend her gardens. Her notebooks are filled with clips about her public and private battles, and her liquor closet still yawns open to reveal where she kept her bottles during the days of America's Prohibition.

The house, today the **Marjorie Kinnan Rawlings State Historic Site**, is open from Thursday through Monday. Rawlings' grave can be visited nearby, at **Island Grove**, south of Gainesville off I-75. Have a look, too, at the historic hamlet of Micanopy, with its quaint shops and a bed and breakfast inn.

The Spanish once ran enormous herds of cattle on these fertile plains, and buffalo were abundant here until they were hunted almost to extinction. Buffalo have

Above: Children at the "Non-smokers of the Year 2000" gathering.

been reintroduced and are thriving here.

Two of Gainesville's tourism treasures are natural phenomena:

Payne's Prairie State Preserve, a 20,000-acre preserve south of Gainesville, is best known for its flocks of sandhill cranes and its herds of buffalo. Climb the observation tower, look out over this vast, featureless prairie, and imagine it as the large lake which it was until a century ago. Suddenly, it dried up – so abruptly that fish, and even a large passenger boat, were stranded. Today a wildlife preserve, Payne's Prairie offers swimming, picnicking, horseback riding, camping, hiking and ranger-guided tours.

Ichetucknee Springs State Park, not far away to the northwest of Gainesville, is best known for its clear, spring-fed stream. Rent an inflatable raft and float the spring run, which takes three to four hours. The waters empty into the Santa Fé, which is a tributary of the Suwannee. The park also offers swimming, scuba diving, nature trails, snorkeling and picnicking.

GAINESVILLE
Area Code 352

Arrival / Transportation
Gainesville Airport, 3400 NE 39th Ave., is served by Delta and US Air.
The city is also served by **Amtrak** trains, (station: SR 24, Waldo, tel. 468-1403), and **Greyhound** buses, (station: 516 W. 4th Ave., tel. 376-5252).

Accommodation
Everyone thinks of the high prices of accommodation in Florida, yet here is another area lacking the costly tourist facilities found elsewhere.
You won't find lavish Disney-style hotels here, and Goofy won't be around to shake your hand when you check in, but then, you won't have to pay for these amenities, either.
What you will find, however, are modest prices, clean, comfortable accommodation, and a quiet break from tourist congestion.
MODERATE: **The Radisson**, 2900 SW 13th Street, tel. 377-4000, each room has its own balcony overlooking a small lake.
Holiday Inn University Center, 1250 W. University Avenue, tel. 376-1661 or 1-800-HOLIDAY, downtown hotel with jogging paths and rooftop pool.
Marriott's Residence Inn, 400l SW l3th Street, tel. 37l-2101 or 1-800-331-3131, suites with cooking facilities, microwave, fireplace, cocktail hour, continental breakfast, newspaper included in rates, lounge, pool, spa, guest laundry, free airport transportation, bus pick-up.
University Center, 1535 Archer Rd., tel. 371-3333, special rates for Shands Hospital patients, suites have refrigerators, free airport or bus transportation, restaurant, bar, beauty salon, famous Fiddler's rooftop restaurant with excellent cuisine.
BUDGET: **Cabot Lodge**, 3726 SW 40th Blvd., tel. 375-2400 or 1-800-843-8735, rates include cocktail hour, continental breakfast.
Super 8 Motel, 4202 SW 40th Blvd., tel. 378-3888 or 1-800-843-1991, basic motel amenities at rock bottom prices, restaurants nearby.
University Inn, l901 SW l3th St., tel. 376-2222, large swimming pool, local shuttle, free continental breakfast.
BED & BREAKFAST: **Herlong Mansion**, 402 NE Cholokka Blvd., Micanopy, tel. 3466-3322, elegant home atmosphere with complete and personal pampering from live-in hosts, some rooms have private baths.

Restaurants
EXPENSIVE: **Sovereign**, 12 SE Second Ave., tel. 378-6307, reservations are recommended for this fine, atmospheric restaurant. Best-quality duckling, veal and beef.
MODERATE: **Great Outdoors Trading Co & Café**, 65 N. Main St., High Springs, tel. 454-2900, gourmet vegetarian and broiled seafood.
Ivey's Grill, 3303 W. University Ave., tel. 371-4839.

Sights
The **Gainesville Northeast Historic District** contains 290 historic buildings from the late 19th century. Many of the structures have been restored and include large public lawns and cool, leafy gardens that were popular in that era.
A self-guided walking tour can be made with the aid of a map supplied by the Visitors and Convention Bureau.
Marjorie Kinnan Rawlings State Historic Site, County Road 335, Route 3, Box 92, Hawthorne, FL 32640, tel. 466-3672, 21 miles southeast of Gainesville.

Museums / Galleries
Florida Museum of Natural History, Museum Road at Newell Dr., tel. 392-1721. The collection comprises the largest natural history museum in the southeast. Objects Gallery contains thousands of specimens, dating back to prehistoric times. Open daily except Christmas. Free admission.
Fred Bear Museum, Archer Road at I-75 (Exit 75), tel. 376-2411. A museum devoted to archery, from earliest man to present day. Open every day except Christmas. Admission fee.
University Art Gallery, on campus, tel. 392-020l. Changing exhibits. Hours vary with the school year. Free admission.

Events
The *Gatornationals Stock Car Races* are held in Gainesville every March.

Parks
The Morningside Nature Center, 3540 E. University Ave., Gainesville, tel. 334-2170, admission free, 9 am-5 pm.
Paynes Prairie State Preserve, Route 2, Box 41, Micanopy, FL 32667, tel. 466-3397.
Ravine State Ornamental Garden, P.O. Box 1096, Palatka, FL 32177, tel. 329-3721.

Tourist Information
Alachua County Visitors and Convention Bureau, 10 SW Second Ave., Suite 220, tel. 374-5231. Among other services that can be arranged through this office, a multilingual staff is available on request for those visitors who speak French, German, Dutch, Italian or Spanish.

NORTHEASTERN FLORIDA

ST. AUGUSTINE
JACKSONVILLE
SUWANNEE COUNTRY

ST. AUGUSTINE

400 years of local history are recorded here, much of it compressed into entire neighborhoods that have been faithfully restored to their origins in one century or another. The first known landing by a European explorer was by Ponce de Leon in 1513, making this America's oldest city. **St. Augustine** was founded in 1565 by Admiral Pedro Menendez de Aviles, who rowed ashore and took possession in the name of Spain. A 208-foot stainless steel cross, the tallest in the nation, rises from a quiet field a few blocks north of downtown to mark this memorable event. Also on the site is the **Nombre De Dios** mission, with the oldest Marian shrine in the country, **Our Lady of La Leche**. Each September, the founding of the city is reenacted on this spot.

In the years 1763 to 1783, when the English drove the Spanish from St. Augustine, the city was already in sad repair. Then a yellow fever epidemic killed many of the newly arrived Britons. Those who survived were kept busy first by the Seminole Wars, then by the Civil War.

Preceding pages: Jacksonville is considered the city with the largest surface area in the U.S. Left: A number of buildings in St. Augustine date back to Henry Flagler's era.

Prosperity did not return to St. Augustine until the 1880s, when Henry Flagler arrived with his railroad, but for the old city that only meant more destruction to make room for the hotels, homes and offices of a brash new era. The final blows were fires that raged through the old Spanish Quarter in 1887 and 1914. Little was left of the old town. Restoration began in earnest in the 1960s, with the goal of recreating the St. Augustine of the period from 1565 to 1821. The years included the First Spanish Period, the English Occupation and the Second Spanish Period.

When restoration was first discussed in 1936, nothing remained of the Spanish period. Researchers went back to original inventories and architectural drawings, many of them in Spain, while archeologists dug for foundations, wells, relics and roadbeds.

Today the past has been brought back to life around the restored buildings in the **Spanish Quarter Living History Museum** (San Augustin Antiguo, St. George Street). The area is alive with people in historical costume who are working, playing, eating and laughing – in short, living everyday lives of the 17th, 18th and 19th centuries.

Stop into a *bodega* for a meal, buy hand-dipped candles, baked goods or a

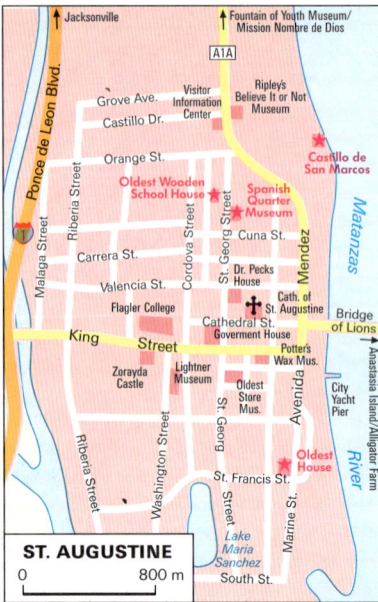

ST. AUGUSTINE

0   800 m

freshly-rolled cigar, or just stroll the streets to bask in the feeling of unhurried yesterdays.

Clusters of costumed characters can be seen here and there; fragments of guitar music steal out from hidden courtyards; on feast days there may be a sudden mustering of men in armor or a parade. At Christmas, carolers roam cobblestone streets by candlelight.

It is rare to find so faithful and complete a 17th-century streetscape, with authentic smells and sounds, and without cars or other modern intrusions. Except for the tourists clad in shorts and sunglasses, this could well be the St. Augustine of 1760 or 1850.

In the restoration area you will see dozens of shops and homes, including the grand **Ribera House** at 22 St. George Street, built by a prominent family. The restored house serves today as an office

Right: America's oldest city sports its ancient cannons.

164

and a starting point for tours of the old town.

In the **Gonzalez de Hita House**, weaving, dyeing and other textile skills are practiced and demonstrated. Further wonderfully-restored houses are the **Gomez House**, the **Sanchez House**, **Dr. Peck's House**, the **Ximenez Fatio House** and the **Oldest Store Museum**. In the **Gallegos House**, a simple Spanish soldier lived with his family in the 1750s. It is that period that has been recreated here.

The **DeMesa-Sanchez House**, one of the colonial homes which survived, has been restored to its early 19th century appearance.

The **Oldest Wooden Schoolhouse** is, indeed, the oldest schoolhouse in the U.S., built of cypress and cedar in the 18th century.

The **blacksmith shop**, where a "Spanish" smithy of the 1700s can be found at work on most days, is made of *tabby* – a building material used widely in early Florida dwellings. Tabby is a mixture of oyster shells and lime, bound with molasses. Other homes were built of *coquina*, a hard coral rock which was cut from quarries. Wood was readily available, and brick was only introduced later. Any stone had to be imported: cobblestones for the streets arrived from Europe as ballast in trading ships.

A tour of the Spanish Quarter can take an entire day; tickets which buy admission to seven homes and the blacksmith's shop are good value. Many other restored buildings contain shops or restaurants and charge no admission.

The oldest of the houses is the **Gonzalez-Alvarez House**, built in the 18th century on a site that had been occupied since the early 1600s. The ground floor is made of coquina; the upper story of wood. Today it is a National Historic Landmark, furnished to show how it looked under Spanish, British and American ownership. The house also has

a beautiful garden for whiling away the time in.

Perhaps the most notable of St. Augustine's landmarks is the great, star-shaped **Castillo de San Marcos**, a powerful symbol of the strength that was Spain in the New World, and a national monument since 1924. It has a deep moat and walls 13 feet thick – and the distinction of never having surrendered.

On a guided tour, you will hear the fort's fascinating and swashbuckling history. In the 16th century there was a series of wooden forts erected on this location, which either burned down or were destroyed by Indians. In the 17th century, the fort was rebuilt of coquina and was the northernmost defender of Spain's vast, gold-hungry Caribbean empire. The fort endured battles between the Spanish and English, then the Seminole and Civil Wars. In subsequent years it was used as a prison for soldiers who deserted during the Spanish-American War.

Start your visit at the **Visitors' Information Center** directly across from the *castillo*. An excellent orientation movie about St. Augustine is shown here, and visitors can pick up free maps here to cover their sightseeing needs.

Parking spaces are almost impossible to find in the inner city, so it is best to make your way on foot. Better still, start with a guided tour, because the city's professional guides are entertaining and well informed. On a tour, you can get oriented and decide where to go later. Sightseeing trains, which include admission to some points of interest, are an excellent idea. So are one-hour tours by horse and carriage, because you have the driver and his narratives all to yourself.

Surviving from the Flagler railroad era at the turn of the century are the ornate, Moorish minarets of **Flagler College** on King Street, originally the luxurious Ponce de Leon Hotel built in 1888, when the equally flamboyant Alcazar Hotel – since 1948 the **Lightner Museum** – was also thrown up in the frenzy of building that hit the city that decade. Today the museum contains a lovely collection of

decorative arts, including glass, Tiffany lamps, toys, musical instruments, paintings and objects from the Victorian era.

Also remaining from this period are neighborhoods of Victorian mansions, some of them incorporating parts of even older structures from the Spanish or English periods. Many of them are now cozy bed and breakfast inns.

There are a number of other museums in St. Augustine, including the **Ripley's Believe It Or Not Museum**, at 19 San Marco Avenue, which shows strange, unusual, horrible and amusing finds by Robert Ripley, for example, an Eiffel Tower made of toothpicks and a copy of a Van Gogh painting made entirely of Gummi Bears. **Potter's Wax Museum**, at 17 King Street, is one of the oldest wax museums in America. There is even a **Fountain of Youth Museum** in town, at 155 Magnolia Avenue, dedicated to Ponce de Leon. Here you get to drink a

Above: History comes alive in the Spanish Quarter of St. Augustine.

cup of water said to be drawn from the original spring discovered by the explorer. Of course, everyone knows that De Leon failed to find a real Fountain of Youth, so take your drink of youth-giving water with a sense of humor.

The oldest alligator farm in the U.S., which opened in 1893, is located outside of town on AIA, two miles south of the Bridge of Lions: the **St. Augustine Alligator Farm**. An educational nature trail leads along a boardwalk through swamps. There are reptile shows here, along with a petting zoo, apes, snakes, turtles and tropical birds.

Farther south on A1A, **Marineland** is the nation's oldest marine attraction and still one of the best. There are diverse aquatic shows, and the shell museum is one of Florida's most complete. Marineland has its own hotel, campground and restaurants. Continuing south on A1A, you will find **Washington Oaks State Gardens**. The gardens themselves are a quiet place to hike and picnic among reedy waterways and towering live oaks.

ST. AUGUSTINE
Area Code 904

Arrival / Transportation
The closest airport is **Jacksonville**, where rental cars are available. Some hotels also offer airport pick-up.

Accommodation
LUXURY: **Ponce de Leon Resort**, 4000 N. US I, St. Augustine, tel. 824-2821, golf, tennis.
Sheraton Palm Coast, 300 Club House Dr., Palm Coast, tel. 445-3000 or 1-800-654-6538, golf.
MODERATE: **Holiday Inn Oceanfront**, 3250 AlA S., St. Augustine Beach, tel. 471-2555.
Topaz Hotel, 1224 S. AlA, Flagler Beach, tel. 439-3301, some units have kitchens.
BUDGET: **Days Inn Historic**, 2800 N. Ponce de Leon Boulevard., St. Augustine, tel. 829-6581, pool, playground, café.
Quality Inn Alhambra, 2700 Ponce de Leon Boulevard., St. Augustine, tel. 824-2883, pool, jacuzzi and restaurant.
BED & BREAKFAST: **Carriage Way**, 70 Cuna St., St. Augustine, tel. 829-2467, Victorian mansion, private baths.
Casa de Solana, 21 Aviles St., St. Augustine, tel. 824-3555, 225-years old, in historic district.
St. Francis Inn, 279 St. George St., St. Augustine, tel. 824-6068, built I79, private baths.
Southern Wind, 18 Cordova St., St. Augustine, tel. 825-3623, Victorian antiques, private baths.

Restaurants
EXPENSIVE: **Raintree**, 102 San Marco Ave., tel. 824-7211, lobster, rack of lamb outdoors on the balcony of this old home, free pick-up at your hotel in the city, lunch and dinner; **Le Pavillon**, 45 San Marco Ave., tel. 824-6202, continental dining.
MODERATE: **Columbia**, 98 St. George St., tel. 824-3341, Spanish paella, black beans, filet salteado, lunch and dinner, Sunday brunch; **Old City House**, 115 Cordova St., tel. 826-0781, seafood with Italian accent; **Topaz Café**, 1224 S. Ocean Shore Boulevard., Flagler Beach, tel. 439-3275, menu includes vegetarian dishes, reservations.

Events
Blessing of the Fleet, Palm Sunday; *Spanish Night Watch,* June; *Greek Festival,* June; *Days in Spain,* mid-August, three nights of entertainment, sword fights, dancing, food, and games in the Plaza area; *Founding Day,* September 8, at the Nombre de Dios mission to recreate the scene when Menendez landed here and claimed the land for Spain; *British Night Watch, Tour of Homes, Christmas Boat Parade* and other events add up to a busy, bright December.

The official Florida State Play, *Cross and Sword,* tells the story of early St. Augustine. It plays in an outdoor amphitheater south of town on AlA, from mid-June to the end of August at 8:30 pm. No performances Sundays. Tel. 471-1965.

Museums / Sights
The **Spanish Quarter Living History Museum** (San Augustin Antiguo), St. George St., is open every day except Christmas, 9 am-5 pm. Tickets buy admission to a number of restored homes, exhibits, and museums, tel. 825-6830. Starting point is the Ribera House at 22 St. George St., which serves as an information center.
The Gonzales-Alvarez House, 14 St. Francis St., is open daily except Christmas. Admission.
The Lightner Museum was built by railroad magnate Flagler as a grand hotel, the Alcazar. There are a number of collections inside. Admission fee. Tel. 824-2874.
Zorayda Castle, built in I883, was patterned after the Alhambra, complete with seraglio. Admission fee. Tel. 824-3097.
The **Castillo de San Marcos National Monument**, 1 Castillo Dr., St. Augustine, on Rt. A1A, is open daily except Christmas for a small admission fee. Tel. 829-6506.
Fort Matanzas National Monument, c/o Castillo de San Marcos National Monument, 1 Castillo Dr., St. Augustine, FL 32084, tel. 471-0116.
Fountain of Youth Museum, 155 Magnolia Ave., tel. 829-3168.
The oldest Marian shrine in the U.S. is **Our Lady of La Leche** at the Nombre de Dios mission, the site where this land was first claimed for Spain. It is free, but donations are expected, tel. 824-2809.
The **St. Augustine Alligator Farm**, Anastasia Island, tel. 824-3337, is the state's oldest, founded a century ago. Animals, reptiles, shows, on A1A, two miles south of the Bridge of Lions.
Sightseeing Trains, tel. 829-6545.
Carriage Tours, tel. 829-0818.

Parks
Anastasia State Recreation Area, camping, swimming, picnicking, mountainous dunes, forests, beaches. Admission fee. Tours, tel. 461-2033.
Faver-Dykes State Park,1000 Faver Dykes Rd., St. Augustine, tel. 794-0997.
Washington Oaks State Gardens, 6400 N. Oceanshore Boulevard., Palm Coast, tel. 446-6780.

Tourist Information
St. Augustine-St. John's Chamber of Commerce, 52 Castillo Drive, St. Augustine, FL 32085, Tel: 904/829-5681.

JACKSONVILLE

Visitors usually hurry through **Jacksonville** because of its heavy traffic and the stink of the paper mill. Those who stay to discover the city will be surprised and amply rewarded. One of the most culturally rich cities in the South, it is abuzz with business travelers, conferences and energy. In the area surrounding Jacksonville are beautiful beaches, historic sites, state parks, forests and rivers, and the number of activities on offer – including sailing, hunting, fishing and camping – is enormous.

French Huguenots settled along the St. Johns River in 1562, founding Fort Caroline – which was soon taken by the Spanish – not far from the mouth of the river. The city developed around the old fort, and was later named after president Andrew Jackson.

After the Civil War, balmy Jacksonville was drawing up to 75,000 tourists

Above: Crossing the St. Johns River by car.

each winter. Then, in 1888, came yellow fever, followed by quarantine. Tourism withered, then died completely after the Great Fire of 1901. Yet Jacksonville's location, with its deep port and benign climate, made up in industry what it could not win in tourism.

By the 1920s, 30 movie studios had moved here, abandoning cold and cloudy New York for Florida's blue skies. Lumber, citrus, pulp products and cigars made the city an import-export hub.

Jacksonville has many facets. The smart, modern city has a number of quaint old neighborhoods – **San Marco**, **Riverside**, **Avondale**, and **Springfield**. Today, the St. Johns River remains not only an important commercial artery, but is also the source of much of the city's recreation.

Take a pleasant stroll along the mile-long **Riverwalk**, with its many shops, restaurants, cafés and street artists; see the gigantic fountain in **Friendship Park**, illuminated at night by colored lights. And, if you are here in October, do

JACKSONVILLE AND ENVIRONS

not miss the Jacksonville Jazz Festival on the river at **Metropolitan Park**. It is one of the nation's best.

In the **Jacksonville Museum of Contemporary Art**, at 4160 Boulevard Center Drive, artifacts from pre-Columbian times can be viewed, and there are also multimedia shows and workshops. The **Museum of Science and History**, at 1025 Museum Circle, contains a natural science collection and a planetarium. The **Cummer Museum of Art and Gardens**, at 829 Riverside Avenue in the Riverside district, is housed in an old mansion, nestled among beautifully-landscaped gardens. Valuable Meissen porcelain, an Oriental collection, and modern works of painting and sculpture are exhibited here.

The **Fort Caroline National Memorial** (12713 Fort Caroline Road, at the mouth of the St. Johns River) marks the location of the one-time Huguenot fort, a true-to-the-original reproduction of which can be seen here. In addition, there are plenty of places around for hiking and picnicking.

Those who feel they need a pause for refreshment after all this culture can visit **Jacksonville Landing** on Independent Drive along the north bank of the St. John's River. You can go make a few purchases, enjoy multinational cuisine or listen to live music in this enormous shopping and entertainment complex.

Kids, however, prefer the **Jacksonville Zoo**, at 8605 Zoo Road, in which animals are kept in well-planned enclosures. Here you will find a miniature railway, elephant and camel rides, a petting zoo and a nature trail.

Jacksonville's sand beaches – **Atlantic Beach**, **Neptune Beach**, **Jacksonville Beach**, and **Ponte Vedra Beach** to the south – stretch out for more than 16 miles, and offer recreation, water sports and fishing.

Route A1A, also known as the Buccaneer Trail, leads to the **Kingsley Plantation State Historic Site**. Built in 1791, this is one of the oldest surviving plantations in Florida, situated on the north shore of Fort George Island. Tour the

169

home and slave cabins with a guide and learn the sordid story of eccentric slave trader Zephaniah Kingsley. A bit further on, the **Little Talbot Island State Park**, with its wild, five-mile-long sand beach, offers unspoiled nature and good opportunities to observe waterfowl and otters.

The A1A continues on to **Amelia Island**, with the quiet vacation town of **Fernandina Beach**. Building boomed here during Victorian times, and many of the showplace mansions remain: bay windows, turrets and stained-glass windows are everywhere. The town's character is marked by arts and crafts and antique shops, galleries, boutiques and restaurants. The **Palace Saloon**, at 117 Center Street, is the oldest in the state.

Further interesting buildings are the red brick Victorian courthouse, with its cast-iron Corinthian columns, and the **Florida House** (22 South 3rd Street), once a posh hotel where guests included

Above: A somewhat peculiar – but very Floridian – Santa Claus.

the Rockefellers and Carnegies. Today it is a fine bed and breakfast inn.

The mansions along south 7th, 8th and 9th streets are among Florida's finest Victoriana. The **Bailey House**, at the corner of 7th and Ash, is a fine Queen Anne style bed and breakfast inn. On South 7th, between Beech and Cedar, is the **Fairbanks House**, a superb Italianate house built in 1885 for a major in the Confederate army.

One of the best gingerbread homes, with its elaborate Chinese Chippendale porch, is on the northeast corner of Beech and South 8th. The **Williams House**, at 103 South 9th, was where the personal belongings of Jefferson Davis, president of the Confederacy, were stored during the Civil War.

St. Peter's Parish Episcopal Church, which dates to 1859, has hand-carved furnishings of Florida cedar and pine, and a Tiffany window honoring two doctors who served during a yellow fever epidemic. The **Presbyterian Church**, one of the oldest churches in Florida, was a garrison during the Civil War. Even the old cemetery, **Bosque Bello**, is worth a visit because it so poignantly records city history; sailors drowned at sea, the many victims of yellow fever epidemics and wars, and names changing from Spanish and English to Portuguese and Greek as waves of immigrants came and went. Fernandina Beach's turbulent history is also brought back to life in the **Amelia Island Museum of History** (233 South 3rd Street).

Fort Clinch is located at the beachside **Fort Clinch State Park**, where you can fish, swim, camp, hike or picnic. This park forms the northern tip of the island. The fort's masonry is a fine example of the bricklayer's art, and the endless tunnels and dungeons of the fort make for interesting exploring on a hot day. Climb the ramparts for a superb view of **Cumberland Sound** and the mouths of the **St. Marys** and **Amelia** rivers.

JACKSONVILLE
Area Code 904

Arrival / Transportation
Jacksonville International Airport is served by American, Continental, Delta, Trans World, United and US Air. **Amtrak** trains, 30 Clifford Lane, tel. 766-5110. **Greyhound** buses, 10 Pearl, tel. 356-9976, toll free 1-800-231-2222.

Accommodation
LUXURY: **Jacksonville Hilton**, 565 Main St., tel. 398-8800, overlooks river, free garage, pool, buffet breakfast; **Marriott**, 4670 Salisbury Rd. at I-4, tel. 296-2222, indoor and outdoor pools, tennis and golf, fitness center, restaurant, lounge with entertainment; **Omni**, 245 Water St., tel. 355-6664, 354 rooms, suites, heated pool, restaurant, lounge with dancing, garage, valet parking extra, located downtown.
MODERATE: **Jacksonville Marriott at Southpoint**, 4670 Salisbury Rd., tel. 296-2222 or 1-800-228-9290, pool, restaurant, bar, exercise room, free daily newspaper; **Doubletree Club**, 4700 Salisbury Rd., tel. 281-9700, I-95 at Turner, Southpoint area, heated pool, exercise room, cozy public room with big-screen TV, library, breakfast, night snacks, van to restaurants.
BUDGET: **Inns of America**, 4300 Salisbury Rd., tel. 281-0198, no-frills l00-room hotel with 24-hour restaurant next door, also at Salisbury Rd., off Butler Rd., exit I-95, tel. 281-0l98; **Red Roof Inn**, 60999 Youngerman Circle, tel. 777-1000, free airport transportation, coffee.
BED & BREAKFAST: **House on Cherry St.**, 1844 Cherry St., tel. 384-1999.

Beach Accommodation
LUXURY: **Lodge at Ponte Vedra Beach**, 607 Ponte Vedra Blvd., tel.273-9500, home of Professional Golf Association, 54 holes of golf, best rooms have fireplace, private whirlpool, casual or gourmet dining; **Amelia Island Plantation**, 3000 First Coast Hwy., Amelia Island, tel. 261-6161; **Marriott** at Sawgrass, l000 TPC Blvd., Ponte Vedra Beach, tel. 285-7777, hotel rooms, suites, villas with kitchen, golf, tennis.
MODERATE: **Fairbanks House**, 277 S. 7th St., Fernandina Beach, Amelia Island, tel. 261-4838; **Florida House**, 22S. 3rd St., Fernandina Beach, Amelia Island, tel. 261-3300, illustrious bed and breakfast inn.
BUDGET: **Comfort Inn**, 2401 Mayport Rd., Atlantic Beach, tel. 249-0313, breakfast included, near fishing boat charters, Mayo Clinic, one mile to beach.

Restaurants
EXPENSIVE: **Augustine Room**, Marriott at Sawgrass, Ponte Vedra Beach, tel. 285-7777, continental cuisine, open daily, reservations. **Mediterranean**

Room at the Lodge, Ponte Vedra Beach, tel. 273-0210, reservations, upscale dining. *MODERATE:* **Café Carmon**, l986 San Marco Blvd., tel. 399-4488, in historic district, closed Sun; **Café on the Square**, l974 San Marco Blvd., tel. 399-4848, open daily except Christmas, New Year's Day; **Dinner Theater**, Alhambra, 12000 Beach Blvd., tel. 641-1212, Tues-Sun, cocktails, buffet, show, Mon closed; **Partners**, 3585 St. Johns Ave., Jacksonville, tel. 387-3585; **Ragtime**, 207 Atlantic Blvd., Atlantic Beach, tel. 241-7877, Cajun seafood, Sunday brunch, reservations; **Café St. Johns**, Marina at St. Johns Place, 1515 Prudential Dr., tel. 396-5100, brightly Floridian with waterfall. *BUDGET:* **Beach Road Chicken**, 4132 Atlantic Blvd., tel. 398-7980, great chicken, great price.

Museums / Sights
Cummer Museum of Art and Gardens, 829 Riverside Ave., tel. 356-6857, Meissen porcelain, Oriental and modern art, admission fee; **Jacksonville Museum of Contemporary Art**, 4160 Blvd. Center Dr., tel. 398-8336, pre-Columbian, Oriental and modern art, closed Mon; **Lighthouse Museum**, 1011 N. 3rd St., Jacksonville Beach, tel. 241-8845; **Museum of Science and History**, 1025 Museum Circle, tel. 396-7062, science museum and planetarium, admission fee; **Museum of Southern History**, 4303 Herschel St., tel. 388-3574; **Jacksonville Zoological Park**, 8605 Zoo Road, tel. 757-4462; **Amelia Island Museum of History**, 233 S. 3rd St., Fernandina Beach, tel. 261-7378.

Parks
Zephaniah Kingsley Plantation, 11676 Palmette Avenue, Jacksonville, tel. 251-3537; **Fort Caroline National Monument**, 12713 Fort Caroline Road, Jacksonville, tel. 641-7155; **Little Talbot Island State Park**, 12157 Heckscher Drive, Fort George, tel. 251-2320; Fort Clinch State Park, Amelia Island, tel. 277-7274.

Events
Pilot Club Antique Show, worldwide dealers, January; *Civil War battle reenactment*, February; *Delius Festival*, March; *Taste of Jacksonville*, April; *Bluegrass Festival, Art Festival*, Sept; *Jacksonville Jazz Festival*, October (tel. 353-7770); *Gator Bowl Festival* and football game, December.

Tourist Information
Jacksonville Convention and Visitors Bureau, 3 Independent Dr., tel. 798-9148. Arts hotline information, tel. 353-6100.
Amelia Island-Fernandina Beach Chamber of Commerce, P.O. Box 472, Fernandina Beach, FL 32034, tel. 261-6997 or 1-800-2-AMELIA.

SUWANNEE COUNTRY

The **Suwannee River**, made famous by Stephen Foster, oozes out of the warm muck of the Okefenokee Swamp in Georgia, and rambles through Florida where it is fed by other springs and rivers before emptying into the Gulf of Mexico near Cedar Key. A long time before the white man came, the river formed a natural boundary between the lands of the powerful Apalachee and the less-well-organized Timucuan Indians.

All along its sunlit, 250-mile length, the Suwannee boasts uncrowded parks, villages, viewpoints, and picnic sites inescapably blessed by the imagined strains of *Old Folks at Home*, perhaps better known from its first line: "Way down upon the S'wannee River."

Since 1935, this has been Florida's official state song, written by the immortal composer, Stephen Foster. The irony is

Above: Relaxing or just being lazy? Right: Watching an alligator show.

that Foster never even saw the river. He needed a two-syllable name, and he liked the sibilant sound of this one. So he changed the spelling to S'wannee to eliminate one syllable, and a legend was born.

The stately and impressive **Stephen Foster State Folk Culture Center Memorial**, overlooking the river at **White Springs**, is a repository of Florida music and culture. On display are several dioramas depicting Foster's short, unhappy life.

Born in 1826, Foster was an early musical success. His talent first surfaced at the ripe old age of four, and his *Tioga Waltz* was written at the age of 15. A chronic alcoholic who was unable to make a go of either his marriage or his career, he died alone in New York City at the age of 37, with only 38 cents in his pocket. Today, his legacy of more than 200 songs, including *Oh! Susanna, Camptown Races, Old Dog Trey* and *My Old Kentucky Home*, are a treasury of Americana known to every school child in the

United States, as well as throughout the world.

In the Foster Culture Center is a 200-foot, 97-bell carillon tower which is open to guided tours. Also on display are Foster's desk and piano, sheet music and other memorabilia. Hauntingly lovely concerts are played every half-hour. As his music steals out across the surrounding park and picnic grounds, it is strange to think that Foster's blessing lies over a spot he never saw.

The Culture Center is also the scene each May of the Florida Folk Festival, in which Florida craftsmen display their wares, while storytellers entertain the crowds with folk tales, folk singers and musicians perform, and old-fashioned Florida foods are served. The center's other annual event is the Jeanie Auditions and Ball, in which women vie for music scholarships. This event is held in early October.

White Springs was a posh spa during Victorian times. Sulphur springs here were held sacred by Indians, and as late as Civil War times the injured from both sides could come here to safely nurse their wounds. The ruins of the bathhouse were later turned into an observation tower. The village of White Springs is a page out of pioneer times, with a few shops, general stores and rustic restaurants.

Nearby **Suwannee Springs** was also a thriving spa during the 19th century, when "taking the waters" was considered the chic – as well as the healthful – thing to do. Today, nothing remains but a ghost town of dilapidated houses, an old gas station, and the ruins of the bathing pool. Gospel singing, three days and nights of it, are celebrated in Live Oak's Suwannee River Jubilee, held each June on the banks of the river.

The Battle of Olustee was a major Confederate victory, fought at Olustee, 15 miles east of Lake City, in 1864. The site, strategically located between Jacksonville and Tallahassee, is now a quiet corner of the Osceola National Forest. Every year in February, "soldiers" in authentic

uniforms reenact this Civil War battle, which involved 10,000 soldiers, of whom more than 100 died and 800 were wounded. Come any time to see the site and hike its nature trails, including the Battlefield Trail, and tour the museum.

North of **Lake City**, the 157,000-acre **Osceola National Forest**, with its cypress swamps, woods and ponds, offers camping, hiking, boating, swimming and fishing. The park is named for Osceola, the greatest Seminole leader and the last to make an effective stand against Washington. Most park activities center around **Ocean Pond**, which lies just inside the park's main entrance east of Lake City.

One of the best spots to enjoy the river is **Suwannee State Park**, near **Live Oak**, which has camping, fishing and hiking. County-operated **Dowling Park** also has campsites. Nearby, at **Falmouth Spring**, 125 gallons of clear 70-degree water

Above: Ospreys – protected birds in Florida.

bubbles out of the earth every second and begins its route into the Suwannee.

At **Hart Springs Park** and **Manatee Springs State Park**, both down river, the Suwannee gets even wider. You can swim all year in the 72-degree waters, or "spring boils," which are pools where water appears to be boiling up out of the earth. Canoes for exploring the river are rented by outfitters, including the Spirit of Suwannee Campground, north of Live Oak.

The canoeing is fairly easy, without whitewater, but it is best to rent from an outfitter who provides drop-off and retrieval service so that you can enjoy a one-way trip with the current. When water levels allow, a paddle-wheel boat offers pleasant sightseeing rides out of White Springs.

Only a century ago, steamboats plied these same waters, bringing travelers and cargo deep into countryside that had no other highways. Another riverfront state park is **O'Leno**, south of Lake City, on the Santa Fé, a river which flows into the Suwannee. Like many other rivers in this region, it is fed by springs which have formed enormous labyrinths of caves.

Scuba divers dote on the dark and dangerous sport of underwater cave exploration. However, even if you are an experienced diver, do not try cave diving without special instruction and the proper equipment. Suwannee County alone has a dozen major springs; **Peacock** and **Ginnie Springs** are among the most popular with divers.

This is a forgotten corner of Florida, untouched by razzle-dazzle theme parks. Tobacco barns and turpentine stills remain from another era. Sap buckets still cling to pine trees. Tobacco is still grown here and the state's only remaining tobacco auction is held in Lake City.

Suwannee country is an ideal area for hiking, bicycling, camping and picnicking along the river with the name that sounds like a melody.

SUWANNEE RIVER AREA
Area Code 904

Arrival / Transportation
The nearest airports are Jacksonville, Gainesville and Tallahassee. Many towns and cities throughout the region are served by Greyhound buses, but this area is not highly developed for tourism as compared with other Florida locales, so a rental car would be an excellent idea for touring.

Accommodation
Far from the high prices of modern Florida, you will not find costly or luxurious accommodation in these parts, but homier, personalized places to stay, family-style motels and cabins that retain a flavor of rural Florida. *MODERATE:* **Holiday Inn**, US 90 at I-75, Lake City, tel. 752-390l, spacious grounds, restaurant, bar, pools, playground, laundry, lighted tennis courts, golf privileges. *BUDGET:* **Howard Johnson**, US 90 at I-75, tel. 752-6262 or toll-free 1-800-654-2000, golf privileges, pool, playground, restaurant; **Ramada Inn**, US 90 at I-75, tel. 752-7550 or toll-free 1-800-2-RAMADA, pool, whirlpool, playground, restaurant, bar; **Colonial House Inn**, I-75 at SR 136, White Springs, tel. 963-240l, bare essentials, nice hosts, pool, playground.

Restaurants
Nell's Steak and Bar-B-Q, Branford, Hwy. 129 N., west of Ichetucknee Springs, tel. 935-1415, downhome comfort, food like Mom used to make – Dixie specialities, including chicken gizzards, deep-fried mullet, greens, cornbread and breaded catfish, all offered as part of a bounteous buffet. Open for three meals every day.
Wayside Restaurant, US 90 at I-75, tel. 752-158l, opens for a fisherman's breakfast at 6 am, closes at ll pm, more hearty southern fare.

Museums / Galleries
Stephen Foster State Folk Culture Center, US 41 North, P.O. Drawer G, White Springs 32096, tel. 397-2733, the museum is set amidst a lush, 250-acre park, open every day, admission fee.
The **Florida Sports Hall of Fame**, honors the achievements of more than 100 athletes who live in Florida or participated in sports in the state. Located on Hall of Fame Drive, off US 90-W. For information contact P.O. Box 1847, Lake City, FL 32056-1847, tel. 758-1310.

Sights
The **Osceola National Forest** is one of the primary remaining wilderness areas in the southeastern US. Camping sites are available at the Ocean Pond area

and the river swimming and boating are idyllic. In addition, the park includes a Civil War battlefield. Route 7, Box 95, Lake City, FL 32055, tel. 752-2577.
Olustee Battlefield Historic Site has hiking trails through another Civil War battlefield. P.O. Box 40, Olustee, FL 32072.
Suwannee River State Park, Route 8, Box 297, Live Oak, FL 32060, tel. 362-2746, offers camping, fishing and hiking along the scenic river.
Ichetucknee Springs State Park, Route 2, Box 108, Fort White, FL 32038, tel. 497-2511, is a great place for river tubing, which is simply floating in an inflated automobile or truck tire tube. Canoeing is also fine, and there are hiking trails which lead to secluded swimming spots.
O'Leno State Park, Route 2, Box 1010, High Springs, FL 32643, tel. 454-1853, is yet another fine site for river activities, camping, fishing, hiking and swimming.

Guided Tours
The **Suwannee Bicycle Association** offers numerous active tours including canoeing on the Suwanee River, bicycle riding and historic tours. Some of the tours combine walking and biking and include an overnight stay in a small country inn. Tel. 397-2347.

Events
Battle of Olustee Reenactment, near Lake City, is held in February. Hundreds of elaborately costumed participants clothed in authentic-looking blue and gray uniforms, complete with period weaponry, act out maneuvers of Confederate and Union forces on the now tranquil spot where the real battle was held. They put on a realistic show for spectators, who come from far and wide to participate or watch. And since this is one battle the Confederacy won, this deeply southern part of the United States carries on with other localized celebrations and special events at this time of year.
The Florida Folk Festival, White Springs, features traditional music and crafts, held in late May.
The Jeanie Auditions and Ball are held in October.
The North Florida Air Show, Lake City, October. This is a big air show with stunt and aerobatic flying, parachuting contests, antique and special interest aircraft, and more.

Tourist Information
Chiefland Area Chamber of Commerce, P.O. Box 1397, Chiefland, FL 32626.
Hamilton County Chamber of Commerce, P.O. Drawer P, Jasper, FL 32052, tel. 792-1300.
Suwannee County Chamber of Commerce, P.O. Box C, Live Oak, FL 32060, tel. 362-3071.
Lake City / Columbia County Tourist Development Council, I5 E Orange St., Lake City, FL 32056-1847, tel. 758-1312.

NORTHWESTERN
FLORIDA

TALLAHASSEE
THE PANHANDLE
PENSACOLA
THE NORTHERN PANHANDLE
APALACHICOLA

TALLAHASSEE

Tallahassee, Florida's capital, is one of the state's most historic cities and is the center of a region of outstanding recreational attraction. Yet because the city is off the beach and far from theme parks, and because its attractions are natural and publicly owned rather than man-made and promoted for profit, visitors vacationing in Florida tend to overlook it.

The region that surrounds Tallahassee has four distinct seasons. Springtime, the most beautiful, is also the busiest. The state legislature meets for at least 60 days, and for much of April and May, timed to the flowering of azaleas and dogwoods, redbuds and magnolias, the city celebrates Springtime Tallahassee, its grandest festival. Summers are hot and humid, though at this time the city's famed "canopy roads" – avenues lined in trees draped with Spanish moss – provide their fullest shade, while springs and beaches only an hour away leave Tallahassee an affordable hub for sampling all the region has to offer. Canopy roads can be found around the capital building, as well as around Park Avenue and Monroe Street.

Preceding pages: Shrimp boats at anchor in the evening. Left: Florida's capitol building in Tallahassee.

Fall brings splendid color to the big Apalachicola National Forest; winter brings cool to cold nights and warm days. The region's numerous woodland trails beckon hikers.

The nearby towns of Havana, Monticello and Quincy spoil visitors with their lovely restored houses and troves of antique shops, farmhouse restaurants and bed and breakfast inns.

The first inhabitants of this region were Native Americans of 12,000 years ago. Their remains and those of a mastodon found in the area are displayed at the **Museum of Florida History**. The oldest evidence of permanent settlement identifies Mississippi Indians who settled by Lake Jackson between 1250 and 1500. In 1539, Hernando de Soto's Spanish expeditionaries invaded the peninsula and set their winter encampment at the site of present-day Tallahassee. Here, De Soto celebrated the first Christmas in North America, though his brutal treatment of the natives was hardly Christian. Artifacts from the encampment are displayed at the **De Soto State Archeological Site**, at 1022 De Soto Park Drive.

In the 18th century, the English did not drive only the Spaniards from the region, but the Indian population as well. In 1823, William Pope Duval, the first civilian governor of the Territory of Florida

179

(newly acquired by the United States in 1821) chose a location for the territorial capital by dispatching explorers east from Pensacola and west from St. Augustine. Where they met was to become the new capital. Their rendezvous occurred at a place the Indians called *tallahassee*, which – auspicously for a new settlement – meant "old town."

A two-story masonry capitol building was erected in 1826, which was enlarged in 1845 and again in 1902. In 1977, the sober 22-story-tall-tower of the **New Capitol** was completed. At the same time, the 1845 **Old Capitol** was restored to its former appearance of 1902. Today, in the Old Capitol, with its "Grecian" columned entrance, cupola-crowned tower and striped awnings, visitors can view a wealth of historical documents. Visitors learn, for example, that the praying mantis was voted in as the state's official insect. In the main lobby, chandeliers are

Right: Old-style transportation through the capital's historic district.

rigged for both gas and electricity, because when Tallahassee was wired in 1902, electricity was available only six hours a day.

The city is best enjoyed by walking through its historic districts. These include Downtown, the Park Avenue Historic District and the Calhoun Street Historic District. The three districts are described in detail in a brochure published by the Historic Tallahassee Preservation Board. A ride on the **Old Town Trolley**, however, a restored streetcar which makes 15 stops in the old town, is a more romantic way to see the city.

One of the oldest commercial buildings in Florida is the **Union Bank** on the Apalachee Parkway, which dates from 1841. It houses a museum on Florida banking history. The historic **Adams Street Commons** was redesigned in the 1970s, with a serpentine street to slow traffic and wide brick walks to encourage pedestrian sightseeing. Adams Street itself, which dates from a century ago, is today lined with offices and saloons, as

well as the **Governor's Inn**, the best hotel in the capital. Gallie's Alley originally provided service access to **Gallie's Opera House**, which, in the last quarter of the 19th century, was a social and cultural center. Today, the alley is the site of special outdoor events, and Gallie's Hall, as the building is called, has been converted to offices.

The **Museum of Florida History**, in the R.A. Gray Building (500 South Bronough Street), provides the best overview of Florida's past. Departments include prehistory – featuring the skeleton of a mastodon – Spanish settlement and the Civil War. The treasures of a Spanish galleon can be seen here. You can even climb aboard a reconstructed steamboat of the kind that opened Florida to vacationers and settlers in the 1870s, visit a recreated "tin-can tourist camp" from the 1920s, and a experience a reconstructed citrus packing house with a display of Florida's colorful citrus packing labels. The Gray Building also houses Florida's State Archives and the State Library.

Some of Tallahassee's oldest and finest homes, dating to Territorial times, were built along today's **Park Avenue Historic District**. **The Columns**, at 100 North Duval, is a white-columned brick home built in the 1830s on land purchased for $5 by William "Money" Williams. Legend has it that he embedded a nickel in each of the bricks baked for construction of the house. Today the building is occupied by the Tallahassee Area Chamber of Commerce.

Churches, cemeteries and parks are clustered in the district. These include the neo-classicist **First Presbyterian Church**, which dates from 1835, the Neo-Gothic **St. James' Church**, one of the first for blacks (it dates from 1899 and now houses offices), and **St. John's Episcopal Church**, once known as "the gentlemen's path to heaven" because of the weighty social standing of its congregants. The city began burials in the **Old City Cemetery** in 1829. Segregation at that time was practiced unto death, and not only between blacks and whites, but

between northerners and southerners as well: during the Civil War, Union dead from the nearby Battle of Natural Bridge were interred in the western half of the cemetery along with blacks.

The most impressive homes of the city are located in the **Calhoun Street Historic District**. A century ago the area was known as Gold Dust Street because of the wealth represented in the district's homes. The **Brokaw-McDougall House** (329 North Meridian Street), dating from 1856, with six magnificent Corinthian columns, is elegantly neo-classicist, with formally-landscaped gardens. The house belongs to the Preservation Society and is open to the public.

The **Governor Bloxham House** (410 N. Calhoun St., dating from 1844) is Tallahassee's only remaining residence from the time before statehood. The **Meginnis-Munroe House** (125 North Gadsden Street), built in 1854, today houses offices and fine art exhibits of the Le Moyne Foundation. The **Knott House Museum** (301 East Park Avenue), built in 1843 and renovated in 1928, was the Tallahassee site for the reading of the Emancipation Proclamation, which freed America's slaves. Visitors enjoy the Victorian furnishings, but especially the simple poetry which Luella Knott wrote and then tied to favorite pieces of furniture, which has earned the house its nickname, "The House That Rhymes."

There are many attractions worth visiting outside of the city center. On the south side of the city is the **Black Archives Museum** at **Florida A&M University**, which houses one of the United States' largest collections of African-American artifacts and memorabilia of notable black American heroes.

For children, the **Tallahassee Museum of History and Natural Science** (3945 Museum Drive, near the airport), is especially interesting. In this outdoor museum, an 1880's farmstead, a 52-acre

Above: In the historic district of Tallahassee.
Right: In the Tallahassee Museum of History and Natural Science, nature is still pristine.

natural habitat zoo and a hands-on Discovery Center can be visited. There is a birds of prey aviary and reptile exhibits, as well as picnic areas and hiking trails. Kids who like to paint enjoy the **Le Moyne Art Gallery**, at 125 North Gadden Street. Admission to the house, built in 1853, is free. Artists from Florida and Georgia are exhibited, and there is a special children's section with pictures hung lower down.

To the north are the **Maclay State Gardens** (3540 Thomasville Rd.), commissioned by New York financier Alfred B. Maclay, with ponds, nature trails and landscaped gardens. Here you can swim, take boat rides or have a picnic. The **San Luis Archeological and Historical Site** (2020 Mission Road) lies on a hilltop to the northwest. An Apalachee village once stood here, and later, in the 17th century, a Spanish mission. Excavations, in which jewelry, pottery and everyday items have been recovered, are ongoing.

Going northeast and leaving the city along Centerville Road, which is shaded by oak trees, you will come to **Bradley's Country Store**. Sausages are made here in the store's own butcher's shop from a traditional country recipe

Surrounding Area

The **Natural Bridge Battlefield State Historic Site**, lies to the south of Tallahassee, six miles from Woodbridge. This site marks the 1865 battle won by a depleted Confederate battalion made up of old men and youngsters who held off advancing Union troops. Their victory allowed Tallahassee to remain the only Confederate capital east of the Mississippi River to remain out of Union hands.

Nearby, 15 miles south of downtown Tallahassee, is the **Wakulla Springs State Park**, with one of the only guest lodges on any of Florida's public lands. Exceptional visitor opportunities include 30-minute boat tours on the Wakulla River, where Tarzan movies were filmed in the 1930s, and where wildlife is abundant. Glass-bottom boat tours glide over

the mammoth spring, one of the largest and deepest in the world. In the wooded park, visitors can swim, picnic or get in some birdwatching.

The Tallahassee-St. Marks Historic Railroad State Trail runs from Tallahassee south along a former railroad bed that has been transformed into a hiking trail. It begins south of the city on Route 363, and is popular with bicyclists, equestrians and hikers, who can enjoy the scenery down to the town of **St. Marks**, on its namesake river, site of **Posey's**, one of the region's favorite seafood restaurants and meeting places.

The **St. Marks National Wildlife Refuge** is situated in the marsh and swamp lands of the coastal section of Apalachee Bay. The refuge is wonderful for hiking, cycling, canoeing and birdwatching. Here various species of eagle are found, as are alligators and other reptiles and mammals. There are a great number of

trails extending through the refuge, the main one of which ends at St. Marks Lighthouse.

Nearby, at the confluence of the Wakulla and St. Marks rivers, is the **San Marcos de Apalache State Historic Site**, a Spanish bastion that dates from 1528. Panfilo de Narvarez, together with 300 men, built and launched the first ships made by Europeans in the New World here. Remnants of fortifications remain from the Civil War and Spanish-American War.

From St. Marks, you can wander onto the **Florida Trail**, which begins near Orlando and extends for a total of more than 1,000 miles. The trail passes through part of the St. Marks Wildlife Refuge, and then crosses the immense **Apalachicola National Forest**, made up primarily of cedar, pine and cypress trees, on its way to Orange.

In the northeast of the Apalachicola National Park is the Silver Lake Recreation Area, with campgrounds and plenty of opportunities for hiking.

Above: The pioneer tradition of building multi-story wooden houses is being revived.

TALLAHASSEE
Area Code 850

Arrival / Transportation

AIR: Delta/ASA and USAir. Flight time to Atlanta is less than one hour; to Miami just over one hour.
LAND: On I-10, 166 miles west of Jacksonville and 244 miles east of Pensacola.

Accommodation

LUXURY: **Governor's Inn,** half block from the State Capitol in the Adams Street Commons area. 209 S. Adams Street, tel. 681-6855; **Las Casas Motor Inn,** 2801 N. Monroe Street, tel. 386-8286; **Killearn Country Club & Inn,** resort with pool, sauna, golf, 100 Tyron Circle, tel. 893-2186.
MODERATE: **Ramada Inn Tallahassee,** quaint, good value, 2900 North Monroe Street,, tel. 386-1027; **Holiday Inn-University Center,** 316 W. Tennessee Street, tel. 222-8000; **Capitol Inn,** 1302 Apalachee Parkway, tel. 877-3141; **Courtyard by Marriott,** 1018 Apalachee Parkway, tel. 222-8822; **Wakulla Springs Lodge,** 1 Springs Rd., Wakulla Springs, tel. 224-5950, attractive rooms in a Spanish-style lodge, amidst state park lands and a wildlife refuge.
BUDGET: **La Quinta Motor Inn-North,** 2905 North Monroe Street, tel. 385-7172; **Cabot Lodge,** 2735 North Monroe Street, tel. 386-8880; **Days Inn South,** 722 Apalachee Parkway, tel. 224-2181.

Restaurants

EXPENSIVE: **Andrew's Second Act,** 228 Adams St., tel. 222-2759, European cuisien; **Silver Slipper,** 531 Scotty Lane, tel. 386-9366, one of the oldest family-run restaurant in the state, a favorite of the political crowd – five presidents of the US have eaten here.
MODERATE TO BUDGET: For Apalachicola oysters and Panacea blue crab, try **Spring Creek** in Crawfordville, tel. 926-3751, or **The Wharf,** 4141 Apalachee Pkwy., Tallahassee, tel. 656-2332. **Barnacle Bill's,** 1830 N. Monroe St., tel. 385-8734, rustic restaurant, their offerings of smoked dolphin and cobia are a rare experience. For a good ol' Southern home-cooked meal complete with beef and fresh baked bread, try **Nicholson's Farmhouse,** Hwy. 12, Quincy, tel. 539-5931, a family plantation home built in 1820. A boot-stomping local hangout is **Rooster's,** 2226 N. Monroe St., tel. 386-8738, guests are allowed to grill their own 32-ounce sirloin. **Chez Pierre** is downtown's best French restaurant, 115 N. Adams St., tel. 722-0936.

Museums / Sights

New Capitol, panoramic views from the 22nd floor, West Plaza, tel. 488-1234; the **Old Capitol** offers vignettes of Florida's political history, South Monroe St. at Apalachee Parkway, tel. 487-1902; **The Museum of Florida History** in the R.A. Gray Building, 500 S. Bronough Street, tel. 488-1673; **The Black Archives Research Center and Museum,** Florida A&M University, tel. 599-3020, these Archives display objects which chronicle the entry of blacks into the United States and their history in Florida; **Tallahassee Museum of Science and Industry,** 3945 Museum Dr., tel. 576-1636.

Parks / Historic Sites

Alfred B. Maclay State Gardens, 3540 Thomasville Rd., Tallahassee, tel. 487-4556; **St. Marks National Wildlife Refuge,** P.O. Box 68, St. Marks, FL 32355, tel. 925-6121; **San Luis Archeological and Historical Site,** 2020 Mission Rd., Tallahassee, tel. 487-3711, free admission; **De Soto State Archeological Site,** 1022 De Soto Park Dr., Tallahassee, tel. 922-6007, free admission, daily 8 am-5 pm.

Tours

No guided tours are offered around Tallahassee for individuals. However, the **Old Town Trolley** provides a 15-stop, cassette-equipped tour – with headphones – that operates every 15 minutes Mon-Fri through the historic districts.

Festivals / Seasonal Events

Springtime Tallahassee is a week-long festival in late March or early April. It includes concerts, home and garden tours and art shows.
The Blue Crab Festival in May at nearby Panacea attracts 20,000 crab lovers annually.
The *Native American Heritage Festival* in September honors the various Indian tribes – it features Indian foods, as well as craft and culture exhibits.

Hospitals

Apalachee Center for Human Services, 2636 NE Capitol Circle, tel. 487-2930.
Capitol Rehabilitation Hospital, 1675 Riggins Rd., tel. 656-4800.
Tallahassee Community Hospital, 2626 Capitol Medical Blvd., tel. 656-5000.
Tallahassee Memorial Regional Medical Center, 1300 Miccosukee Rd., tel. 681-1155.

Tourist Information

Tallahassee Area Convention & Visitors Bureau / Leon County Tourist Development Council, 200 W. College Ave., Tallahassee, tel. 413-9200 or 1-800-628-2866.
Tallahassee Area Visitor Information Center, New Capitol, West Plaza.
Visitor Information Center, 200 W. College Ave., Hospitality Sq., tel. 413-9200.

Chumuckla Baker Liberty Ponce de Leon
Blackwater River De St. Rec. Westville
State Park Crestview Dorcas Mossy Head Funiak Area Ponce
Allentown Milligan Sprs. de Leon
Molino Blackwater 11 15
Harold Eglin Air Force Redbay
Cottage Hill Wallace Base 13
Gonzalez Pace Milton Eglin Air Force
Avalon Base 15
Beach Amusement Freeport
Ensley Park Valparaiso Fred Gannon Bruce
East Niceville Rocky Bayou
West Bay Holley St. Rec. Area Portland
Pensacola Pensacola Navarre Florosa Shalimar Choctawhatchee Bay
Bay Mary Destin Santa Rosa
Warrington Oriole Beach Esther Fort Beach Grayton
Gulf Breeze Walton Mus. of the Beach Eden Gardens
Pickens Pensacola ROSA Gulfarium Beach Sea and Grayton Beach
SANTA Beach ISLAND Indian St. Rec. Area Seagrove
Gulf Island Nat'l Seashore Seaside Beach Inlet Beach Westbay
Laguna Beach
Miracle Strip
Amusement Park
Panama City
Gulf V
St. An
State

GULF OF MEXICO

GULF COAST – MIRACLE STRIP

0   10   20   30   40   50 km

0   15   30 miles

THE PANHANDLE

Florida's Panhandle, once a secret known to but few initiates, is gradually being discovered by the the masses. The Apalachicola River, flowing north to south, forms the "border" between the Eastern Time Zone and the Central Time Zone. It is only a hop, skip and a jump from the Panhandle to the neighboring states of Alabama and Georgia. Broad plantations and grand columned mansions are hallmarks of the Panhandle, where the lifestyle is relaxed and Southern hospitality comes straight from the heart.

Exploration of the Panhandle began with Navarez and De Soto in the 1520s and 1530s. From Europe, culture came to the New World along with the Renaissance. By contrast, lower Florida cities, such as Boca Raton and Venice, date only from the 1920s. The climate of the Panhandle is not all sunshine and beach weather, though; snow sometimes falls in winter, water pipes can freeze and fireplaces take on a fundamental importance when the mercury dips.

Summer, however, is *the* season here, as in all of Florida. Those who enjoy staying at the beach, but who prefer to avoid the crowds and tumult of the summer months, should come here in the autumn, after school has started: the beaches are less packed, the waters in the Gulf are still warm enough for pleasant swims, and the prices drop noticeably.

that will not result in destruction of property or bodily harm. Motels are overfilled, and traffic becomes hopelessly snarled. Unless you are a teenager yourself, or else a voyeur, coming here in the spring should be avoided at all costs.

In summer, vacationers flood four-lane Route 231 out of Alabama and Georgia. At the Gulf they move into their private condos or else head en masse further along Highway 98. Motorists stuck in fumy traffic either lose their temper or, if they have endured this form of torture before, lethargically observe the situation as if it were a huge TV spectacle.

From Panama City Beach to Destin, Panhandle summers for a million young parents recall their own childhoods here, as each new generation continues to return. Retirees on fixed incomes love the economy of weekly and monthly rates, as no place in Florida is more affordable than the Panhandle. Food – especially seafood – is less expensive here than anywhere else in the state. Seafood in the restaurants on the coast is freshly-caught and will satisfy even the most finicky gourmet.

But the Panhandle is also made up of historic cities along with its modern way of life, as well as one-of-a-kind state parks and a large selection of lodgings, from luxurious to basic comfort. Many of the hotels along the beach that were damaged or destroyed by Hurricane Opal are back in business, and new hotels have also opened.

The three most popular vacation areas in the Panhandle are relatively close to one another: **Panama City Beach** to the east, the coastal area around **Destin** in the center, and **Santa Rosa Island** to the west. Each boasts a share of the best beaches in the continental U.S., formed of fine white quartz sand. These beaches are doubly appealing: the dunes near the coast are protected areas and remain generally undisturbed and beautiful, helping keep the beaches intact.

In winter, the beaches are deserted, a lot of restaurants are closed, and the nightlife, so charged with energy during the summer, hardly exists at all. Dressed warmly, hikes along the bays can be undertaken during the day, when the mild sun and sea breezes can be enjoyed. In the evening, the day can be ended with a nightcap in front of the fireplace.

When spring arrives, so do the college students. Whereas "spring break" has been harrassed out of Florida cities lower down the coast by police who enforce behavior codes to the letter, Panhandle towns – especially Panama City Beach– continue to turn a blind eye to teenage misbehavior. In fact, the police are instructed to tolerate almost any behavior

All three resort areas, however, suffer from unattractive strips of motels, fast food restaurants, and all kinds of rip-off joints which, with ever-bigger and more obtrusive glaring neon signs, try to outdo each other in the quest for the tourist dollar. Yet each also has its outstanding undeveloped beach parks where, especially in the off-season, sun, sand and surf can be peacefully enjoyed.

Panama City Beach

All the beaches are, of course, open to the public, but the big hotels and condominiums set between road and beach, and the motels elsewhere aligned cheek-by-jowl, effectively block views of the sea for miles. And, although "spring break" pumps big money into the economy, many properties that cater to the college teens are left shabby and in need of repair just before summer. Paved parking lots line the roadside, trees are few. Neon signs are everywhere announcing T-shirt bargains, early-bird dinners, miniature golf and go-kart rides. Aesthetically, the resort area suffers from an excess of entrepreneurship unbalanced by civic restraint.

The phenomenon is well known in Florida, from Miami Beach to Daytona Beach, along Highway 192 to Kissimmee, on the beaches of St. Petersburg, and especially here in Panama City Beach. Enjoyment of this Panhandle resort area requires the suspension of critical faculties or a stocial or Zen detachment. Or, of course, simply a degree of naïveté. For too many, unfortunately, Panama City Beach is the true face of America.

One after another the **Miracle Strip** hauls out its big-league attractions. The biggest of these is the **Miracle Strip Amusement Park**, which features a

Left: A hundred miles of white beaches – enough to make you forget the Caribbean!

first-class wooden roller coaster, the Starliner, plus an assortment of 30 other rides and attractions, arcade games, carnival pastimes, and live entertainment. The **Sea Dragon**, which is shaped like a Viking ship, rocks passengers high up into the air.

Nine acres of things to do at Miracle Strip Park include a log flume ride, the Abominable Snowman, ferris wheels, small-scale rides for chidren, continuous entertainment, contests, games and special events. During the tourist season, from late May to early September, the park is open daily. The rest of the year it is only open on weekends.

If the amusement park eventually gets boring, there is **Shipwreck Island** next door, a six-acre water park complete with a 35-mile-per-hour water slide, a 370-foot White Water Tube, wave machines, river floats and rope swings. The park offers attractions for younger children, too (open daily from June to September; Saturdays only in April and May).

Close by the City Pier is **Gulf World**, where bottle-nosed dolphins, sea lions and parrots perform. Set in tropical gardens, this attraction also includes the **Coral Reef Theater**, and a tide pool where visitors can pet a real stingray. Entertainment here includes underwater shows, such as shark feedings and scuba demonstrations.

Just back of the beach area is the **Museum of Man in the Sea**, which tells the story of human efforts to live, work and play underwater. Marine life sciences, underwater exploration, marine salvage and construction, oceanography, and underwater archeology are some of the fields about which visitors are informed by divers.

The **Zoo World Zoological and Botanical Park**, on Front Beach Road, features big cats, primates, an aviary and a petting zoo – altogether about 100 different species of animals can be seen here. The zoo is a participant in the Species

Survival Plan, an international zoological association for protecting the world's most endangered species and, wherever possible, for reintroducing them into the wild.

Back on the strip, you come across shopping arcades that invite you to spend some of your hard-earned vacation money, and miniature golf courses where you can test your coordination and skill. Miniature golf, which was introduced in the 1920s, has lost none of its popularity in Panama City Beach, where six large courses draw in the crowds. One of these is the size of a football field and is laid out in the form of a labyrinth. The course even challenges competition players in a race against time.

Panama City offers the most active night scene along the Panhandle. Dog racing, which started in the United States in 1919, is represented here at the **Ebro Greyhound Park**, where visitors can enjoy dinner and drinks, and wager on the races. The **Southern Elegance** offers romantic evening dinner cruises around the bay, as well as day-long "cruises to nowhere" for those who just want to get away from it all for a few hours.

The younger generation favors the discos. Popular clubs here include the **La Vela** and the **Spinnaker**, both of which are located on the beach, and which offer everything you could possibly want: from multi-level sun decks and swimming pools to performing stages and big dance floors. Both of these clubs book top acts in the spring.

Night spots that cater to a somewhat older and quieter age group include **Pineapple Willie's**, with comedy acts and live bands, and the **Ocean Opry Show**, which specializes in country and western music.

When nothing will do but relief from the hustle and bustle, respite is as close as the **St. Andrews State Recreation Area**. This park, at the eastern tip of Panama City Beach in the section called Land's End, is one of the most-visited in Florida, encompassing 1,063 acres of forests and marshes, and renowned for its pristine beaches and clear waters. Nature trails cross the dunes and woodlands. On the **Grand Lagoon**, campers and backpackers can always find a nice spot for themselves. Alligators, wading birds, deer, raccoons and smaller animals find shelter here. The jetties formed of granite boulders that extend into the gulf and protect the beach will bring back memories for many adults, who climbed over these same rocks as youngsters.

Shell Island lies somewhat further to the southeast in St. Andrews Bay. This island was formed in the early 1930s, when an artificial pass was cut through the eastern tip of the peninsula and jetties were built. The island is accessible by boat only (there are trips twice daily except Mondays on the *Island Queen* from Marriott's Bay Point Resort).

As the island has no shops or commercial facilities, it is a wonderful place for a picnic. Plan a good half day for the relaxing trip to Shell Island, where the only thing that might bother you is the fact that life is not always as peaceful and enjoyable as it is right here.

Not surprisingly, the best resort in the area – indeed, the best resort in the entire Panhandle – is far removed from the hectic action of the strip, here at the far east end of Panama City Beach along St. Andrews Bay. This is **Marriott's Bay Point Resort**, an exclusive and protected enclave. The resort offers two 18-hole golf courses including the par 72 Lagoon Legend, acclaimed by golfdom as one of the new signature courses of the South. After the festivities of the Fourth of July, the Bay Point Billfish Invitational Tournament takes place here, a sport-fishing contest with $350,000 in prize money up for grabs.

Right: Thousands of greyhounds run during the racing season.

Marriott guests can enjoy twelve tennis courts, four of which have floodlights, five swimming pools, and a private marina. There are seven restaurants, including the **Terrace Court**, the most elegant on the coast. The Yacht Club's lounges are open to hotel guests and outsiders.

Also worth a visit is the **Downtown Art District** in Panama City, a historic area on St. Andrews Bay which, in recent years, has been upgraded with arty and inexpensive bars, with more than a dozen attractive galleries. In the **Visual Arts Center**, year-round exhibitions, classes, and tours take place. On special occasions, works by regional artists are often available most affordably at the Arts Center, as well as at the various galleries.

Seaside and Grayton Beach

West of Panama City Beach, just half an hour by car but light years away in its atmosphere, is **Seaside**, a combined vacation resort and celebrated "new town." In stark contrast to the garish Miracle Strip, Seaside restores confidence in the concepts of order and scale, proportion and style. The little village is the work of city planner Robert Davis, who inherited these few hundred acres by the beach and decided to build here, inspired not by the immense proportions of most modern buildings, but rather by the straightforward architecture of the American North, where he grew up.

The result is a community with houses that are pleasing to the eye, and which offer "old-fashioned" comfort. Small Queen Anne style vacation houses have been built here, painted in joyful pastel colors. Seaside's honeymoon cottages are especially charming: there is a bedroom downstairs that opens to the beach, and a living room upstairs which has a kitchenette with a wood stove in it.

Seaside's guests are supplied with the very best, from fresh vegetables to imported beer, by the **Modica Market**. Three restaurants, including the award-winning **Bud & Alley's**, fashionable

shops, an excellent bookstore among them, a weekly flea market, and occasional dance and theater performances provide for a high quality of life. Architects Andres Duany and Elizabeth Plater-Zyberk, who built Seaside for Davis, have provided a breath of fresh air for vacationers who demand style – and who are able and willing to pay extra for it.

Grayton Beach, further west, is perhaps Florida's most beautiful beach of all. Restless dunes shift with the tides, rearranging the shorefront. Beach houses, clustered together here more like a village, do not interfere with the view. The tiny community surrounded by trees lies beyond the east-west road hidden between patches of forest and salt-water ponds. Art galleries and unconventional restaurants are run by people who care more about the village than they do about lining their pockets.

Above: Having a rest at a beach gallery.
Right: Plea and warning at the same time –
dunes are an important ecological factor.

In Grayton Beach, one of Florida's 20 best restaurants, **Criolla's**, can be found. Local gourments, however, generally head for the **Picolo Restaurant** and **The Red Bar**, which features live jazz bands during dinner every night of the week.

Destin

Destin is the newest of the Panhandle resort areas. In contrast to Panama City Beach it is more stylish and high-class. Here there are more privately-owned condos than motels, more upscale restaurants and shops, making Destin an improbable host to future wild spring break parties. A number of wealthy retirees have settled here. Motor boats fill Destin's marina, which is also home to Florida's largest charter boat fleet, underscoring the conclusion that well-to-do people must live here.

Since the 1950s, the fishing village of Destin has developed into a popular center of tourism. Despite its rapid development, however, the beaches were spared

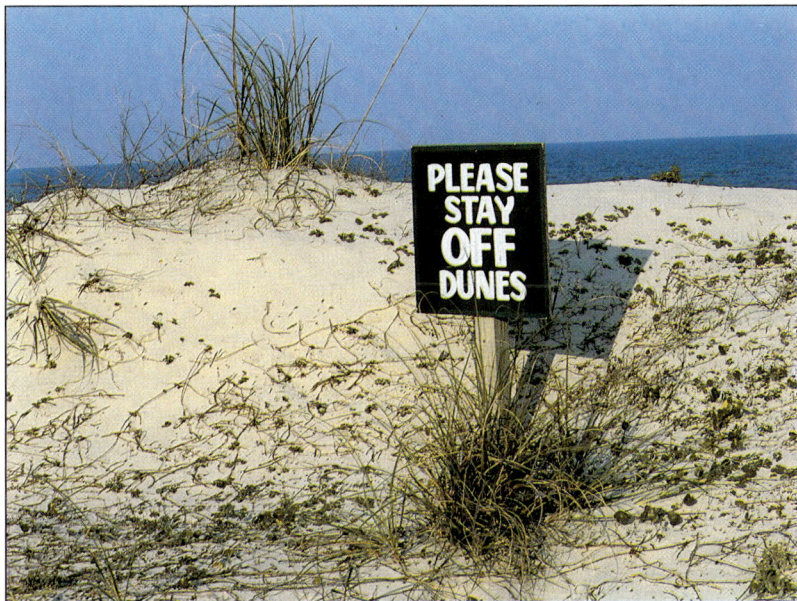

the effects of the building boom. Fully 60 percent of the shore of Okaloosa County has been set aside as public parks or belong to the mammoth **Eglin Air Force Base**, one of the largest in the world. A small section of the base liest to the west of Destin and on the eastern tip of Santa Rosa Island. The rest of the base stretches across an immense section of the interior to the north. The base can be visited year-round. The **U.S. Air Force Armament Museum** at the east gate exhibits weapons and aircraft, among them a reconstructed ST-71 Blackbird spy plane.

Henderson Beach State Park effectively separates the more touristic build-up of Destin from the quieter condominium and private home areas to the east. A number of good seafood restaurants edge the eastern beaches, built up on pilings behind the dunes, with beautiful views of the gulf. To the west, **Sandestin**, with its immaculate private homes and apartment buildings on a wonderful beach, is likewise separated from the hustle and bustle of the tourist area.

Visitors come to Destin for the fine white sand beaches, no doubt, and for the uncomplicated lifestyle here, without the crowds of teenagers on the beach promenade.

This is one of the top shell-collecting destinations in the world. But unlike other destinations, shell collectors here don't simply walk the beach. A boat runs to the sandbar a mile away called **Sand Dollar City**, and to the limestone reef three miles out where the rarer horse conchs, lion's paws, tulips and queen helmets are found. Though these graceful creatures can be seen and observed in the clear waters, live animals ought to be admired but not taken. Snorkeling and diving are popular among the artificial reefs. Dive shops offer excursions and diving certification.

Destin also attracts anglers, who try their luck from off the 1,200-foot Okaloosa Pier, as well as from the outer pier and jetties. Twenty-seven miles offshore, sailfish, white and blue marlin, dolphin, and wahoo can be caught.

Nowhere in the Gulf does the offshore shelf drop so precipitously to 100 fathoms as here off Destin, attracting some 20 species of game fish in seasonal runs conveniently close to shore.

For golfers, ten excellent courses are located here, chief among these is the Golf Club at **Bluewater Bay**, hailed by *Golfweek* for six consecutive years as the top course in northwest Florida. Tennis fans have 104 courts to choose from. Two stables rent horses. The **Destin Fishing Museum** looks at the history of this city, which calls itself the "world's luckiest fishing village."

The **Indian Temple Mound and Museum** in neighboring **Fort Walton Beach** to the west tells the story, through interesting exhibits, of life on the Gulf Coast from prehistoric times to the present. The **Gulfarium**, on Okaloosa Island near Fort Walton, is home to sea dwellers such as dolphins, seals and sharks, some of which can be seen in shows. West of Fort Walton Beach, in Gulf Breeze, is the **Gulf Breeze Zoo**, with some 700 animals and a petting zoo with elephant rides.

A string of modern houses on stilts can be seen along the beaches to the west as far as Navarre, where, fortunately, the usual crowds of tourists tend to be absent. Near Navarre, there is a bridge to the island of Santa Rosa.

Santa Rosa Island

Santa Rosa Island stretches from Fort Walton to Pensacola Bay. This section of beach constitutes the Florida portion of **Gulf Islands National Seashore**. Every year, thousands of tourists stream onto **Pensacola Beach** to the west, with its fine white sand beaches, hiking trails and the laid-back way of life that can be enjoyed in this paradise. The water is ideal for swimming, and the high waves in winter draw a large number of surfers here. Portions of the island, especially wildlife preserves and protected areas, as well as a spectacular sand dune landscape, cannot be commercially developed, so that, now and then, you can still happen upon a remote, unspoiled stretch of beach. **Fort Pickens**, erected on the western tip of the island in 1829, is open to the public.

PENSACOLA

Pensacola, 191 miles from Tallahassee, is Florida's largest city in the west. In 1559, Tristan de Luna settled a colony of about 1,500 people at Pensacola Bay and reported to King Philip II that this was "the best port in the Indies." Two years later the settlement was devastated by a hurricane and abandoned, and so Pensacola, though founded six years before St. Augustine, lost the distinction of being the oldest continuously occupied settlement in North America. The area later belonged to France and England before becoming part of the U.S. in 1821.

After the Civil War, the region's vast forests of oak, cedar, cypress and pine led to a timber boom, from which the shipping and railroad industries benefited enormously. The **Museum of Industry** in the **Pensacola Historic District** – also known as the **Seville Historic District** – depicts this period of Panhandle history (Zarragoza and Tarragona streets).

Across the street, the **Museum of Commerce** offers a completely reconstructed old-time Pensacola street, with many businesses common to Victorian times. Included are a print shop, pharmacy, toy store and hardware store. Some are more than just museum exhibits and are open for business. The museum also includes horse-drawn buggies and an early gas station.

Another popular attraction nearby is **Julee Cottage**. This house was purchased in 1805 by Julee Panton, a "free woman of color," and was later owned by

Right: Modern "stilt" houses like these skirt the beaches.

a succession of free black women. The cottage has been reconstructed as the **Black History Museum**.

Pensacola's old town is charming, with its antique shops, art galleries and museums. This was once the center of the young town, where wealthy merchants built their homes along the bay. They were Scottish, Spanish and English. Their restored houses are a mixture of styles: half-timbered country, Victorian and Creole – all early 19th-century.

The **Palafox District** was the commercial heart of old Pensacola. A number of the old wooden buildings survived fires, hurricanes and urban renewal, and have been restored to their original beauty. Noteworthy is the old city hall (built in 1908) on Jefferson Street across from **Plaza Ferdinand**, which is now the **T.T. Wentworth State Museum**. The Neo-Renaissance building houses a huge local history collection. The third floor contains a section called **Discovery**, a hands-on museum experience for children. Another good adaption of a former gov-

ernment building is the **Pensacola Museum of Art**. This building once housed the Pensacola City Jail. The **Old Christ Church**, Florida's oldest Protestant church, on Seville Square, is today home to the **Pensacola Historical Museum**. Not to be missed is the **North Hills Preservation District**, near the old town, made up of 50 blocks with 500 fashionable houses from the turn of the century. In **Hopkins Boarding House**, opulant Southern breakfasts, lunches and dinners are served daily except Mondays.

West of downtown, *Top Gun* fans will enjoy the **National Museum of Naval Aviation** (Naval Air Station, Navy Blvd., via US 98). This is one of America's outstanding military museums, illustrating the history of warfare and military-inspired inventions. The NC-4 airplane built by Glenn Curtiss, which made the first transatlantic flight in 1919, and the 1973 Skylab space module can be seen here. Admission is free.

The top event in Pensacola in May is the Five Flags Fiesta, when the landing

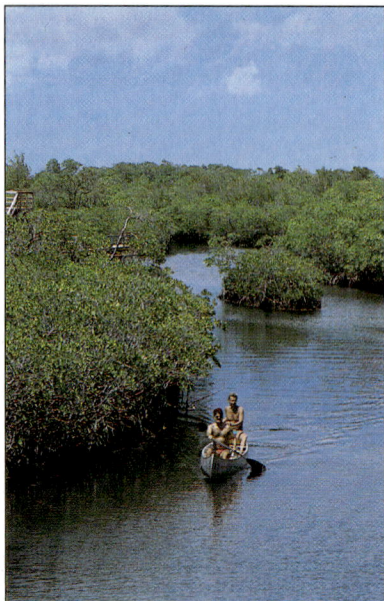

by Tristan de Luna y Arellano in 1559 is celebrated by young and old.

Farther west is the beach town of **Perdido Key**, which is the last resort area before the Alabama state line. The last stop in the state is the **Flora-Bama Lounge & Package Store**, an open-deck oyster bar on the Gulf.

THE NORTHERN PANHANDLE

Northeast of Pensacola, on the west bank of the Blackwater River, is the town of **Milton**, the "canoe capital of Florida." US 90 narrows to a respectful two lanes through the historic district, where the town has lately built a boardwalk beside the river's edge.

A typical Old South town with pretty Victorian houses is **De Funiak Springs**. The **H & M Café**, run by the Griggs sisters, Maggie and Merle, puts out the best hot dog in the South, so locals claim. The

Above: Paddling through untamed nature.
Right: In the Marianna Caverns.

196

little library on the lake is the oldest in Florida. The former home of Governor Sidney J. Catts has become the **Sunbright Manor Bed and Breakfast Inn**.

Northwest of De Funiak Springs is the highest natural point in Florida, **Lakewood Park**, at an altitude of 345 feet.

Inland Parks and Canoeing

The Panhandle's inland parks are truly wonderful. At **Falling Waters**, below Chipley, a stream drops 100 feet into a sinkhole, somewhat similar to **Caverns State Park**, 20 miles northeast outside **Marianna**. In this gigantic system of caverns, with its dry as well as water-filled caves at different levels, under-water ponds and stalactites glisten. In the park there are nature trails, and places for swimming, canoeing and fishing.

Eden Mansion and State Park is a stately 1895 mansion and its grounds on Choctawhatchee Bay, northeast of Destin. Walking through the house, with its fine old furnishings, and through the gardens, with their azaleas and camelias, you feel yourself transported back in time to the glory days of the Old South.

Torreya State Park lies to the north of the small town of Bristol, where the steep cliffs of the Apalachicola River tower above the water. The park features the restored antebellum **Gregory Mansion**, but it is the unique **Botanical Garden** that makes the park worth visiting. During the last Ice Age, as the glaciers moved slowly south, cold weather flora and fauna moved south ahead of the icy flow. As the glacier receded, the flora and fauna typically retreated with it. But not at Torreya: here there is a marvellous collection of vegetation unknown elsewhere in the South – and in the case of the Torreya pines, hardly anywhere else in the world.

Canoeists find much to enjoy in the Blackwater River and the **Blackwater River State Park**. Another favorite is

Holmes Creek to the east, fed by water from **Cypress Springs** and an excellent place to fish. This 16-mile-stretch, marked by gently flowing waters, lush swamp lands, and high sand banks, is ideal for beginners. Cypress Springs also offers cave diving to those holding proper certification.

Econfina Creek offers up to 22 miles of canoeing streams rated moderate to strenuous. Various tube and canoe outfitters operate along these canoe runs.

APALACHICOLA AND VICINITY

In **Apalachicola**, in the southeast corner of the Panhandle, artists and oystermen live compatibly in a seafaring town reminiscent of early Key West. Once an important southern port, the town during much of this century has been the hub of Gulf Coast oyster harvests. Its historic district shines with more than a hundred late-Victorian houses. The **John Gorrie Museum** honors a country doctor who late in the 19th century invented the ice-making machine. The **Gibson Inn** at the bridge into town is one of Florida's best restaurants. In the area around the town are some lovely, quiet beaches, and in many of the restaurants along the coast, fresh seafood is always on offer.

The offshore island of **St. George** can be reached by way of a dam from **Eastpoint**. In this state park you will find simple lodgings and more than six miles of white sand beaches, as well as many species of birds and nature trails.

From Apalachicola, trips can be made to the **Apalachicola National Forest** and, to the west, to the **St. Joseph Peninsula State Park**.

To the south, on St. Vincent Island, is the remote **St. Vincent National Wildlife Refuge**, with its marshlands, dunes and fresh-water lakes. Endangered animal species have found a safe haven here.

From **Carabelle** to the east, there is a ferry to **Dog Island**, although this service is suspended in winter. The mangrove covered island has the highest sand dunes in the state.

The Area Code for the Panhandle is 850

PANAMA CITY BEACH / DESTIN / FORT WALTON BEACH

Arrival / Transportation

AIR: Just one hour's flight from Atlanta or 90 minutes from Miami with Delta/ASA Northwest Airlines. The airport is 15 minutes from the beach area.
LAND: Follow the I-10 (Tallahassee-Pensacola). A number of highways turn off south to the coast. Then take US 98, which runs along the coast. This highway goes through downtown Panama City and across the bridge to Panama City Beach and continues east to Destin, Fort Walton Beach, and further.

Accommodation

LUXURY: **Marriott Bay Point**, 4200 Marriott Dr., Panama City Beach, tel. 234-3307; **Seaside Cottage Rentals**, County Rd., 30 A between Grayton and Seagrove, tel. 1-800-277-8696; **Edgewater Beach Resort**, 11212 W. Front Beach Rd., Panama City Beach, tel. 235-4044 or 1-800-874-8686; **Hilton Sandestin Beach**, 4000 Sandestin Blvd. S., Sandestin, tel. 267-9500 or 1-800-367-1271.
MODERATE: **Tops'l Beach and Racquet Club**, 5550 Hwy. 98E, Destin, tel. 267-9222; **The Inn at St. Thomas Square**, 88730 Thomas Dr., Panama City Beach, tel. 234-0349 or 1-800-874-8600; **Sheraton Inn**, 1325 Miracle Strip Parkway, Fort Walton Beach, tel. 243-8116 or 1-800-874-8104; **The Gibson Inn**, Market St. and Ave. C, Apalachicola, tel. 653-2191.
BUDGET: There are many campsites, trailer parks, and economy motels.

Restaurants

Shuckums Oyster Pub & Seafood Grill, 15614 Front Beach Rd., Panama City Beach, tel. 235-3214; **Treasure Ship**, 3605 Thomas Dr., Panama City Beach, tel. 234-8881, a delicacy is *scampi*, whose juicy white meat melts in the mouth; **Boar's Head**, 17290 Front Beach Rd., Panama City Beach, tel. 234-6628; **Billy's I**, 3000 Thomas Dr., Panama City Beach, tel. 235-2349; **Billy's II**, one mile west of Philipp's Inlet, tel. 231-5487.

Museums / Art Galleries

The Museum of Man in the Sea, 17314 Hutchinson Rd., Panama City Beach, tel. 235-4101; **Junior Museum of Bay County**, 1731 Jenks Avenue, Panama City, tel. 769-6128; **John Gorrie State Museum**, 6th Street and Avenue D, Apalachicola, tel. 653-9347; **Gulf World**, 15412 West Highway 98A, Panama City Beach, tel. 234-5271; **Indian Temple Mound Museum**, 139 Miracle Strip Pkwy., Fort Walton Beach, tel. 243-6521; **Institute of Diving**, 17314 Hutchinson Rd. (Highway 98), Panama City, tel. 235-4101; **Destin Fishing**

Museum, 4801 Beach Highway, Destin 32541, tel. 654-1011; **Visual Arts Center of Northwest Florida**, at the corner of 4th St. and Harrison St., Panama City, tel. 769-4451. Ask for a map of the Downtown Art District.

Hospitals

Gulf Coast Hospital, tel. 769-8341; **Bay Medical**, tel. 769-1511 – both in Panama City.

Festivals / Events

Snowbird Golf Tournament, end of January and beginning of February; *Spring Break,* end of February until the beginning of April, attracts thousands of college students during their spring holidays; the *Offshore Classic Power Boat Races* are held in April; the *Indian Summer Seafood Festival* takes place in October.

Tourist Information

Emerald Coast Convention & Visitors Bureau, P.O. Box 609, Fort Walton Beach, FL 32549, tel. 651-7131; **Panama City Beach Convention Visitors Bureau**, P.O. Box 9473, Panama City Beach, FL 32417, tel. 233-6503 or 1-800-PC-BEACH; **Bay County Chamber of Commerce**, P.O. Box 1850, Panama City, FL 32402, tel. 785-5206; **South Walton Tourist Development Council**, P.O. Box 1248, Santa Rosa Beach, 32459, tel. 267-1216; **Greater Fort Walton Beach Chamber of Commerce**, 34 SE Miracle Strip Parkway, Fort Walton Beach, tel. 244-8191; **Apalachicola Bay Chamber of Commerce**, 128 Market St., Apalachicola, tel. 653-9419; **Port St. Joe-Gulf Chamber of Commerce**, P.O. Box 964, Port St. Joe, FL 32456, tel. 227-1223

PENSACOLA AND PENSACOLA BEACH

Arrival / Transportation

LAND: The I-10 runs east-west through the Panhandle; US 98 runs along the coast. *AIR:* Airports are in Tallahassee, Panama City and Pensacola.

Accommodation

PENSACOLA: *LUXURY:* **The Pensacola Grand Hotel**, 200 E. Gregory Street, Pensacola, tel. 433-3336 or 1-800-348-3336. *MODERATE:* **Best Western Village Inn**, 8240 N. Davis Highway, tel. 479-1099 or 1-800-528-1234; **Hampton Inn**, 7330 Plantation Rd., tel. 477-3333 or 1-800-HAMPTON; **Holiday Inn Express**, 6501 Pensacola Blvd., tel. 476-7200; **Holiday Inn-University Mall**, 7200 Plantation Road, tel. 474-0100; **The Homestead Inn**, 7830 Pine Forest Road, tel. 944-4366; **New World Inn**, 600 S. Palafox St., tel. 432-4111. *BUDGET:* **Red Roof Inn**, I-10 at

SR 291, tel. 476-7960; **Econo Lodge**, 7194 Pensacola Blvd., tel. 479-8600.
PENSACOLA BEACH: *LUXURY:* **Holiday Inn Pensacola Beach**, 165 Fort Pickens Rd., tel. 932-5361. *BUDGET:* **East Side Resort**, 14 Via De Luna, tel. 932-5331.

Restaurants

Pensacola boasts a large selection of good restaurants in various price categories. **Capt'n Jim's Seafood**, 905 East Gregory, is very popular with the locals, tel. 433-3562, as is **Marchelo's Italian Restaurant**, 620 South Navy Blvd., tel. 456-5200; **McGuire's Irish Pub and Brewery**, 600 East Gregory St., tel. 433-6789, for an authentic Irish night; **1912 Restaurant** in the Pensacola Grand, tel. 433-3336; **Casino Restaurant** in the Holiday Inn Pensacola Beach, 165 Fort Pickens Rd., tel. 932-5361; **Flounder's Chowder and Ale House** offers seafood grilled on hickory wood, 800 Quietwater Beach Rd., Pensacola Beach, tel. 932-2003; **Jubilee Restaurant and Oyster Bar / Captain Fun's**, 400 Quietwater Beach Rd., tel. 934-3108.

Museums

Pensacola Museum of Art, **T.T. Wentworth State Museum**, **Museum of Industry** and the **Museum of Commerce** are all in Pensacola's historical quarter. The **National Museum of Naval Aviation** is in the Naval Air Station.

Parks

Big Lagoon State Recreation Area, 12301 Gulf Beach Highway, Pensacola, tel. 492-1595; **Blackwater River State Park**, Route 1, Box 57-C, Holt, FL 32564, tel. 623-2363; **Grayton Beach State Recreation Area**, Rte. 2, Box 6600, Santa Rosa Beach, FL 32459, tel. 231-4210; **Gulf Islands National Seashore**, P.O. Box 100, Gulf Breeze, FL 32561, tel. 934-2604.

Tourist Information

Pensacola Area Chamber of Commerce, 117 Garden Street, Pensacola, tel. 438-4081; **Pensacola Convention & Visitors Information Center**, 4081 East Gregory St., Pensacola, tel. 434-1234 or 1-800-343-4321 (within Florida), 1-800-874-1234 (from outside the state); **Gulf Breeze Area Chamber of Commerce**, 913 Gulf Breeze Parkway, Suite 17, Gulf Breeze, tel. 932-7888; **Santa Rosa Country Chamber of Commerce**, 501 Stewart Street SW, Milton, tel. 623-2339; **South Walton Tourist Development Council**, P.O. Box 1248, Santa Rosa Beach, FL 32459, tel. 267-1216 or 1-800-822-6877; **Walton County Chamber of Commerce**, Chatauqua Building, Circle Drive, DeFuniak Springs, tel. 892-3191.

NORTHERN PANHANDLE

Arrival / Transportation

LAND: The I-10 runs in east-west-direction through the Panhandle from Tallahassee to Pensacola; various state roads branch off and run north and south.
AIR: Airports in Tallahassee, Panama City and Pensacola.

Accommodation

In the northern Panhandle, motels, campsites and trailer parks are the only means of accommodation. It is therefore advisable to stay in Tallahassee, Panama City Beach, Destin or Fort Walton Beach in one of the numerous beach colonies, or find accommodation in Pensacola.
CRESTVIEW: *LUXURY:* **Pelican Inn**, 5030 Dog Island, tel. 1-800-451-5294. *MODERATE:* **Holiday Inn**, 800 yards south of I-10 exit 12, P.O. Box 1355, Crestview, FL 32236 tel. 682-6111. *BUDGET:* **Econo Lodge**, 400 yards north of I-10 exit 12, P.O. Box 1466, Crestview, FL 32236, tel. 682-6255.
DEFUNIAK SPRINGS: *LUXURY:* **Sunbright Manor**, 606 Live Oak, tel. 892-0656. *BUDGET:* **Best Western Crossroads Inn**, at the junction of I-10 and US 331, tel. 892-5111.
MARIANNA: *LUXURY:* **Hilltop Inn**, three-quarters of a mile northwest of I-10 exit 21 at Hwy 90E, tel. 526-3251. *MODERATE:* **Best Western Marianna Inn**, south of junction I-10 and SR 71, tel. 526-5666. *BUDGET:* **Econo Lodge**, a mile and a half northeast on US 90 from I-10 exit 20, 1119 W. Lafayette Street, tel. 526-3710; **Days Inn**, eleven miles northeast on US 90 from I-10 exit 20, 1114 W. Lafayette Street, tel. 526-4311.
NICEVILLE: *LUXURY:* **Bluewater Bay Resort**, 1950 Bluewater Blvd., tel. 897-3613 or 1-800-874-2128; **Comfort Inn**, 101 Highway 85N, tel. 678-8077.
PORT ST. JOE: *MODERATE:* **Old Salt Works Cabins**, P.O. Box 526, Port St. Joe, FL 32456.
WAKULLA SPRINGS: **Wakulla Springs Lodge & Conference Center**, Wakulla Springs State Park, 1 Springs Drive, tel. 224-5950.

Restaurants

A recommendable restaurant in the northern Panhandle is **Golf Clubhouse Restaurant** in Niceville, in the Bluewater Bay Resort, tel. 897-2583. *BUDGET:* **Nichols Restaurant** in Milton – near I-10, exit 8 at Robinson Point Road, tel. 623-3410.

Tourist Information

Florida Department of Commerce / Division of Tourism, Tallahassee, FL 32399-2000, tel. 487-1462. Information about canoeing and state parks is available from the **Department of Environmental Protection**, Division of Recreation and Parks, tel. 488-9872.

Map labels:
Mobile
Pensacola
Blackwater River State Park & Forest
Panama City
Tallahassee
Apalachicola Nat'l. Forest
Okefenokee Swamp
Osceola N. Forest
Jacksonville
Lake City
ATLANTIC
Cape San Blas
Apalachee Bay
Gainesville
Marjorie Kinnan Rawlings St. Hist. Site
Ocala
Ocala Nat'l. Forest
Blue Springs St. Park
Daytona Beach
Canaveral Nat'l. Seashore
Titusville
Cape Canaveral
Orlando
Merritt I. Nat'l. Wildlife Refuge
Melbourne
Tampa
OCEAN
St. Petersburg
Tampa Bay
Sarasota
Myakka River State Park Wilderness Preserve
Ft. Myers
Lake Okeechobee
Palm Beach
Boca Raton
J. N. "Ding" Darling Nat'l. Wildlife Refuge
GULF OF MEXICO
Ft. Lauderdale
Florida City
Miami
Everglades Nat'l. Park
Cape Sable
Biscayne Nat'l. Park
John Pennecamp Coral Reef S. Park
Indian Key Hist. Site, Lignumvitae Key State Botanical Site
Bahia - Honda St. Rec. Area
Key West
Fort Jefferson Nat. Monument
Key West Nat'l. Wildlife Refuge
FLORIDA KEYS

NATIONAL AND STATE PARKS
0   100km
0   60miles

NATIONAL AND STATE PARKS / UNDERWATER PARKS

First impressions to the contrary, Florida is not all man-made entertainment like Walt Disney World, concrete canyons like Miami Beach, or the never-ending sub-divisions seen throughout the state. With 900 new residents arriving every day and millions of visitors a year, it is sometimes hard to get away from all these people, their houses and shopping centers.

Still, Florida has many natural treasures, another excellent reason for coming here: coral reefs, barrier islands and mangroves, pine lands and hardwood hammocks, cypress swamps, fresh- and salt-water marshes, and the Everglades, unique in the world.

Seasonal changes are subtle, with an annual average temperature range be-

tween 65° and 85° F. Generally, summers are humid and wet, winters cool and dry, with possible night frost in the north and central sections, while frost is rare in the southern regions.

Spring through fall is the optimal time for camping in northern Florida. In the south, from late fall to the first rains of summer in June is the best time to pitch your tent and explore the territory. Fishing is outstanding year-round.

For diving, the calm mornings of summer are best, with warm water temperatures and almost unlimited visibility. Summertime, too, can bring violent and potentially dangerous thunderstorms, and in densely foliated woods and mangroves, lots of mosquitoes. Mosquitos, like sand flies, are most active in the early evening hours, so it is easy to schedule activities around them.

Almost without exception, all natural areas have adequate lodging facilities nearby. A plethora of private campgrounds, geared mainly toward recreational vehicles, can be found throughout

Preceding pages: Typical scene at the J. N. "Ding" Darling National Wildlife Refuge. Right: An underwater sermon.

the state. For many out-of-the-way places, though, you might need a tent and camping equipment. Once you have set up camp, a canoe is a great way to explore nearby rivers and waterways. Outfitters throughout the state provide rental, drop-off and pick-up services.

Typically, the best tent and trailer sites are found in the public domain: the national and state parks, forests and recreational areas. Camping in wilderness areas generally requires a back country permit, available at no cost at the park office, and you should be well versed in wilderness skills and etiquette. Of the hundreds of possible wilderness areas to choose from, we have selected a number of well-loved sites for a sampling.

Since most first-time visitors choose Miami, Orlando or Tampa as gateways, our choices are concentrated around those areas. In so doing, we have had to neglect some very scenic but harder to reach natural lands like the Blackwater River State Park and Forest in the northwest corner of the state; the Okefenokee

Swamp and Osceola Forest in the north, and most of the 27 top-quality freshwater springs, like Wakulla Springs near Tallahassee.

Miami Area

From Miami, the Everglades National Park and the Florida Keys, with unparalleled diving and fishing opportunities, are within easy reach. The closest to Miami is **Biscayne National Park**, Canal Drive, Homestead (tel. 305-247-7275). This park is made up of a group of islands in South Biscayne Bay and the reef of the Upper Keys. Divers and snorkelers find a fascinating and colorful underwater world here.

Though islands like **Elliott** and **Boca Chita Key** are popular with Miami boaters, with a little luck you may be the only one there during the week.

Biscayne Aqua Tours, the Park's concessionaire (tel. 305-247-2400), offers glass-bottom boat sightseeing, snorkeling, scuba diving and island tours. The

203

reefs are as beautiful as Pennecamp's, which they adjoin and which are less crowded on weekdays.

John Pennecamp Coral Reef State Park, mile marker (MM) 102.5, on Key Largo (tel. 305-451-1202), is only a 90-minute drive from Miami. The area shelters a large and beautiful segment of the coral reef that defines the Keys.

The park concessionaire, Coral Reef Park Co. (tel. 305-451-1621 or toll-free in Florida 1-800-432-2871), provides access with a large assortment of tours: full and half-day snorkeling, scuba diving or glass-bottom boat, as well as rental boats and a fully-equipped dive shop. Reservations are necessary. The best conditions in the summer usually prevail in the morning hours before the afternoon breeze starts to pick up.

If it is too windy for the reef, you can rent a canoe and explore the mangrove

Above: Taking a siesta in the swamps.
Right: When it comes to fishing, father always knows best.

channels, or a Hobie-cat to sail Largo Sound. The most popular reefs are **Grecian Rocks**, with elkhorn, staghorn, brain coral and old Spanish cannons. **French Reef** has canyons, ledges and caves. **Molasses Reef** is popular, as is *Christ of the Deep*, which is a 4,000 pound, nine-foot-tall replica of the Genoese *Il Cristo Degli Abissi*.

The **Indian Key State Historic Site** and **Lignumvitae Key State Botanical Site** lie offshore, surrounded by turquoise waters south of Islamorada. The Park Service pontoon boat picks up visitors on Indian Key Fill at MM 79, Thursday through Monday, for morning and afternoon tours. Reservations are necessary (tel. 305-664-4815). Indian Key is what early Florida history is all about: Calusa Indians preying on Spanish shipwrecks, the first government seat of Dade County, home to Jacob Housman and his high-rolling and hard-playing men who found plenty of work and prosperity salvaging sailing vessels that were driven onto the reefs.

Lignumvitae Key, on the bay side of Indian Key Fill and rising to 16 feet, is the highest point in the islands. A naturalist's paradise, the fossilized coral rock harbors a healthy tropical hammock, the type that once covered most of the Keys until man's thoughtless intrusion.

Lignumvitae, mastic, ironwood, pigeon plum, gumbo limbo and the three mangroves, red, black and white, grow here. Among the fauna you will find the Key Largo wood rat, golden orb spider, over 20 different kinds of butterflies, rare tree snails, a host of bird species, and, especially during the rainy season, hordes of mosquitoes. In a small clearing, a typical Keys house of 1919 vintage with cistern and hurricane shelter recalls simpler times.

Boat rentals, too, are readily available at nearby marinas, but note that Lignumvitae Key is closed every Tuesday and Wednesday.

The **Bahia Honda State Recreation Area**, MM 37, Big Pine Key, (tel. 305-872-2353), has the finest swimming beach in the Keys. Campsites, cabins (high-priced and too close to the road), a marina with launch facilities, plenty of pavilions and cooking grills are available. At the south end of the area is the old Bahia Honda Bridge, where the original road was laid precariously above the railroad trestle.

Nature trails along the shore and a tidal lagoon offer insights into the tropical fauna and flora, brought ashore long ago by wind, waves and birds. Rare botanical species include the satin wood tree, spiny catesbaea and dwarf morning glory. The shore and lagoon are favorite fishing grounds for white-crowned pigeons, white herons and roseate spoonbills.

The **Looe Key National Marine Sanctuary**, only six miles from land, is accessible by dive boat from either Marathon or Ramrod Key (MM 27). In 1744, the British frigate *HMS Looe* ran aground here. In recent years, this rather isolated reef has become enormously popular with snorkelers and divers alike because of its great depth and unsurpassed water clarity. The 115-foot canyon walls are a challenge to experienced scuba divers, while the reef crest offers safe snorkeling for novices.

Fort Jefferson National Monument in the **Dry Tortugas** is a favorite spot, but is somewhat expensive to get to. It combines the historical and the natural. Located 70 miles west of Key West, it is a 40-minute flight by seaplane; an overnight voyage by boat. Fort Jefferson, on Garden Key, belongs to the seven-island group known as the Dry Tortugas. Ponce de Leon made landfall here in 1513 and found an abundance of sea turtles – hence the name.

Designed to be the largest fort in a line of U.S. Atlantic seacoast defenses, it was never used as part of the obsolete defense system. It was turned into the infamous

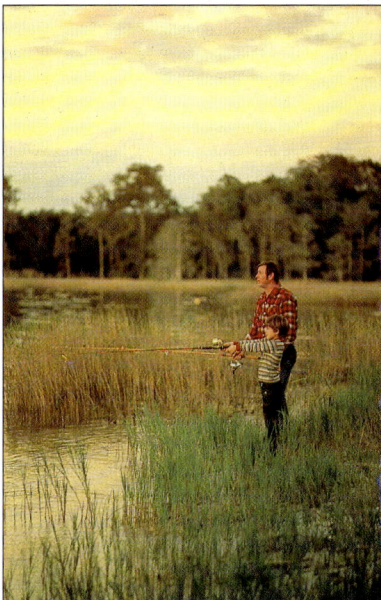

"Devil's Island," part of the U.S. prison system. Its most famous prisoner was Dr. Mudd, the physician implicated as a co-conspirator in President Lincoln's assassination.

Flying in at an altitude of 500 feet, you might see large sharks cruising the shallows. Your pilot will point out the **Marquesa Islands**, the only Atlantic atoll, and the shoals where many treasure ships have gone down over the centuries, among them the Spanish galleon *Atocha*, whose recovered riches are now on view at **Mel Fisher's Key West Treasure Museum**.

After an introductory slide show at Fort Jefferson, you are on your own to explore or snorkel. The parapet affords an incomparable view of the powder magazines, cistern, moat and surrounding islands.

Overhead, frigate birds with seven-foot wingspans soar, cormorants and royal terns occupy the pilings. Across the channel is **Bush Key**, with its nesting colony of sooty terns and brown noddys.

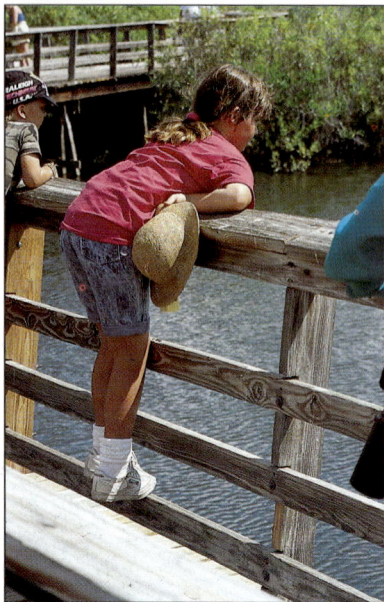

In the clear water, blue and grey angelfish, striped sergeant majors, snapper and grouper feed around moat openings, and conch and welk crawl over the sandy sea bottom while urchins hide in the turtle grass.

During spring migration, from March to early May, the fort bustles with activity, not only from the birds, but also from bird watchers, who come here hoping to be able to add a few new species to their lists. The island's isolation and lack of services – you have to bring your own drinking water with you, for example – preserve it for a select few.

Environmental groups, such as the Sierra Club and the Audubon Society, run late-spring boat trips of two to three days. Non-members are also welcome on a space available basis. Key West Seaplane Service offers half- or full-day and overnight trips.

Above: There is plenty to see along nature preserve paths. Right: Landscape at the. "Ding" Darling Wildlife Refuge.

Orlando Area

From Orlando, it is not far to **Ocala National Forest** and the rolling hills and lakes of central Florida.

A very different habitat is the **Merritt Island National Wildlife Refuge** and **Canaveral National Seashore** (tel. 407-867-0667), just north of the Kennedy Space Center. Access is via Route 402, east of Titusville, to a bird-watcher's heaven, from fall through spring. Expect to see snipe, avocets and wintering ducks in the marshes and lagoons. Pick up a map at the visitors' center and enjoy a beach picnic with a backdrop of wild dunes. Some beach areas are closed during space shuttle pre- and post-launch periods.

Blue Springs State Park, in Orange City (tel. 904-775-3663), is situated off I-4 as you drive towards Daytona Beach. If you have never seen a manatee, visit between December and mid-March, when a herd of about 60 sea cows gathers here to escape cold waters elsewhere. Plan on an early morning visit to avoid the crowds. There are camp sites, canoe rentals, scuba diving and trails.

The **Marjorie Kinnan Rawlings State Historic Site** (tel. 352-466-3672) is located 20 miles south of Gainesville, on FL 325, between FL 20 and US 301. Author Rawlings' house, a "small place of enchantment" which can be visited, tells of a simpler, more authentic life. Fortunately, development has been slow in this little outpost of old Florida, where the renowned author wrote *Cross Creek* and *The Yearling*.

Tampa Area

From Tampa-St. Petersburg, outdoors investigations lead to the long beaches and islands of Florida's west coast. In spite of a burgeoning population, areas such as **Caladesi Island** and **Cayo Costa** offer prime outdoor recreation in rela-

tively unspoiled natural settings. With its easier access, we favor the **Myakka River State Park** and adjacent **Wilderness Preserve** (tel. 813-924-1027), southwest of busy Sarasota-Bradenton yet a world removed. The Civilian Conservation Corps built the first facilities here in the 1930s. The campground tends to get crowded in the winter months, but you can escape to the primitive sites if you can do without some of civilization's amenities for a while. Do some hiking or canoeing, go fishing, or just sit down somewhere and take in the beauty of the river, marshes, pine lands and prairies. Wildlife sightings, especially in winter, are outstanding.

The Visitors' Center and entrance to the **J. N. "Ding" Darling National Wildlife Refuge** (tel. 813-472-1100) are about six miles west of the Causeway on Sanibel Island. A five-mile road winds through the refuge, named after a 1930s journalist famous for his conservation-minded cartoons that twice won him the Pulitzer Prize. Take one of the trails,

climb the observation tower or rent a canoe at Tarpon Bay Marina (tel. 813-472-8900). You might find flocks of roseate spoonbills, and, with luck, observe manatees and alligators. The best time for observation is low tide.

Over 250 bird species make this refuge their home or stop over during spring and fall migration. In addition, large numbers of reptiles and amphibians, and 32 mammal species, reside here year-round.

Additional information on Florida's natural lands, camping and underwater parks is available from: The Department of Natural Resources, Information Office, 3900 Commonwealth Blvd., Room 613, Tallahassee, FL 32399 (free information on camping, hiking and canoeing). The Florida Audubon Society, 1101 Audubon Way, Maitland, FL 32751, specializes in bird-watching and nature trips. The Florida Division of Tourism, Tourist Information, Department of Commerce, Tallahassee, FL 32399-2000, provides free listings of private campgrounds and free maps.

EVERGLADES DAY TRIPS

The **Everglades National Park**, which takes up most of the southwestern tip of Florida, has been declared a World Heritage Site. Cycles of nature produce a winter season of impressive bird concentrations and rich opportunities for walking and canoeing through semi-aquatic wildlife habitat. For more than a century, humans intruded into this natural landscape due to cultivation and the building of cities. It was only through the intervention of conservationists that they could be stopped from completely destroying this unique region with its mangrove swamps.

Lake Okeechobee, which historically overflowed southwards in summer, spreading a vast, shallow sheet of water that flowed in what naturalist Marjory Stoneman Douglas described as a "river of grass" across a no-man's land, ulti-

Above: The Everglades at dusk. Right: Snake enjoying a sunbath.

mately inching into Florida Bay. Its ecosystem sustained huge populations of fowl, fish and mammals, all of which adapted to the flow of alternating wet and dry seasons.

As human intervention into this cycle of nature began to leave a noticeable impression, the establishment of the Everglades National Park in 1947 became a first step toward protecting this sensitive and threatened region. Reclaiming the Everglades will only be possible when people understand and agree that their future, too, lies in maintaining a balanced ecosystem; in a time of increasing ecological awareness, the number of people who love and will fight for the protection of the quiet expanses of the Everglades is growing.

Drainage of the Everglades, begun late in the 19th century, led to the diking of Lake Okeechobee and the construction of flood-control canals after the hurricane-driven overflow of Okeechobee in 1928 caused 2,000 deaths. The new flood-control system diverted water away from

the drainage-dependent Everglades agricultural area. Water that once washed naturally across the Glades now flowed through canals into huge pools that supplied fresh water for the coastal cities, or was allowed to spill directly into the ocean. The seasonal cycle that Everglades wildlife depended upon was disrupted. Water released into the Everglades now had a high phosphorous content and was polluted with pesticide residues from the huge cattle ranches and sugar plantations. Bird populations declined. Florida Bay became increasingly saline, which killed sea grasses and led to vast algae blooms. Shrimp fisheries suffered, and reefs off the Florida Keys became threatened.

A series of new laws have produced a truce among government agencies and agricultural interests, which is likely to improve the quality and quantity of water flowing through the Everglades. Science has focused more intensely on the issues; economic interests that depend on the fisheries and tourism of Florida Bay have now challenged economic interests that farm the region arround Lake Okeechobee.

What will happen in the future is hard to say: the public is not yet sufficiently aroused to act decisively. Disney World, the many amusement parks, and the Art Deco District of Miami all attract more attention than do questions of preserving the "river of grass." Meanwhile, visitors can still enjoy the Everglades and hope for the ecosystem's improvement.

Visitors have a choice of three different day outings. From Miami, we suggest an all-day trip to **Flamingo**, by way of the main visitors' entrance near Florida City. For those with less time available, a half-day trip to **Shark Valley**, the northern entrance to the park, about 30 miles west of Miami, gives an introduction to the wide grasslands. At the main visitors' center, stop for an orientation program, guides and maps. Along the way, the landscape includes pinelands, hardwood hammocks in a sawgrass prairie, dwarf cypress forests and mangrove coasts.

Leave your car to look for alligator hatchlings on a sunny canal bank, anhinga feeding their young, hummingbirds or snowy egrets. The park service has provided many trails and boardwalks.

Favorite walks include **Royal Palm Hammock**, four miles from the Visitor Center. The **Gumbo Limbo Trail** leads inside a hardwood hammock, where slightly elevated ground provides ideal conditions for plants such as the gumbo limbo, red maple, live oak and strangler fig. On the **Anhinga Trail**, the namesake waterfowl swim snake-like underwater. Alligators make their home here. They have survived for eons without extra feeding. In fact, the feeding of all wildlife is prohibited.

The **Pa-hay-okee Overlook**, situated twelve miles into the park, affords a good view of the "river of grass." Sights are

Above: During spring the Everglades show their true colors. Right: These vultures seem to be interested in today's television schedule.

undramatic: just the play of sky and clouds over the prairie. After 19 miles, **Mahogany Hammock** is where you can see what the typical hardwood hammock looked like before loggers destroyed most old growth. **Paurotis Pond**, about five miles further on, is a good spot for a lunch picnic by the shore.

At **West Lake**, another five miles or so along, fresh and salt water mingle. All three kinds of mangroves and the related buttonwood are found here. The latter provided the means for making charcoal to the early settlers.

Flamingo is situated on **Florida Bay**. On calm days, distant islands seem to float above the water. You will find a ranger-staffed visitors' center, viewing scopes, a marina with houseboat, skiff and canoe rentals, a motel, a restaurant, a campground, and an amphitheater for campfire programs on winter evenings.

Arrive by mid-afternoon and take the tram tour to **Snake Bight**. It departs winters only from the visitors' center. Florida Bay stretches before you. On a quiet afternoon, hundreds of waterfowl reflect in the calm few inches of water. Early evening is good for dining on the catch of the day at the second-floor restaurant overlooking the bay. White and brown pelicans, cormorants, egrets and herons, large sandpipers and little pips crowd the sandbar, perhaps with an occasional eagle aloft. As an alternative, you might want to take a sunset cruise into Florida Bay on the concessionaire-operated boat. Self-sufficient types tend to prefer the comfort of their own campsite.

Day travelers to **Shark Valley** drive across the **Tamiami Trail** (US 41). A 15-mile loop road leads into the heart of this sawgrass-covered, slow-flowing region. You can rent a bike or take the ranger-guided tram which operates year-round. At the southern end of the road you can climb the observation tower for a birds-eye view of this sea of grass and hammocks. Alligators bask on the banks of a pond or swim quietly. You may surprise a family of white-tailed deer along the road, observe snail kites, turkey vultures and red-shouldered hawks, or see the limpkin or the green heron. Allow two hours for the tram ride, three to four hours if you decide to bicycle. Bring food and drink because only water is available at the tower. Don't forget mosquito repellent no matter when you come.

Depending on the time of year, the Everglades always looks different, but is always beautiful. Sharp contures and brilliant colors are prevalent in the winter months, while in summer enormous clouds float by overhead. In the early evening the sky is filled with mauve, orange and pink tones.

The **Miccosukee Indian Village** near the Shark Valley entrance provides a glimpse of life lived in the Glades by a people forced to adapt to these harsh conditions after being chased from their upper Florida lands 140 years ago by invading whites. Miccosukees are famous for colorful jackets and skirts in brightly colored patchwork and zigzag patterns. Try their pumpkin and fry bread in the native restaurant, but the fare is otherwise run-of-the-mill American. If you want to ride an airboat, this is the place. Although less damaging than the popular off-road vehicles, airboats in the fragile ecosystem of the Everglades are still controversial.

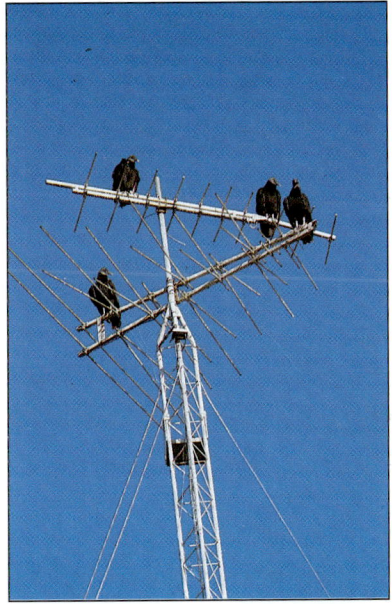

On the Naples-Ft. Myers side of the Everglades, drive to the **Gulf Coast Ranger Station and Visitors' Center** of Everglades National Park south of Everglades City on Highway 29. The new visitors' center has been redesigned and contains an exhibit on mangrove forests, fish life from Chokoloskee Bay and the back-country region between Everglades City and Flamingo. The park's excursion boats take you for an introductory tour of the **Ten Thousand Islands**, the mangrove islands that form the southwestern side of the Everglades. Dolphins, sea turtles, and osprey are possible sightings. Here, too, is the start of the 100-mile-long wilderness waterway that connects through the back country to Flamingo.

THEME PARKS

There is always something new to discover in the wonderland of Florida theme parks. In addition to world-renowned Walt Disney World, there are many other appealing attractions, some of which are new, others long-time favorites. Often, they are less crowded and less expensive. Travel agents should have the latest information about tour package plans featuring the parks of your choice.

Orlando and Disney

Since its opening in 1971, Walt Disney World has become the world's most-popular man-made attraction. The **Magic Kingdom**, **Epcot** and **Disney-MGM Studios** are its major areas, with **Disney's Animal Kingdom** newly opened in 1998. At Epcot Center's **Future World**, new ideas in communications, energy, transportation, land and the imagination are presented. One of Epcot's newest attractions is **Innoventions**, showcasing the latest technology. In Epcot's **World Showcase**, eleven nations exhibit their cultures with shows, attractions, restaurants and shops. The nighttime light and laser show, **Illumi-Nations**, is one of the best at Disney.

Disney-MGM Studios is an actual motion picture studio. A guided backstage tour is also offered, along with lively shows and attractions, the newest of which, **Tower of Terror**, is a thrilling, 13-story drop in a runaway elevator. **Star Tours** takes visitors into outer space in a flight simulator.

Walt Disney World also includes three water parks. In **Typhoon Lagoon**, five-foot waves slam onto the sand beaches, you can glide through caves on a water slide, go white-water rafting or dive to coral reefs in Shark Reef. **Discovery Island** is a large park with unusual plants, trees and lots of animals.

Pleasure Island, near **Downtown Disney**, is the place to go for after-dark dining and dancing. **Disney Institute** is the latest resort experience, with more than

40 learning programs, from rock climbing to animation.

Universal Studios Florida, the state's newest entertainment-themed attraction, opened in 1990, and is currently being expanded. A state-of-the-art motion picture and television production facility, it is the largest, most complete film studio outside of Hollywood. The park's back lot features entertainment based on popular motion picture and television locations.

Located at the park entrance is one of America's most popular rock 'n' roll establishments, the **Hard Rock Café**, the world's largest. Live shows enable visitors to travel *Back to the Future* with Dr. Brown from the popular movie or narrowly escape King Kong as he attacks a New York City elevated railway. Guests can also tremble in a simulated earthquake, or soar on flying bicycles to E.T.'s planet.

Sea World, in Orlando, is among Florida's most popular parks. It features a variety of marine animals in themed productions. *Shamu: New World Vision*, in Shamu Stadium, stars an entire killer whale family. In *New Friends*, Beluga whales and dolphins perform at the Whale and Dolphin Stadium. Hotel Clyde and Seamore stars otters and walruses.

Guests get close-up views of hundreds of penguins at Penguin Encounter, a large science center which also serves as a living laboratory of polar life. Shark Encounter, Wild Arctic Flight Simulator, Shamu's Happy Harbor and the new Key West themed area add to the excitement of a Sea World visit. The park also features a nightly Polynesian *luau* dinner show (additional cost).

Orlando's **Wet 'n' Wild Water Park** has more than a dozen exciting slides, flumes and pools. Visitors experience such challenges as Der Stuka, called the world's fastest water slide; the Raging Rapids white water thrill ride through torrential rains and waterfalls; the Kamikaze, where brave explorers plunge down a water chute more than six stories above pool level; and the thrilling Black Hole, an enclosed flume ride with space-age effects. Here, also, visitors discover the new Fuji Flyer water roller coaster, as well as such aquatic oddities as Mach 5 and Hydra-Maniac.

Other popular features include wavepools, a beach, cable-operated kneeboard rides, a picnic area, food stands and miniature golf.

Aside from the big attractions, central Florida also has its share of offbeat attractions. **A World of Orchids** in Kissimmee showcases 3,000 orchids in a half-acre garden; **Blue Springs State Park** is home to dozens of manatees in the winter months; **Lakeridge Winery & Vineyards** produces and sells wines, and visitors can taste a spectrum of reds, whites and bubblies.

Cypress Gardens

Bordering Lake Eloise near Winter Haven is central Florida's famed **Cypress Gardens**, magnificent botanical gardens that bloom year-round, where sightseeing boats wind along waterways bordered by flowers, exotic shrubs and cypress trees. Flower-lined paths also lead through the gardens with over 8,000 plant varieties from 75 countries. During the Chrysanthemum Festival in November, more than two million of these flowers blossom here, and at Christmas time, 5,000 poinsettias reveal their bright red petals.

Other floral showcases include the **All-America Rose Gardens**, displaying more than 500 varieties of the state's official flower. The park's live entertainment features an ice-skating revue and a water-skiing extravaganza showcasing high-powered boat racing and ski jumping.

Visitors can also shop and see elaborate model railroads at **Southern Crossroads**, a replica antebellum town; enjoy

panoramic views from a platform atop **Kodak Island's** Sky Tower; and tour an animal forest with walk-through aviary, house pet zoo, alligator- and snake-handling demonstrations, and a treatment center for injured birds.

Silver Springs

Florida's **Silver Springs**, outside Ocala, is the area's oldest major theme park and site of many Hollywood films, including the original *Tarzan* movies. The popular glass-bottom boat ride floats on crystal clear water where deep springs form the Silver River.

The Jungle Cruise Safari, aboard quiet electric boats, glides past wildlife preserves inhabited by Barbary sheep, giraffes, zebras, llamas and monkeys. Other popular attractions include Cypress Point, an island plaza inhabited by turtles, flamingos and waterfowl, a rep-

Above: Dolphin show at Marineland. Right: Life-like Tyrannosaurus.

tile institute, a petting zoo, and an antique car collection. Silver Springs Wild Waters includes a huge wave pool, eight flume rides, a children's water play area and miniature golf.

Weeki Wachee

At **Weeki Wachee Springs**, about 47 miles north of Tampa-St. Petersburg, the park's famed swimming "mermaids" perform behind the glass walls of an underwater theater. The park also features an aviary, where injured birds are rehabilitated and returned to natural environments whenever possible, and an "orphanage" for injured sea birds.

Trained macaws and cockatoos perform their own show daily, and an electric boat cruise explores the Weeki Wachee River for views of native wildlife and plants. There's also a petting zoo.

The park's adjacent **Buccaneer Bay** includes a beach with river swimming, flume rides and volleyball courts. **Fantasy Island** is a big hit with kids.

Marineland

On the Atlantic coast south of St. Augustine is **Marineland**, Florida's first marine park. A multi-dimensional film, *Sea Dream*, is presented in the Aquarium Theater. Walkways lead thtough semi-tropical jungles, and the **Margaret Herrick Shell Museum** displays over 6,000 rare specimens from around the world. In the park's most popular feature, continuous shows star performing dolphins, and over 1,000 sea species can be viewed in an aquarium and two huge Oceanarium tanks. Also in St. Augustine, Humboldt penguins are at home in **Whitney Park**, where visitors can also view sea lions feeding. Two newer aquariums showcase two unique marine habitats: **Secrets of the Reef** features Pacific fish, while **Wonders of the Spring** displays Florida fresh-water fish.

Tampa's Busch Gardens

In Tampa's **Busch Gardens**, **The Dark Continent** is an African-inspired section combining a mixture of wildlife park, Hemmingwayesque atmosphere and amusement center.

Visitors ride through the park's Serengeti in a futuristic electric train, viewing African big game roaming freely across a veldt-like plain. The animals can also be seen from a steam locomotive, sky ride or promenade.

Other areas include **Timbuktu**, an "ancient desert trading center," with its Scorpion coaster, the Phoenix thrill ride and the 1200-seat *Das Festhaus* dining-entertainment complex with German food, music and dancing.

Morocco is home to the Moroccan Palace Theater, staging Broadway-style musical reviews. At **Nairobi**, baby birds and animals are tended in a nursery, and the **Nocturnal Mountain's** simulated night environment allows visitors to observe species which are active in the dark.

The **Congo** offers Kumba, the largest and fastest roller coaster in the Southeast, the Congo River Rapids white-water raft ride and the Python roller coaster with double spiral. **Bird Gardens**, the park's oldest segment, displays over 2,000 exotic birds; some perform in a trained show and others are at home in natural habitat aviaries.

Stanleyville, a bustling African village, includes the Stanley Falls log flume ride and thrill-packed Tanganyika Tidal Wave, a water safari ride through a dense jungle culminating in a 55-foot drop into a lake, thus creating a giant wave that drenches riders.

Montu, the world's highest and longest inverted steel coaster, is in **Egypt**, a whole new area of the park.

Adventure Island, a separate water park, is adjacent to Busch Gardens. It features a triple-tube looping water slide, as well as a number of other aquatic attractions popular with young and old alike. In addition, the park has swimming and diving pools especially for children.

215

Map labels:
GEORGIA
Mobile
Bluewater Bay Resort
Pensacola
Tallahassee
Lake City
Jacksonville
Plantation Racquet Park
Amelia Island Plantation
Marriott Golf
Marriott's Bay Point Resort
Panama City
Cape San Blas
Apalachee Bay
Gainesville
ATLANTIC
Ocala
Daytona Beach
Indigo Lakes Resort
Orlando
Titusville
Cape Canaveral
Saddlebrook Golf & Tennis Res.
Grand Cypress Resort
Luxurious Marriott
Tampa
Innisbrook Sports & Leisure Res.
Grenelefe Resort
Melbourne
OCEAN
St. Petersburg
Tampa Bay
Palm Aire
Indian River Plantation
Sarasota
Longboat Key Club
Ft. Myers
PGA Sheraton Resort, The Breakers
Palm Beach
Boca Raton Hotel & Spa
South Sea Plantation
Lake Okeechobee
Boca Raton
Sheraton Bonaventure Resort & Spa
Sundial Beach & Tennis Res.
Ft. Lauderdale
Florida City
Miami
Doral Resort & Country Club
Don Shula's Golf Club
GULF OF MEXICO
Cape Sable
Cheeca Lodge
Key West
FLORIDA KEYS
BAHAMAS

GOLF
0   100 km
0   60 miles

GOLF AND TENNIS RESORTS

The Sunshine State's benign climate beckons golf and tennis vacationers with some incomparable resort hideaways. Adding to their appeal, most offer cost-effective packages which may include lodging and some meals. Some are self-contained communities, where you might happily spend an entire vacation.

Tucked away at **Islamorada** in the Florida Keys is **Cheeca Lodge**. Best known as an anglers' haven, the resort also has a challenging nine-hole executive golf course designed by Jack Nicklaus. There are six lighted all-weather tennis courts on the beautifully landscaped 27-acre site, an ocean beach and a fishing pier.

Some of Florida's most famous resorts have sprung up along the "American Riviera," the south Atlantic coast. In northwest Miami, **Doral Resort and**

Right: Preparing to take their first steps into the world of tennis.

Country Club is set amid palm trees, lakes and softly rolling hills. Its Blue Course is home of the prestigious Doral Ryder Open PGA Tournament; there are four other championship courses and a par-27 nine-hole beginners' course.

Doral's Arthur Ashe Jr. Tennis Club contains 15 courts, including stadium seating for 400, and is home of the Rick Day Tennis Academy. Additionally, the resort includes an equestrian center and Olympic-size pool.

Also in the northwest, **Miami Lakes Inn Athletic Club Golf Resort** nestles in an elegant country club community. There is an 18-hole championship golf course, a lighted executive course and driving range, nine lighted tennis courts and a racquetball center with a glass-enclosed championship court. The Athletic Club also includes a gymnasium and spa.

At **Palm Beach Gardens**, the **PGA Sheraton Resort** is the home of the Professional Golf Association of America and the U.S. Croquet Association. Site of

the PGA Seniors' Championship Tournament, its Champion Course was recently reopened, following redesign by Jack Nicklaus. The PGA National Golf Academy offers championship golf schools. There are four additional championship courses, 19 clay tennis courts, five croquet courts, a health and fitness center and 26-acre sailing lake.

In neighboring **Fort Lauderdale**, the **Sheraton Bonaventure Resort and Spa** overlooks two championship courses managed by PGA professionals in an exclusive residential community. The resort's spa is one of the nation's largest, and there are 24 all-weather tennis courts, squash and racquetball courts, an equestrian center, indoor roller skating and bowling.

Another internationally-renowned spa and celebrity retreat, **Palm-Aire**, at **Pompano Beach**, has now emerged as a major golf and tennis center. Its owners recently purchased a neighboring golf and racquet club, bringing the complex a total of five 18-hole golf courses and 37 tennis courts. Health and fitness programs are available year-round.

At **Boca Raton**, the award-winning **Boca Raton Hotel and Club**, one of America's grand retreats, has two championship 18-hole golf courses on its 200-acre estate. Other amenities: a 29-court tennis center, site of the All American Sports Tennis Academy, fitness center, beach and marina on the Intracoastal Waterway.

Another legendary retreat, **The Breakers**, in **Palm Beach**, has undergone a $50-million renovation, with rooms refurbished by interior designer Carleton Varney. Home of the state's oldest 18-hole golf course, a Donald Ross design, it is also the site of the championship Breakers West layout. There are 19 tennis courts, a croquet court and a fitness center.

The **Palm Beach Polo and Country Club** is perhaps best known for 7.5 minute-long chukkers and the Piaget World Cup of Polo. After all, Prince Charles has stayed here several times, as have other assorted royalty, and they

217

probably came more to take advantage of the ten polo fields, clubhouse and equestrian center than for the golf or tennis.

Northward, on the "Treasure Coast," a serene, lesser-known region, **Indian River Plantation** on **Hutchinson Island** is an idyllic retreat bordered by the Atlantic Ocean and the Intracoastal Waterway. There is golfing on an 18-hole par-61 course with lakeside club house, and tennis on 13 courts, seven of them lighted. Other amenities here include an outdoor spa, private Atlantic beach, deep-sea fishing charters and full service marina.

Further up the coast, **Indigo Lakes Resort** is near the internationally-renowned Daytona Beach Speedway. Its par-72 golf course consistently ranks among Florida's best. The new headquarters resort for the Ladies Professional Golf Association, Indigo Lakes added a

Above: Golf – a game for individualists.
Right: Many of the major hotels have their own golf courses.

new LPGA designed course and resort facilities in 1992. It also includes ten lighted tennis courts, racquetball courts, an Olympic pool, fitness center-spa and Parcourse Fitness Trail.

One of the United States' largest golf resorts is luxurious **Marriott** in **Sawgrass**, at Ponte Vedra Beach, about 26 miles southeast of Jacksonville. One of two resorts in the world with two Tournament Players Club (TPC) courses, it is also home of the PGA Tour. The resort's five championship 18-hole courses include the TPC at Sawgrass Valley and TPC at Sawgrass Stadium, home of the famous par-3, 121-meter island hole and site of The Players Championship tournament.

The tennis center offers ten clay courts; guests also have privileges at the new eleven-court Association of Tennis Professionals (ATP), international headquarters of the prestigious organization. Sawgrass also includes two fitness centers; advanced corporate conditioning programs are available through St. Vin-

cent's Wellness Center and the Jacksonville branch of Mayo Clinic.

There's more fine golfing at nearby **Amelia Island Plantation**. Its new Long Point Course challenges with highly elevated fairways and large bodies of water; the other 37 holes mingle island greens with salt marshes and ocean dunes. The **Plantation Racquet Park** has 23 tennis courts scattered amid live oak trees. All American Sports operates the instructional program. There is also a fitness center with racquetball courts and heated indoor lap pool.

The "world's theme park capital," central Florida, is also the capital of fine golf and tennis resorts. At Orlando's 1,500-acre **Grand Cypress Resort**, 45 holes of Jack Nicklaus-designed golf include the New Course, inspired by the Old Course at St. Andrews, Scotland. True tennis enthusiasts can polish their game at the twelve-court racquet club. There's also a nine-wicket croquet court and an equestrian center offering English as well as Western trail rides.

Near **Haines City**, **Grenelefe Resort** on the shores of Lake Marion has three 18-hole championship golf courses. Its 20-court tennis center includes a 1,700-set stadium and is featured on the Grand Prix Tennis Circuit. There's a full service marina and staff can organize complete fishing tournaments.

At **Niceville**, in the northwest Panhandle, **Bluewater Bay Resort's** 27-hole golf courses are the site of the International Invitational and Florida Cup golf tournaments. Highlights are presentations of the $10,000 Goebel Trophy and the Herman Tissies Memorial "Spirit of the Game" award, honoring the memory of the famed German amateur. Bluewater Bay's active tennis program is on 21 courts with three different surfaces. There is also an Olympic pool and a full-service marina.

At nearby **Sandestin**, there is more championship golf on 81 holes. One of the few U.S. resorts offering grass courts, Sandestin also has hard and composition tennis courts, making a total of 16. There

is a fitness center, full-service marina and deep-sea fishing.

Marriott's Bay Point Resort at neighboring **Panama City Beach** features golf on two par-72 courses, and there is a twelve-court tennis center, site of the Men's Intercollegiate Clay Championship. For passionate sport fishing fans, the Yacht Club serves as a base for the famous $350,000 July Bay Point Billfish Invitational.

On the southwest Gulf Coast, at **Tarpon Springs**, **Innisbrook Sports and Leisure Resort** offers 63 holes of golf on three recently restored championship courses, meandering amid lakes, woodlands and low hills. Its Tennis and Racquetball Center, home of the Australian Tennis Institute, includes 18 tennis courts and four racquetball courts. In addition, there is a separate children's recreation center.

Above: Hats for every occasion. Right: This building boasts being the smallest post office in the world.

At **Wesley Chapel** on nearby Tampa Bay, **Saddlebrook Golf and Tennis Resort** has two Arnold Palmer golf courses. Its huge 37-court tennis complex is headquarters of the U. S. Professional Tennis Association. The "Superpool," which is as long as a football field, features racing lanes. There is also a fitness center.

On **Longboat Key**, near Sarasota, luxurious **Longboat Key Club** has an 18-hole golf course in a tropical setting and 27 holes bordering Sarasota Bay. There is an 18-court tennis center along a quiet lagoon and another 20-court complex beside an idyllic inland waterway. Southward, there is tennis on two idyllic hideaway islands.

On serene **Captiva Island**, **South Seas Plantation**, one of the Gulf Coast's top tennis facilities, has 22 courts. There is golf on a nine-hole par-36 course, along with a deep-water yacht basin. On adjacent **Sanibel Island**, world famed for its shelling beaches, **Sundial Beach and Tennis Resort** has seven composition and six clay courts.

FLORIDA TRAILS

As Florida becomes increasingly urbanized – its surging numbers will make it the third most populous state by the turn of the century – recreational planning seeks to link remaining green and open spaces. Visitors will find the state's growing network of recreational trails appealing for mild adventure, for wildlife sightings, and for fitness.

Trails within Parks and Forests

Short hiking trails can be found just about everywhere, from the beaches of **Cayo Costa** along the mid-Gulf Coast to the five-mile saltwater marsh trail of the **Merritt Island National Wildlife Refuge**, with its observation tower which is excellent for viewing bird life. **Everglades National Park** and **Highlands Hammock State Park** near Sebring offer the best of park trails through tropical hammocks.

Leisurely trails that traverse, in part, formal gardens can be enjoyed through **Fairchild Tropical Gardens** south of Miami, through **Washington Oaks State Gardens** south of St. Augustine, through **Maclay State Gardens** north of Tallahassee, and through **Eden State Garden** near Panama City. The short trail through **Sugar Mill Gardens** in Port Orange leads visitors through "Bongoland," an unsuccessful theme park from the 1950s with concrete Dinosaurs. **Ravine State Gardens** near Palatka offers a surprisingly steep trail for Florida, best enjoyed timed to the peak flowering of azaleas during March and April.

Gamble Place, west of Daytona Beach, offers a more-than-mile-long trail through its 150 acres and the surrounding **Spruce Creek Preserve** that can be combined with visits to a country house and to a cottage fashioned after the house featured in the Walt Disney film, "Snow White and the Seven Dwarfs."

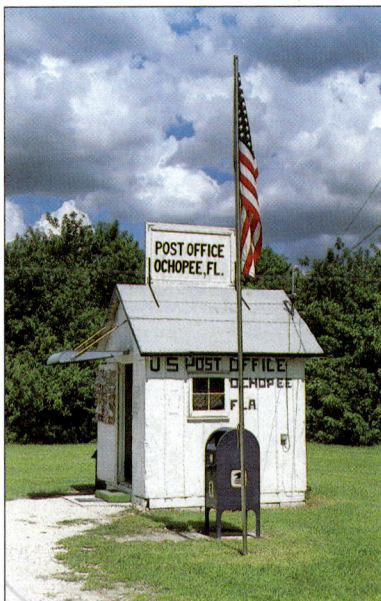

The best forest cycling in the state takes place through lands of the **Suwannee River Water Management District** in rural north Hamilton County. More than 100 miles of off-road trails have been mapped here by the Suwannee Bicycle Association (tel. 904-397-2347), including narrow beachfronts along modest rapids of the famed Suwannee River.

Canoe trails in parks and forests are especially popular in northeast Florida, where rentals are widely available, and trails lead through the salt marshes special to this part of the state. Popular parks include the **Anastasia State Recreation Area** near St. Augustine, **Big Talbot** and **Little Talbot Island State Park** north of Jacksonville, the **Bulow Plantation Ruins State Historic Site** at Bunnell, the underutilized **Faver-Dykes State Park** also near St. Augustine, and **Tomoka State Park**, north of Ormond Beach, moss-draped and evocatively Southern.

For information about these trails and trails described in the next two sections, contact **Office of Greenways & Trails**,

325 John Knox Road, Building 500, Tallahassee, FL 32303-4124.

Bicycling Trails

Florida enjoys the most progressive bicycling administration in America. However, the state suffers one of the highest accident rates among cyclists. As an accident-reduction measure, recent years have seen road-building policies that require new and retro-fitted state highways to include paved shoulders. Three recently-mapped trails cover 711 miles of largely quiet and scenic rural roads. The tours are designed for cyclists riding 50 to 70 miles a day. These tours include the Everglades to the upper Florida Keys, a broad loop through the springs of north-central Florida, and a tour called Seven Hills to the Sea along the upper Atlantic coast. Tours are mapped so that days end at state parks with camping facilities.

Above and Right: In Florida, windsurfing and cycling dreams come true.

Bridle Paths

There are seven bridle paths ranging from eleven to 35 miles between north and south Florida. However, horses are not available for hire. Arrangements can sometimes be made privately through **AHOOF** (Affiliated Horse Organization of Florida, P.O. Box 448, Laurel, FL 34272, tel. 813-484-6449). AHOOF can provide a list of stables around Florida. One opportunity for riding along Florida's beaches is through **Sea Horse Stable**, Highway A1A at the south end of Amelia Island in far northeast Florida (904-261-4878). Rides last approximately 75 minutes, horse rentals are $30, riders may not weigh more than 200 lbs.

Rail Trails

Chief among some 200 miles of these flat abandoned railbeds are: the 42-mile paved **Pinellas Trail** through metropolitan St. Petersburg-Clearwater; the 15-mile paved **St. Marks Historic Railroad**

State Trail, which begins south of Talla-hassee and ends at Apalachee Bay; the 17-mile **Gainesville-Hawthorne Trail** (unpaved) along the edge of Payne's Prairie; the 47-mile unpaved **Withla-coochee Trail** in upper west-central Florida; the 28-mile unpaved **Van Fleet Trail** through mid-state's important Green Swamp watershed; the 15-mile un-paved **Jacksonville-Baldwin Corridor**; and the nine-mile paved **Blackwater Heritage State Trail** in Florida's far west Panhandle. For information, contact **Rails-to-Trails Conservancy of Flo-rida**, 2545 Blairstone Pines Drive, Talla-hassee, FL 32301, tel. (904) 942-2379.

Florida Trail

This extraodinary trail now traverses 1,000 miles through virtually every type of topographic, biological and scenic landscape, protected almost everywhere from urban intrusion. Portions of the trail are open only to members of the **Florida Trail Association**. Contact the FTA for de-

tails at P.O. Box 13708, Gainesville FL 32604, tel. (904) 378-8823 (toll free: 1-800-343-1882, within Florida only).

Scenic Trail Lake Okeechobee

This trail is 30 feet up in the air atop the dike around the 130 miles of the lake that is at the heart of the Everglades, and is considered to be *the* adventure trail for cyclists. The entire trail is unpaved, and along much of the way offers exceptional views of the lake, as well as vistas across immense sugar and vegetable plantations and ranches. There are restaurants, lodg-ings and campsites every ten to 20 miles. For details, contact: **U.S. Army Corps of Engineers**, 525 Ridgelawn Rd., Clewis-ton, FL 33440-5399, tel. (813) 983-3335.

Greenways

A system of green corridors linking Florida's major parks, forests and other preserved natural sites will become ac-cessible to the public through the rest of

223

Above: Southermost House, Key West. Right: Must be the home of a harness-racing fan.

224

this decade. Some corridors will extend more than 100 miles. For updated information contact: **The Florida Greenways Program**, P.O. Box 5948, Tallahassee, FL 32314-5948, tel. (904) 222-6277.

BED AND BREAKFAST INNS

Florida has grown from only a few dozen B&B inns just a decade ago to some 250 today. They're found in former stores, such as the Governor's Inn, Tallahessee, stables (the Island City House in Key West), bridgetender houses (the Riverview Hotel in New Smyrna Beach), carriage houses (Old City House Inn in St. Augustine), and even a house of ill repute (a portion of the Merlinn Guest House, Key West).

B&B inns include the oldest homes in town, such as the Live Oak Inn in Daytona Beach; the grandest homes in town, such as the Herlong Mansion Inn in Mi-

canopy; mayors' homes (Hibiscus House in West Palm Beach), and homes of Florida governors (Sunbright Manor in De Funiak Springs and the Allison House Inn in Quincy). From former youth hostels (the Riverview) to former retirement homes (Indian River Inn), and from a one-time parsonage (Coquina Inn), to stately mansions (Curry Mansion Inn, home of Key West's first millionaire), the state's B&B inns represent the vanguard of historic preservation in Florida.

Visitors find B&B inns in all parts of the state, including directly on beaches, where you can step from your room onto the sand (Elizabeth Pointe Lodge on Amelia Island and Harrington House in Holmes Beach), and where donkey carts transport guests through fields to breakfast (Wits End Farm near Ocklawaha). At least two offer horseback riding (Cypress House B&B in Bushnell and L&M Paso Fino Ranch in Brooksville); one offers canoeing (the Great Outdoors Inn in High Springs). The Phoenix Nest on Amelia Island started by looking after stressed out women. The largest concentrations of B&B inns are in northeast Fernandina Beach and St. Augustine, and in far south Key West. If metro areas have few, numbers are nonetheless increasing, and local governments are finally awakening to this lodging sector's appeal by enacting ordinances for their encouragement.

Among cities, the Orlando area has five, including The Perri House, only minutes from Disney World, and is likely to get more. Metro Jacksonville has several, including three that front on the broad St. Johns River (Club Continental, House on Cherry Street and The Willows). The Himmarshee Village Historic District of newly-revived downtown Fort Lauderdale is about to open four, but otherwise Florida's big cities are meagerly represented: at latest count, the metro areas of Miami, Tampa and St. Petersburg together only have seven.

Rural Florida has B&Bs scattered around places that tell much about the history of the state. Many reveal connections with Florida cattle (Historic Parker House in Arcadia), Florida horse ranching (Wits End Farm), Florida railroading (The Crown Hotel in Inverness), earlier stages of Florida tourism that centered around healing springs and along rivers that were once the principal routes for reaching inland (the inns of High Springs, and Sprague House Inn in Crescent City) – even Florida under an earlier flag (Casa de Solana in St. Augustine).

Presidents and celebrities have stayed in Florida's B&B's: Eisenhower and Nixon at the Rod & Gun Club in Everglades City; suffragette Susan B. Anthony at what is now JD's Southern Oaks in Winter Haven; and milliner Lily Dache at Harrington House. Five are substantially on their own islands: Little Palm Island in the Florida Keys; Keewaydin Lodge in Naples; Cabbage Key off Fort Myers; Indigo Inn on Drayton Island; and the Pelican Inn on Dog Island. One is partly on a yacht (Southern Wind

in St. Augustine); another is in a whimsical castle (Solomon's Castle in Ona).

Florida's B&Bs provide hospitality in sharp contrast to the state's large numbers of chain hotels and motels. Maybe they're Victorian, grandly turreted and bay-windowed, such as Bailey House in Fernandina Beach or Sunbright Manor, or maybe rustic or darkly cypress, such as the Lakeside Inn in East Lake Weir or the Lake Morton B&B (one of Florida's best buys) in Lakeland. Heron House in Key West features the best modern interiors, though many are older Art Deco, including the Wellborn Apartments, now part of the Courtyard at Lake Lucerne in Orlando, and numerous choices in the Art Deco District of Miami Beach. Typically, inns reflect hosts' tastes.

A few modern onces fit well into their districts and are typically very well situated. These include, for example, Henderson Park Inn, a "late Victorian" directly on Destin Beach in the Panhandle, Josephine's, in the brillant new town of Seaside, Elizabeth Pointe Lodge, on

Amelia Island, and side-by-side beach-front Barnacle and Casa Grande in the Florida Keys.

Walls generally have been insulated to provide privacy, but it's good to ask about this. Only a few inns have elevators. Parking in most places is available on the premises.

Breakfasts range from store-bought doughnuts and coffee at the St. Francis Inn in St. Augustine to elaborate gourmet spreads at the Inn By The Sea in Naples. Almost everywhere, hosts are happy to let you store your drinks or food in their refrigerators.

More and more B&Bs provide meals in addition to breakfast. In some cases, B&Bs operate dining rooms which are open to the public, and their kitchens have achieved some renown (e.g., the Marquesa Hotel in Key West, the Florida House Inn in Fernandina Beach, the Old City House Inn, Keewaydin Lodge, the Bay Harbor Inn near Miami Beach, Chalet Suzanne and Hotel Place St. Michel in Coral Gables). In other cases, as at the Seven Sisters Inn in Ocala, hosts themselves will prepare dinners booked in advance. Such meals can often be arranged for couples romantically alone, served in guest rooms or outdoors on porches. Picnic lunches can often be prepared on request. Curry House Mansion in Key West serves evening cocktails with a pianist by the pool.

Florida B&Bs tend to charge rates higher than in many other states. In general, though, rates fall well below those of luxury hotels.

The two best sources for more detailed information about bed and breakfast inns in Florida are Inn Route, a non-profit organization that represents more than 75 inns in Florida (c/o Elizabeth Pointe Lodge), and two books: *Florida Country Inns* by Robert Tolf and *Guide to the Small & Historic Lodgings of Florida* by Herbert Hiller.

Above: One of many bed and breakfast inns in lovely historic buildings.

BED & BREAKFAST INNS

ARCADIA: Historic Parker House, 427 W. Hickory Street, Arcadia, FL 33821, tel. (941) 494-2499.
BROOKSVILLE: L&M Paso Fino Ranch, 5114 Spring Lake Highway, Brooksville, FL 34601, tel. (850) 544-0299.
BUSHNELL: Cypress House B&B, RR 1 Box 70 W. E, Bushnell, FL 33513, tel. (850) 568-0909.
BIG PINE KEY: Casa Grande, Rt. 1, Box 378, Big Pine Key, FL 33043, tel. (305) 872-2878; **The Barnacle**, Rt. 1, Box 780A, Big Pine Key, FL 33043, tel. (305) 872-3298.
CARRABELLE: Pelican Inn, Box 5030 Dog Island, Carrabelle 32322, tel. 1-800-451-5294.
CASSADAGA: The Cassadaga Hotel, 355 Cassadaga Road, Cassadaga, FL 32706, tel. (904) 228-2323.
CRESCENT CITY: Sprague House Inn, 125 Central Avenue, Crescent City, FL 32012, tel. (904) 698-2430.
DAYTONA BEACH: Coquina Inn, 544 S. Palmetto Avenue, Daytona Beach, FL 32114, tel. (904) 254-4969; **Live Oak Inn**, 448 S. Beach Street, Daytona Beach, FL 32114, tel. (904) 252-4667.
DE FUNIAK: Sunbright Manor, 606 Live Oak, De Funiak Springs, FL 32433, tel. (850) 892-0656.
DESTIN: Henderson Park Inn, 2700 Highway 98, Destin, FL 32541, tel. (850) 837-2434.
EVERGLADES CITY: Rod & Gun Club, 200 Riverside Drive, Everglades City, FL 33929, tel. (941) 695-2101; **Ivey House B&B**, 107 Camelia Street, Everglades City, FL 33929, tel. (941) 695-3299.
FERNANDINA BEACH: Bailey House, 28 S. 7th Street, Fernandina Beach, FL 32034, tel. (904) 261-5390; **Elizabeth Pointe Lodge**, 98 S. Fletcher Avenue, Fernandina Beach, FL 32034 tel. (904)277-4851; **Florida House Inn**, 20 & 22 S. 3rd Street, Fernandina Beach, FL 32034, tel. (904) 261-3300; **The 1735 House**, 584 S. Fletcher Avenue, Fernandina Beach, FL 32034, tel. (904) 261-4148 or 1-800-872-8531.
GEORGETOWN: Indigo Inn, Drayton Road, Box 5, Georgetown, FL 32139, tel. (904) 467-2446.
HIGH SPRINGS: Great Outdoors Inn, 65 N. Main Street, High Springs, FL 32643, tel. (904) 454-2900.
HOLMES BEACH: Harrington House, 5626 Gulf Drive, Holmes Beach, FL 34217, tel. (941) 778-5444.
INVERNESS: The Crown Hotel, 109 N. Seminole Avenue, Inverness, FL 34450, tel. (352) 344-5555.
JACKSONVILLE: House on Cherry Street, 1844 Cherry Street, Jacksonville, FL 32205, tel. (904) 384-1999; **The Willows**, 1849 Willow Branch Terrace, Jacksonville, FL 32205, tel. (904) 387-9152.
KEY WEST: Curry Mansion Inn, 511 Caroline Street, Key West, FL 33040, tel. (305) 294-5349; **Heron House**, 512 Simonton Street, Key West, FL 33040,

tel. (305) 294-9227; **Island City House**, 810 Eaton Street, Key West, FL 33040, tel. (305) 294-5702; **Wicker Guest House**, 913 Duval, Key West, FL 33040, tel. (305) 296-4275; **Merlinn Guest House**, 811 Simonton Street, Key West, FL 33040, tel. (305) 296-3336.
LAKELAND: Lake Morton B&B, 817 South Blvd, Lakeland, FL 33801, tel. (941) 688-6788.
LAKE WALES: Chalet Suzanne, 3800 Chalet Suzanne Drive, Lake Wales, FL 33853-7060, tel. (941) 676-6011.
LITTLE TORCH KEY: Little Palm Island, Route 4, Box 1036, Little Torch Key, FL 33043, tel. (305) 872-2524.
MIAMI: Miami River Inn, 118 SW S. River Drive, Miami, FL 33130, tel. (305) 325-0045.
MICANOPY: Herlong Mansion Inn, 402 NE Cholokka Blvd., Micanopy, FL 32667, tel. (352) 466-3322.
NAPLES: Inn By the Sea, 287 11th Avenue, Naples, FL 33940, tel. (941) 649-4124; **Keewaydin Lodge**, 260 Bay Road, Naples, FL 33940, tel. (941) 262-4149.
NEW SMYRNA: Indian River Inn, 1210 S. Riverside Drive, New Smyrna Beach, FL 32168, tel. (904) 428-2491; **Riverview Hotel**, 103 Flagler Avenue, New Smyrna Beach, FL 32169, tel. (904) 428-5858.
OCALA: Seven Sisters Inn, 820 SE Ft. King Street, Ocala, FL 32671, tel. (352) 867-1170.
OCKLAWAHA: Wits End Farm, Box 964, Ocklawaha, FL 32179, tel. (352) 288-4924.
ONA: Solomon's Castle, Rt. 1, Ona, FL 33865, tel. (941) 494-6077.
ORLANDO: Courtyard at Lake Lucerne, 211 N. Lucerne Circle E, Orlando, FL 32801, tel. (407) 648-5188; **Perri House**, 10417 SR 535, Orlando, FL 32836, tel. (407) 876-4830.
PINELAND: Cabbage Key Inn, Box 200, Pineland, FL 33945, tel. (941) 283-2278.
QUINCY: Allison House Inn, 215 N. Madison Street, Quincy 32351, tel. (850) 875-2511.
SEASIDE: Josephine's, 101 Seaside Avenue, Seaside, FL 32459, tel. (850) 231-1940.
ST. AUGUSTINE: Casa de Solana, 21 Aviles Street, St. Augustine, FL 32084, tel. (904) 824-3555; **Old Powder House Inn**, 38 Cordova Street, St. Augustine, FL 32084, tel. (904) 824-4149; **Southern Wind**, 18 Cordova Street, St. Augustine, FL 32084, tel. (904) 825-3623; **St. Francis Inn**, 279 St. George Street, St. Augustine, FL 32084, tel. (904) 824-6068.
TALLAHASSE: Governors Inn, 209 S. Adam Street, Tallahassee, FL 32301, tel. (850) 681-6855.
WEST PALM BEACH: Hibiscus House, 510 30th Street, West Palm Beach, FL 33407, tel. (561) 863-5633.
WINTER HAVEN: JD's Southern Oaks, 3800 Country Club Road, Winter Haven, FL 33881, tel. (941) 293-2335.

© Zbyszek: Conversations

HAND-
PAINTED
15

© Zbyszek - Until Tomorrow KEY WEST

HISPANIC INFLUENCE

Miami International Airport is one of the few airports in this country in which airline announcements are sometimes aired first in Spanish. Some travelers are stunned by this – Miami is, after all, still in Florida, which at the last count was still one of the United States.

But this Spanish first, English second order is not surprising given the pervasive Hispanic influence in the area. In Miami, 900,000 residents of the city's 1.9 million total are Hispanic, with that number growing every day. Small Cuban markets proliferate throughout southeast Florida, and shoppers are commonly spoken to in Spanish. This can be disconcerting to Americans purchasing a carton of milk or a pack of cigarettes. Bowing to the numbers and the political impact, more Hispanic politicians have been

Preceding pages: Artist in Key West. Above: A Hispanic immigrant at work. Right: Exotic friendship.

elected in recent years. In 1992, Florida elected its second Hispanic-American to the U.S. Congress. A recent governor of the state, Bob Martinez, was Hispanic, as is former Mayor Xavier Suarez of Miami.

In one recent, hotly-contested Congressional election, a Cuban woman, Ileana Ros-Lehtinen, was elected primarily because of her ethnic base; she felt that the seat should be a Cuban seat. The base in Miami is strong because it is pretty homogeneous; more than 75% of Greater Miami's Hispanic population is Cuban. As a result, they feel more united and more powerful, although other Hispanics of Central or South American heritage are calling Florida their home, yet without the political base the Cubans have forged in the years since Castro took power. Miami residents hear more Spanish stations on the radio, more Spanish spoken in the street, and there has been resistance on the part of some immigrants to learning English. To some older residents of the area, this is frightening: some are leaving Miami and moving north to Broward and Palm Beach counties. Some Hispanics are, too. Broward County is quieter, less urban, and less political than Miami, and some who prefer to be out of the fray live in Broward and drive to their jobs in Miami.

There have been tensions in these areas as well for some time. Census taking in Broward County has come under attack for under-counting the number of Hispanic residents; the Hispanic voters feel they are being undercut politically; that politicians who have seen the Hispanic vote rule in Miami do not want the same thing to happen up north. But others are reminded that 10% of Broward County's 1.3 million residents are now Hispanic, and that number is expected to increase. The Hispanics living in Broward County are not as militant as their compatriots in Greater Miami, but they warn that they represent serious numbers and want to be taken seriously.

SOCIAL PROBLEMS IN THE SUNSHINE STATE

The first wave of violence here occurred in 1965, just as Civil Rights legislation in this country was finally opening up opportunities for blacks. Instead of having the field to themselves, however, blacks found themselves in competition with the recently-arrived Cubans from Fidel Castro's airlift: 260,000 of whom came to south Florida over the next six years. 125,000 more refugees came in the Mariel boatlift of 1980, a boatlift that was roundly criticized later because Castro had seemingly cleaned out his mental hospitals and jails and sent their occupants to the United States.

More recently, Nicaraguan refugees have come to the area at the rate of some 200 a day. Once the Hispanic immigrants come to the area, many set to work trying to achieve the American Dream by starting up and owning their own businesses, and later buying a house.

In contrast, black residents of the area tend to feel that they have somehow been left behind; their rate of joblessness is higher than that of the Hispanics, which is, in fact, dropping.

Local police are continually being accused of uncontrolled racist behavior. Since 40 percent of the police force is made up of Hispanics, who also patrol black neighborhoods, it is no surprise that there are occasional eruptions of violence.

Riots in a black section of Miami in 1989 shocked the city. Arson, looting and violence escalated. The catalyst for the rioting– the shooting of a young black man by a Columbian police officer – was the result of years of increasing tension between the two communities. These problems will certainly continue to exist until there equal rights for all of Miami's citizens.

The hit TV show *Miami Vice* showed a Miami in which flashy drug dealers

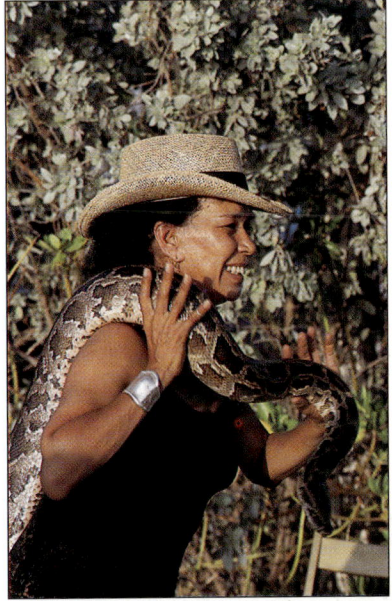

lurked behind every palm tree and yacht. To many residents the show, despite its scenes of brutal violence, misrepresented and downplayed the reality of Florida's drug scene.

And the way the Coast Guard and Drug Enforcement Administration see it, that assessment is not far wrong. That Miami has been a major drop-off point for cocaine and other drugs coming into the country has long been well known. After all, it is perfectly situated near Central and South America and Mexico. Since the early 1980s, however, the federal government has been trying to do something about putting an end to these criminal activities – with varying degrees of success.

If you are driving in the vicinity of Cape Canaveral, or near Cudjoe Key in the Florida Keys, and see a large balloon tethered to a stationary point, you will see one aspect of these drug combating efforts at work. The balloons (the Keys balloon is nicknamed "Fat Albert" by the locals) contain radar devices to help

guide Coast Guard and Customs boats sweeping for smugglers.

Smugglers, though, have been using superfast boats that can reach speeds of up to 80 mph, so that while the Coast Guard may see them and catch some, many more easily slip away. Over the years, there have been reports that these efforts have annoyed the drug smugglers to the degree that they have shifted some operations to Texas and California. That may well be, but south Florida seems unlikely to lose them for good.

Bales of marijuana jettisoned by smugglers continue to wash up on Florida's shores. Enormous ships' holds packed with cocaine cause nary a ripple in the news when intercepted by legal authorities. In their wake are often violent shoot-outs as drug deals go bad, and the untrustworthy are eliminated.

But as menacing as drug violence can be, Florida violence does not always have

Above: Watching out for drug dealers?
Right: Jogging on the beach.

something to do with drugs. The state has one of the loosest gun control laws in the country, and although there may be a short waiting period when buying a gun, there is no law against carrying a concealed weapon, a *de rigueur* statute in other places.

A few years ago, after a rash of children getting their hands on their parents' guns and shooting other children made the news, the legislature made it illegal to keep a gun any place where children can get at it. But that is all. Having the gun itself is not a problem. However, introducing the law has not cut down on children being shot; since it was enacted, more children have been accidentally gunned down, but no one has pressed charges using the new law.

Therefore, Florida may not be exactly Dodge City, but it is not a place where a person looks to get into a fight with a stranger either, or even to cut another car off in traffic, which has been known to precipitate gunfire. And watch your head on New Year's Eve: at midnight, Floridians like to shoot guns into the air. The next day's news almost always contains a report of some poor soul being killed by a stray bullet while sitting in his home.

Throughout the 1990s, an increasing number of foreign tourists have been robbed or even murdered in Florida. The murder of Italian fashion designer Gianni Versace in front of his villa, in the summer of 1997, made for headlines in newspapers all over the world.

No one wants to have to forego a vacation in the Sunshine State because of this, though. Visitors from abroad have become noticeably more careful, and they generally stick to a few basic rules of behavior to help keep them out of harm's way (see "Safety" in the *Guidelines* section). The safety of tourists to Florida – especially in Miami and Miami Beach – has been addressed in the form of more stringent laws and controls on the side of the police.

THE GOLDEN YEARS IN FLORIDA

The stream of elderly visitors from the frigid north to the sunny south is hardly a new phenomenon: retirees have been moving to the Sunshine State since the 1930s. The numbers add up: residents 65 and older represented one out of six in the 1988 census; by the year 2000, this is expected to be one in five. A great many retirees come here to spend their golden years in a warm, sunny climate and in a quiet, relaxed atmosphere.

The repercussions of this older population are manifold: politically, areas with concentrations of retirees – and especially the lower three counties, Dade, Broward and Palm Beach – have very status quo laws. No new taxes are enacted in these areas, despite municipal need. People on fixed incomes do not want to pay out, especially for services many of them do not need.

Municipal ordinances also change when a large block of the elderly are voters. One reason given for the departure of the college students' Spring Break from Fort Lauderdale was the large number of wealthy retired people in the city: they moved here for a life of peace and quiet and did not appreciate the raucous goings-on that occured each year when the teenagers took over.

The ambience of the area also changes when the elderly move in. Entertainment, food stores and restaurants all gear services to over-65s' needs. Many of them enjoy robust physical and mental health: it is not unusual to see a group of "Grey Panthers" happily jogging or working out in a fitness center. Another aspect of being in an area of so many retirees is that, as has been known to happen, an elderly person at an adjacent table in a restaurant may suddenly suffer a heart attack or stroke.

Driving can also be risky; elderly people who have always driven and need to drive in order to get around are reluctant to surrender their licenses – even though many should.

METRIC CONVERSION

Metric Unit	US Equivalent
Meter (m)	39.37 in.
Kilometer (km)	0.6241 mi.
Square Meter (sq m)	10.76 sq. ft.
Hectare (ha)	2.471 acres
Square Kilometer (sq km)	0.386 sq. mi.
Kilogram (kg)	2.2 lbs.
Liter (l)	1.05 qt.

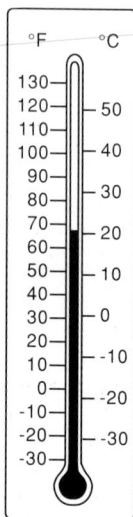

°F   °C

130—
120—   — 50
110—
100—   — 40
90—
80—   — 30
70—   — 20
60—
50—   — 10
40—
30—   — 0
20—
10—   — -10
0—
-10—   — -20
-20—   — -30
-30—

TRAVEL PREPARATIONS

Visa Requirements

Visitors from Australia, as well as from the U.K., Ireland and most other European countries, can enter the U.S. without a visa under the Visa Waiver Pilot Program (VWPP), if your stay is for no more than 90 days, is for a holiday or business, and if you have a return or on-going ticket. Passports must be valid for at least six months from date of entry. Visitors to the U.S. under the VWPP may not work during their stay. Contact the nearest U.S. embassy or consulate for further details.

For those arriving without a return or ongoing ticket, or for those who intend to stay for longer than between three and six months (the maximum stay allowed), visas must be obtained either by post (special delivery) or in person. They are available through U.S. consulates and are generally processed quickly and unbureaucratically. During certain times of year, however, especially during the summer peak tourist season, the waiting time can be as much as six weeks.

Visa applications should be filled out carefully and to the best of your knowledge in order to avoid possible misunderstandings later on. Tourist visas are only denied in certain cases (e.g., criminal record, drug offences, etc.).

Entry and Customs Requirements

All passengers traveling to the U.S. are given a customs declaration form in the airplane, which must be filled out before arrival. The so-called 194W (green form) requests the usual information: the purpose of your visit, addresses of friends or relatives in the U.S. (be sure to give the name and address of a hotel, or a friend or relative!), whether you are a member of an outlawed party or organization, etc. The bottom copy of this form will be attached to your passport by an immigrations officer in the airport, marked with the date and place of entry. On departure, it will be removed (normally by a representative of the airline). During your stay in the U.S., be careful not to lose this form.

In general, there are no problems with arrival, and passengers are processed quickly. On occasion, a passenger might be asked about his or her financial situation or travel plans. Those who can provide proof of sufficient resources on request – as cash in U.S. dollars or traveler's checks – should not have any problems. If you have stamps in your passport from communist countries, such as Cuba or North Korea, or certain Arabic countries, such as Libya, Syria, Iraq or Iran, for example, you might arouse the suspicions of immigrations personnel. Even in such a case, however, you will probably only be asked a few questions and asked to show your return ticket and your cash or traveler's checks.

After entry formalities are completed, passengers then go through customs clearance. As a rule, customs officers just stamp the papers of passengers arriving from central or western European countries. If bringing an amount of more than $10,000 per person into the country, this must be declared.

Finally, it should be mentioned that the import of fresh foodstuffs (for example, meat or sausage, bread, fruits and vegetables) is strictly forbidden. Those who are on regular medication should be sure to obtain a written verification (in English) of this from their physician. Otherwise, there is the possibility that medication could be confiscated during a routine control.

Cash, Traveler's Checks, Credit Cards

For safety's sake, as a rule, it is a good idea to take as little cash as possible with you when traveling to the U.S. The denomination of bills should not be above $50. Foreign currencies can only be exchanged in larger cities and in some banks.

It is safer and more practical to get your traveler's checks in U.S. dollars from American Express or Visa, for example. These are accepted at all hotels, shops and businesses in the country. Just as safe, and even more practical, are credit cards. Whoever has Eurocard/Mastercard, Visa Card or an American Express card will never have problems using them in Florida. In fact, with some hotels and car rental agencies, a credit card is an absolute necessity!

Medical Insurance

If you travel to Florida without adequate medical insurance, you could find yourself facing financial ruin: the U.S. is well behind European health insurance standards – whoever gets ill here can pay heavily for any treatment rendered.

Before leaving home, be sure to check with your insurer to find out whether or not you are covered while in the U.S., and what the extent of this coverage is. If you are not fully covered, a supplementary travel insurance policy is strongly recommended. This should have unlimited full coverage guaranteed (preferably with accompanying accident insurance). Credit card holders, especially those with EuroCard Gold, can assume that their annual credit card fee includes travel insurance. Check with your credit card company to be sure.

In any case, if visiting a doctor, hospital or clinic while in the U.S., keep in mind that bills must be paid on the spot either in cash, or by traveler's check or credit card.

Climate / Travel Seasons

Florida's climate is generally predictable. There is very little seasonal change, leaves do not fall off trees in winter and for the most part temperatures can be expected to stay above freezing, even in January, the coldest month. In recent years, however, climatic changes have been pronounced, with winter temperatures falling below the freezing point as far south as Tampa. These cold spells are generally short-lived, and it would not be uncommon for a cold snap to dissipate in a day or so, with normal temperatures returning promptly.

Although most visitors will pack their swimwear and tennis outfits for a south Florida vacation in winter, recent temperatures have dropped into the 30-40° F range, so travelers should pack a sweater or jacket, too. Rain is a much more common occurrence than freezing temperatures. Summers provide the most rainfall, on an almost daily basis, though these sometimes violent soakings have the added benefit of cooling things down. At other times of year, though, rain falls on a more irregular basis, although the farther south you go, the more likely wet weather is.

Average low winter temperatures range from around 40° F in the northern Panhandle to around 65° F in the Florida Keys. Daytime highs, however, can be quite pleasant, averaging 20° F higher than recorded low temperatures. Average high summer temperatures range from 85 to 90° F. throughout the state, with average lows dropping only about 10° F. Because of the relatively high humidity, it often seems to be much hotter than it actually is.

Peak-season pricing has everything to do with Florida's weather, so you can expect to pay more for accommodation during winter in south Florida, and during summer in the Florida Panhandle. Many places of interest and national parks are packed with American tourists between Memorial Day (end of May) and Labor Day (beginning of September).

Travelers should be aware during their Florida vacation that the forces of nature in the New World can be much more extreme – and at times more dangerous – than in most European countries. Warnings of storms, tornados, hurricanes and tidal waves should be taken extremely seriously!

Clothing

Clothing styles are becoming more and more casual throughout most of Florida, except for the Palm Beach area, which tends toward the formal. Light, loose-fitting clothing of natural fibers is recommended. Bring shorts, T-shirts, sandals or sneakers. Swimwear is always acceptable at beach resorts or coastal areas during the day, although not always in the evening. Evenings sometimes call for a jacket for men, slacks or a dress for women. Only the most posh resorts or restaurants will require formal attire.

Taking light rain gear with you is probably a good idea, though it is not always necessary; because of the heat, rainfall can sometimes actually be quite refreshing. Unfortunately, due to the high levels of humidity, once you get wet it might take quite some time to dry out again, even after the sun comes out. This is not a problem if you are in your swimsuit, but some people, particularly the elderly who so love Florida, easily catch colds from darting in and out of air-conditioned buildings while wet.

Caps or sun hats are recommended. Suncreams with a high screen factor should be used. A warmer jacket or a sweater is recommended for winter travel in Florida.

Warning: Do not go barefoot in places other than the beach. Florida is largely covered in cement and asphalt that can get very hot in the sun.

Departure

Allow at least 90 minutes for departure formalities, such as ticketing, seat assignment and security checks. Allow longer at Miami International Airport, particularly if traveling during peak season or holiday periods. Always reconfirm international flights 24 hours prior to departure. Consult your carrier for any additional departure fees that may be required.

U.S. Embassies and Consulates in Australia, Ireland and the U.K.

AUSTRALIA: U.S. Embassy, Consular Section, Moonah Place, Canberra, A.C.T., tel. (6) 270-5000, fax. (6) 270-5970; U.S. Consulate General, 553 St. Kilda Road, O.O. Box 6722, Melbourne, Victoria 3004, tel. (3) 526-5900, fax. (3) 510-4646; U.S. Consulate General, 16 St. Georges Terrace, 13th fl., Perth WA 6000, tel. (9) 231-9400, fax. (9) 231-9444; U.S. Consulate General, MLC Centre, 19-29 Martin Place, 59th fl., Sydney NSW 2000, tel. (2) 373-9200.

IRELAND: U.S. Embassy, Consular Section, 42 Elgin Road, Ballsbridge, Dublin, tel. (1) 668-7122, fax. (1) 668-9946.

U.K.: U.S. Embassy, Consular Section, 24 Grosvenor Square, London, W1A 1AE, tel. (171) 499-9000 – Visa Information Line, 891-200-290 (for recorded information; calls charged at 50p per minute) or 991-500-590 for operator assisted information (calls charged at £1.50 per minute); Consulate General, 3 Regent Terrace, Edinburgh, Scotland EH7 5BW, tel. (131) 556-8315, fax. (131) 557-6023 (Visa Information Line as for London); Consulate General, Queen's House, 14 Queen Street, Belfast, Northern Ireland BT1 6EQ, tel. (1232) 328-239, fax. (1232) 224-8482.

TRAVELING IN FLORIDA

Airlines

A confusing number of airlines serve Florida from within the United States and internationally, and these lines change somewhat as routes are frequently added or dropped. In even more of a constant state of flux than routes are fares. These vary dramatically according to the time of year, the particular route you travel, special promotions and package fares.

Airfares from heavy traffic areas such as the northeast U.S. are often competitively priced as airlines fight for the lucrative traffic. Shop around for bargains. Likewise, as international traffic continues to grow, good fares can be found, particularly through connections to the Caribbean, Central and South America, as well as an increasing number of direct flights from European capitals. The tax on tickets for domestic flights is ten percent.

For those who prefer to deal with airlines directly, the following is a partial listing of major airlines serving Florida's major airports. All have toll-free numbers which can be dialed from within the

U.S: **American Airlines** (AA), tel. 1-800-433-7300; **Continental Airlines** (CO), tel. 1-800-525-0280; **Delta Air Lines** (DL), tel. 1-800-221-1212; **Northwest Airlines** (NW), tel. 1-800-225-2525; **Southwest Airlines** (WN), tel. 1-800-435-9792; **Trans World Airlines** (TWA), tel. 1-800-221-2000; **United Airlines** (UA), tel. 1-800-241-6522; **USAir** (US), tel. 1-800-428-4322.

The most important airports in Florida are: **Miami International**, P.O. Box 592075, tel. (305) 871-7090; **Fort Lauderdale / Hollywood International**, 1400 Lee Wagener Blvd., tel. (954) 357-6100; **Jacksonville International**, tel. (904) 741-2000; **Orlando International**, 1 Airport Blvd., tel. (407) 826-2001; **Palm Beach International**, Bldg. 846, West Palm Beach, tel. (407) 471-7400; **Sarasota/Bradenton International**, Sarasota, tel. (941) 359-5200; **Southwest Florida International**, 1600 Chamberlin Parkway SE, Fort Myers, tel. (941) 768-1000; **Tampa International**, tel. (813) 276-3400.

Regional Airports: **Marathon Airport**, 9000 Overseas Highway, tel. (305) 289-6060; **Daytona Beach Regional Airport**, 700 Catalina Dr., tel. (904) 248-8030; **Key West Airport**, South Roosevelt Blvd., tel. (305) 296-5439; **Naples Airport**, Terminal Drive, tel. (941) 643-0733; **Pensacola Regional**, 2430 Airport Blvd., tel. (850) 435-1746; **Tallahassee Regional**, 3240 Capitol Circle, tel. (850) 891-7800; **Panama City/Bay County Airport**, 3173 Airport Rd., tel. (850) 763-6751. **Destin/Fort Walton Okaloosa County Air Terminal**, Hwy. 85, Eglin Air Force Base, tel. (850) 651-7160.

Car Rentals

Arranging your rental car from your home country can save you as much as 60 percent of what you will pay if you book after arriving in Florida. The regular rates of the big rental companies – Hertz, Avis and Budget – are pretty much alike, but careful comparison is still recommended, especially as regards special offers. Often there are special daily, weekly or monthly rates, or package deals which combine hotel stays with rental cars.

In order to rent a car in Florida, the driver must be at least 21 years of age and in possession of a valid driver's license. For drivers under the age of 25, many rental companies add a per-day surcharge. Get all the information you need regarding additional costs when renting the car, such as insurance, tax, pick-up costs, miles driven above the free mileage limit, etc.

Most travel agencies can arrange so-called Fly-and-Drive vacations, in which the price of the flight and the cost of a rental car (normally by the week) are economically combined into a single package

A number of rental agencies also offer campers and RV's (recreational vehicles). These can also often be arranged through a Fly-and-Drive package.

In Florida, information can be obtained from the following companies at their toll-free numbers:

Alamo Rent-A-Car, tel. 1-800-327-9633; **Avis Reservations Center**, tel. 1-800-331-1212; **Budget Rent-A-Car**, tel. 1-800-527-0700; **Dollar Rent-A-Car**, tel. 1-800-800-4000; **Hertz Corporation**, tel. 1-800-654-3131; **National Car Rental**, tel. 1-800-CAR-RENT; **Thrifty Rent-A-Car**, tel. 1-800-367-2277.

Driving in Florida

Most foreign travelers to Florida are allowed to operate a motor vehicle provided they are holding a valid license issued at home. Residents of certain countries may need to produce an International Driver's permit issued at home. For details and information regarding specific requirements, contact: **Florida Highway Safety and Motor Vehicles Department**, Driver's Licenses Division, Neil Kirkman Building, Tallahassee, FL 32399-0575, (850) 488-3144.

Driving on American roads is much simpler and more relaxing than driving in Europe: the roads are wider, in rural areas they are often empty, and Americans generally drive according to the principle of "Safety First." Driving here is much more defensive than in Italy, for instance, or even the U.K. Aggressive driving or tailgating can easily result in a traffic ticket. And you can be certain that the local Highway Patrol will be after you in a flash if they see any infractions of local traffic laws.

Americans expect tourists to drive in a civilized fashion, especially in cities. That Americans drive more carefully is not simply a question of mentality, it is also a question of money: many U.S. drivers only carry the bare legal minimum of insurance coverage (about $20,000 damages per person) – and this in a country famous for horrendous hospital bills!

International travelers should familiarize themselves with certain important Florida driving rules:

Stoplights: Red light: Stop. Yellow light: Warning, signal is changing from green to red. Green Light: Proceed. Green arrow: Proceed in direction of arrow from appropriate lane. Flashing red light: Come to a full stop, then proceed with caution. Flashing yellow light: Slow down, then proceed with caution.

Traffic Regulations: Drive on the right: Motorists must stay to the right of the road. On the highway, the passing lane is on the left. Right turn on red: Following a full stop, it is legal to turn right at a red light unless otherwise posted.

Speed Limits: In cities and congested areas, the speed limit is generally between 20 and 40 mph. The speed limit on highways is 70 mph; though on some it may be less. Posted signs on roadways indicate specific speed limits. All limits are enforced.

If you are stopped by the Highway Patrol, keep both hands on the steering wheel until the officer has asked to see your papers. Only then should you reach for your wallet: and do this slowly; otherwise you might give the impression that you're going for a weapon!

Beware of fire hydrants when parking. Make sure you park at least the prescribed 13 feet from a hydrant: the ticket and towing charges if you park too close to one can be very expensive!

Street signs that aren't known in Europe include the *No U-Turn* sign, which prohibits turning around, and the *Crossover* sign, which allows turning around on a highway. "Xing" stands for crossing. *Gator Xing* lets you know that alligators could be crossing the road at this point. Some lanes of multiple-lane streets in cities often have *HOV* signs posted (for High Occupancy Vehicle). These lanes can only be used by cars that have at least two (*HOV-2*) or three (*HOV-3*) occupants during rush hours.

Accidents: All traffic accidents must be reported to the local police department, county sheriff's office or Florida Highway Patrol.

School Buses: Traffic moving in both directions must stop while a school bus is loading or unloading, except if the bus is stopped on the opposite side of a divided highway.

Emergency Vehicles: All traffic must yield to police vehicles, fire engines, ambulances and all other emergency vehicles which display flashing lights or use audible alarms, or both.

The **Interstate Highway System** provides major access to Florida. Interstate 95 covers Florida's east coast. I-75 runs down the west coast of the state. I-10 runs from Pensacola eastward to its terminus at I-95 in Jacksonville. I-4 runs from Daytona Beach on the Atlantic Coast to Tampa on the Gulf Coast.

The **Florida Turnpike** is generally less crowded than the Interstates, probably because there is a toll charge. It runs north-south out of the Miami area to Wildwood, in central Florida.

Florida Toll Roads: *Airport Expressway*: Downtown Miami to Miami International Airport, nine miles; *Bee Line Expressway*: Orlando to Cape Canaveral, 53 miles; *Dolphin Expressway*: Downtown Miami to Palmetto Expressway, nine miles; *Everglades Parkway*: Naples to Andytown, 78 miles; *East-West Expressway*: South Orlando business district, 13.5 miles; *Central Florida Greeneway*, SR 417 to Sanford, 35 miles; *Florida Turnpike*: Wildwood to Homestead, 318 miles; *J. Turner Butler Expressway*: S.R. 115 to Jacksonville Beach, ten miles; *Sawgrass Parkway*: Northwest of Fort Lauderdale, 22 miles; *South Crosstown Expressway*: Tampa, 18 miles.

To keep up to date with Florida's expanding highway system, request a free *Florida Official Transportation Map*, from the Florida Department of Commerce, Collins Building, Tallahassee, FL 32399.

Breakdown Assistance

If you have a breakdown in a rental car, contact the rental agency first. Otherwise, help is available from the American Automobile Association (AAA, known as "Triple A"). Their toll-free number is_ 1-800-222-4357. This is America's largest automobile club. Some European auto clubs have reciprocal arrangements with the Triple A. Inquire at yours as to whether this is the case.

Motorcycles

To ride along the wide highways of America on a Harley-Davidson is the dream of many a motorcycle fan. And you can rent a Harley – or another make – in many places in Florida.

Some airlines even offer a "Fly & Ride" program for those who want to bring their own motorcycle along with them. Check with travel agencies in your area to find out what companies offer such a package.

In Florida, Harleys can be rented from: **EagleRider Motorcycle Rentals**, 527 Miller Street, Orlando, FL 32805, tel. (407) 316-8687, fax. (407) 316-8678 (starting at $75/day); **Street Eagle of Sarasota Florida**, 6216 28th St. East, Bradenton, FL 34203, tel. (941) 752-4600, fax. (941) 739-6410; **Street Eagle of Pinellas County**, 12477 66th St. North, Largo, FL 34643, tel. (813) 524-7999, fax. (813) 524-7997.

Buses

Local bus lines connect many of Florida's cities. The Chamber of Commerce can provide visitors with schedules and route information. Larger bus companies also offer luggage and package services.

Greyhound is the biggest bus company in the U.S. You can call their toll-free number for fare and schedule information at 1-800-231-2222.

You can purchase the economical Greyhound *Ameripass* at any Greyhound station in the U.S., and abroad from many travel agencies. Passes are for 7, 15, 30 and 60 days and are good for unlimited travel on Greyhound and other authorized bus lines. A 15-day pass, for example, costs $299; a 30-day pass $409.

Trains

AMTRAK serves most Florida cities, from Jacksonville to Key West, from Miami to Pensacola. Here is is small selection of their sales representatives abroad: *AUSTRALIA:* Thomas Cook World Rail, Level 8, 130 Pitt Street, Sydney, tel. (2) 9320-6566; Rail Plus, Level 8, 114 William Street, Melbourne, tel. (3) 9642-8644. *IRELAND:* USIT, 19/21 Aston Quay, O'Connell Bridge, Dublin 2, tel. (1) 602-1600. *U.K.:* Trailfinders Limited, 215 Kensington High Street, London, tel. (171) 937-5400; Trailfinders Limited, 254-284 Sauchiehall Street, Glasgow, tel. (141) 353-2224.

The Amtrak North American Rail Pass costs $450 off-season and $645 peak season, and is good for 30 days of unlimited travel. Ask your travel agent for information, or from inside the U.S. contact Amtrak at their toll-free number: 1-800-USA-RAIL.

Houseboats

Small groups of up to ten people, and honeymooners as well, can enjoy a river trip on the St. Johns River in a houseboat. These roomy houseboats are luxuriously furnished and come equipped with everything from a kitchen with refrigerator and microwave oven to a shower and television. Food can and sometimes must be brought on board. The sun deck has room for all passengers. Along the way you can "drop anchor" free of charge at marked piers. Swimming and fishing opportunities are unlimited. No boat license is necessary; you'll be shown the ropes by staff. Excellent maps help you with your orientation. Contact: **Three Bouys Houseboat Vacations**, 2280 Hontoon Rd., DeLand, FL, 32720, tel. (904) 736-9422 or 1-800-262-3454; **Florida Boaters Assoc.**, 1900 79th St. Causeway, Bay Village, FL 33141, tel. (305) 868-4117.

PRACTICAL TIPS FROM A TO Z

Accommodation

Accommodation in Florida runs the gamut from ultra-expensive, ultra-luxurious resort hotels, to old-fashioned motor courts and inexpensive motels, YMCAs, YWCAs and American Youth Hostels, with every extreme and everything in between well-represented. Accommodation listed in the *Guidepost* sections of this book are meant to be among the best in each price range, although there are many more to choose from in most areas of Florida. A wise travel agent is a good bet for sifting through the voluminous possibilities in accommodation, as well as in planning other trip details.

Most Florida accommodations have swimming pools and air conditioning. Color TVs in all rooms are *de rigueur*, with cable-TV an increasingly common free feature. Pay-for-view in-room broadcasts of first-run movies are found mostly in expensive to luxury properties. Many accommodations have in-room service bars, but prices are high for this convenience. Rooms overlooking the ocean are naturally more expensive than similar rooms facing an interior courtyard or a parking lot.

Most rates are adjusted seasonally, with the highest prices generally from December through April, and the lowest rates in summer. Buffer seasons sometimes offer bargains, and the savvy traveler realizes that although summers can be extremely hot and humid, there is little difference in the sublime climate conditions of the peak season and those found in May or November, when substantial savings are available. Package prices combining accommodation with air transportation or activity schedules are frequently offered. Accommodation for handicapped travelers is increasingly found throughout the state.

Many hotel and motel chains offer centralized reservation systems through toll-free phone numbers that may be called from within the U.S. or Canada free of charge. The following is a list of these phone numbers for major chains represented in Florida.

Best Western International, 1-800-528-1234; **Choice Inn**, **Comfort Inn**, **Quality Inn**, **Clarion Hotel**, **Sleep Inn**, **Rodeway Inn**, **Friendship Inn** and **Econo Lodge**, 1-800-228-5151; **Days Inn**, 1-800-325-2525; **Courtyard Inn**, **Fairfield Inn**, **Residence Inn**, 1-800-228-2800; **Doubletree** and **CP Hotel**, 1-800-528-0244; **Econo Lodge of America**, 1-800-446-6900; **Embassy Suite**, 1-800-362-2779; **Friendship Inn of America,** 1800-453-4511; **Hampton Inn**, 1-800-HAMPTON; **Hilton Hotel**, 1-800-HILTONS; **Holiday Inn**, 800-HOLIDAY; **Howard Johnson**, 1-800-654-2000; **Hyatt Corporation**, 1-800-233-1234; **La Quinta Motor Inn**, 1-800-531-5900; **Marriott Hotel**, 1-800-228-9290; **Preferred Hotel**, 1-800-323-7500; **Quality Inn**, 1-800-228-5151; **Radisson Hotel**, 1-800-333-3333; **Ramada Inn**, 1-800-2-RAMADA; **Red Carpet**, **Scottish Inn**, **Downtowner**, **Master Host**, **Passport Inn**, 1-800-251-1962; **Red Roof Inn** and **Master Host Inn**, 1-800-843-7663; **Resident Inn**, **Fairfield Inn**, **Marriott Hotel**, 1-800-331-3131; **Rodeway Inn International**, 1-800-228-2000; **Sheraton Hotels and Inns**, 1800-325-3535; **Sonesta Hotel**, 1-800-766-3782; **Travelodge International / Viscount Hotel**, 1-800-255-3050; **Westin Hotel**, 1-800-228-3000.

Alcohol and Cigarettes

For most Americans, the consumption of alcohol is considered to be somewhat reprehensible. This is not so much because of their puritanical past, the Prohibition or the drug problem in the country: it has more to do with the exaggerated heatlh movement there than anything else. A lot of Americans start the day with a handful of vitamin pills; alcohol and tobacco are accepted less and less by society.

Those who don't want to go without a few drinks on their Florida vacation have to keep in mind that you must be at least 21 years old in order to purchase alcoholic beverages (including beer) or to be allowed into a bar or disco where alcohol is served.

Drinking alcoholic beverages in public is illegal, which is why you may see people on the sidewalk drinking something from a brown paper bag. Drinking while driving is against the law, as is having an open bottle of alcohol in the passenger compartment of a car; store open bottles in the trunk when driving!

Drunk driving is a very serious offense in the U.S. In case of an accident, or at random control points, "breathalyzer" tests may be made. Even tourists can quickly wind up in the local jail if driving under the influence.

Smoking is strictly prohibited in many public buildings, as well as on domestic flights, in buses and trains. Movie theaters with smokers' areas in the foyer are almost unkown. In smaller cafés smoking is generally prohibited; restaurants, as a rule, have a smoking section.

Banks

Most banks are open Monday through Friday from 9 a.m. to 4 p.m. When cashing traveler's checks or picking up cash on a credit card, you must show your passport and often a second piece of identification (driver's license, national identity card, etc.).

Cruise Directory

The following cruise lines are currently serving the Florida ports under which they are listed.

Port of Miami, 1015 North America Way, Miami, FL 33132, tel. (941) 371-7678: Carnival Cruise Lines; Commodore Cruise Line; Dolphin Cruise Lines; Fantasy Cruises; Ivaran Lines; Majesty Cruise Line; Norwegian Cruise Line; Royal Caribbean Cruise Line; Sea Escape, Ltd.; Starlite Cruises.

Port Everglades, 1850 Eller Drive, Fort Lauderdale, FL 33316, tel. (941) 523-3404: Carnival Cruise Lines; Celebrity Cruises; Costa Cruises; Crystal Cruises; Cunard Line; Discovery Cruises; Epirotiki Lines; Holland America Line/Westours; Princess Cruises; Royal Viking Line/Kloster Cruises Ltd.; Seabourn Cruise Line; Sea Escape Ltd., Sun Line Cruises.

Port Canaveral, P.O. Box 267, Cape Canaveral, FL 32920, tel. (407) 783-7831: Carnival Cruise Line, tel. (407) 799-0638; Premier Cruise Line, tel. (407) 783-7831; Disney Cruise Line, 210 Celebration Place, Celebration, FL 34747, tel. (407) 566-3687.

Port of Palm Beach, P.O. Box 9935, Riviera Beach, FL 33419, tel. (407) 842-4201: Palm Beach Cruise Line; Crown Cruise Line.

Port of St. Petersburg, Port Director Office, 107 8th Ave. SE, St. Petersburg, FL 33701, tel. (813) 893-7053: Odess-America.

Port of Tampa, 811 Wynkoop Rd., Tampa, FL 33605, tel. (813) 248-1924: Holland America Line; Regency Cruises.

Currency and Exchange

Foreign currency is readily exchanged at the Florida port of entry, or at most banks. Some Florida hotels provide currency exchange services, but possibly at a rate less favorable than a bank. Despite the prevalence of many sources for exchanging foreign currency, including larger shops and department stores, U.S. dollars traveler's checks are probably going to be easier to deal with for the foreign traveler.

The U.S. dollar, the "Greenback," comes in bank notes of the following denominations: 1, 2, 5, 10, 20, 50, 100, 500, 1,000, 5,000 and 10,000 dollar bills. However, you probably won't see anything larger than a hundred. All bills are the same size and color: so pay attention when making purchases!

In many shops and restaurants large bills are not accepted; you'll have to change them at a bank. If you can, try to keep cash on hand in bills of $50 or less.

A dollar is made up of 100 cents. Coins are the penny (one cent), the nickel (five cents), the dime (ten cents) and the quarter (25 cents). Occasionally an old half-dollar or dollar coin may turn up.

The quarter is the most important of these coins, as these are needed for pay phones, parking meters, vending machines, etc.

Doctors, Emergencies

Whoever has good medical insurance can go to any doctor as a private patient for treatment – provided you have enough cash on you, or else a credit card. Payment is expected on the spot, either in cash or by credit card. Just how much of this cost will be picked up by your insurer at home should be cleared up before you travel.

The emergency phone number for the police, fire department and ambulance is 911.

Electricity

A 110 volt Alternating Current (AC) system is used in the U.S. Conversion kits are available at appliance stores and at some hotels that cater to a large international clientele. An increasing number of electrical appliances can be switched directly from 220 to 110 volts.

Festivals and Holidays

Festivals and special events in Florida are too numerous to mention. Virtually every community that caters to tourists also offers art, music, film, culinary or cultural festivals. For a complete listing of Florida festivals contact: Department of Commerce, Division of Tourism, 126 W. Van Buren Street, Tallahassee, FL 33299-2000, (850) 487-1462.

The following official public holidays are celebrated in Florida. Local, state and federal offices, as well as most banks and some businesses, are closed.

New Year's Day . . . . January 1
Martin Luther King Day . . January 15
President's Day . . . . Third Monday
in February
Memorial Day . . Last Monday in May
Independence Day . . . . July 4
Labor Day . . . . First Monday
in September
Columbus Day . . . . Second Monday
in October
Veteran's Day . . . . . . November 11
Thanksgiving Day . . . Last Thursday
in November
Christmas Day . . . . . . December 25

In addition to these holidays, which are celebrated throughout the state, individual localities may celebrate other dates as well. Religious holidays are celebrated widely in certain areas.

Food and Drink

The United States still has a reputation abroad for being backward when it comes to the culinary arts. When most people think of American food, they think of Hamburgers, hotdogs, steaks and chili. Florida's culinary strength, however, lies in its delicious regional specialties, a strong Cuban influence, and the variety of fresh fish and seafood available throughout the state (see "The Flavors of Florida" on page 52).

Americans like to have a hearty breakfast, a light lunch (often cold) and a hot meal for dinner.

Breakfast in America, which is, incidentally, rarely included in hotel stays, is best enjoyed in a coffee shop. Breakfast normally starts with orange juice and cereal, followed by eggs with bacon or sausage and toast or pancakes. Lunch, generally between noon and 2 p.m., is usually a sandwich and soup or salad. Dinner is the biggest meal of the day.

Restuarants in America are somewhat different to those in Europe. Even in more exclusive restaurants, no one seems too concerned about jackets and ties or formal clothing. The relationship between staff and customers is more relaxed and familiar than in Europe, and etiquette is more lax (it is not uncommon to see women putting on their makeup right at the table, for example).

Customers are normally greeted by a host or hostess – or by the mâitre d' – on entering an establishment, and are almost always asked if they want to sit in a smoking or non-smoking section. If the restaurant is full, your name will be taken and added to the list of those already waiting for a table. As tables become free, guests are called in the order in which they appear on the list. While waiting for a table, guests can go to the bar or cocktail lounge for an aperitif.

Once you are at your table, the waiter or waitress will bring you the menu, and will generally introduce him- or herself ("Hi, my name's Brandy and I'll be your server this evening..."). Portions in the U.S. are considerably larger than in Europe, so you might want to pass on the appetizer and order the main course straight away.

Ice water (tap water) is always on hand in American restaurants. Coffee refills are free, as many as you want, as refills often are on many soft drinks. American coffee tends to seem sort of watery to foreigners, and it may take a few days for you to get used to it. If you don't want ice in your Coke of Fanta, make sure to order it that way.

Most restaurants offer a Daily Special meal at a special price. Most restaurants have self-service salad bars, which are much bigger and more complete than any you'll have seen in Europe. For those who are really hungry, a lot of places have all-you-can-eat specials. Most restaurants also have a special children's menu and senior's menu, with smaller portions at smaller prices.

American beer has a bad reputation abroad. While it is true that some of the beers made by the mega-breweries are not especially good, there are dozens if not hundreds of smaller breweries that produce extremely palatable brews. Better-known import beers (e.g., Heineken and Beck's) are avialable just about everywhere. While European wines are on offer in many restaurants, California wines prevail, some of which are quite good.

After dinner, you will almost always be asked if you'd like dessert. The assortment of these sweet delicacies is generally extensive, and many restaurants have their own home-made special treats. When the check is brought to you, it is generally put on the table. In some restaurants you pay at the table, though in general you pay at the cash register on your way out. The tip, which should be between 15 and 20 percent, is left on the table, not handed to the waiter or waitress. Keep in mind that service is not included in the bill; food servers in the U.S. earn most of their money from tips – their hourly wage is negligable. If paying by credit card, there is a space on the form for the gratuity.

Once your bill has been brought, you are expected to pay and leave within a few minutes: especially if the place is crowded and others are waiting for a table. Again, keep in mind that the service personnel make their money from tips, and the longer a table is tied up, the less money they will earn. In some instances, if it is thought that you are spending too much time relaxing after a meal, you might even be asked to leave. This is not necessarily being unfriendly, it is simply a matter of business.

Those who want to forego dining in restaurants and prefer to fend for themselves, will find more than you could ever possibly want in the supermarket, almost all of which have their own bakeries and delicatessen sections.

If you want to try some indigenous cheeses, New York and Vermont cheddars are excellent, especially the sharp ones, as are most varieties from Wisconsin (known as America's Dairyland).

A number of foods are much cheaper in the U.S. than in Europe, especially beef and seafood. Although Americans tend to eat mostly white bread, a variety of whole grain breads are available; albeit these are generally pre-packaged.

Ground coffee, sold in cans, is extremely coarse ground and not very good. Instant coffee is commonly drunk in many American homes. Good fresh ground coffees are generally available in bigger supermarkets, and in natural food and specialty shops.

Americans don't drink much mineral water, especially since tap water is free.

Opening Hours

Most shops and department stores are open Monday through Saturday from 9 a.m. to 9 or 10 p.m. On Sundays and holidays, many are open from 9 a.m. or noon until 9 p.m. Many supermarkets and corner stores and delis are open 24 hours a day. Only banks and post offices close on Sundays and holidays.

Postal Services

Most post offices are open Monday to Friday from 8 a.m. to 5 p.m., though many in larger cities stay open later, as well as on Saturday mornings. Postage stamps are often available at super markets, hotels and drug stores, as well as at most air, sea and bus terminals. Mailboxes can be found at all post offices, on many street corners, and often in hotels.

Express deliveries and packages can be sent through the U.S. Post Office, as well as through firms such as Federal Express and United Parcel Service.

Safety

If for a time tourists vacationing in Florida seemed like easy prey, they are no longer. Everyone considering a trip to Florida by now knows about keeping doors locked, not stopping if someone suddenly bumps your car from behind, and making sure that on arrival you know exactly where you are going between airport and hotel. Special care needs to be taken at night. Taxis are recommended if not driving your own car. The emergency number for the police, fire department and ambulance is 911.

Regrettable as the idea may be for vacationers, you must behave as if you were being watched. At any time, malefactors may have you under surveillance and they may have rehearsed how to make the hit. Don't walk alone at night or in couples where there's no one else around, espe-

cially where the street or beach is unlit. Ask reliable persons about safest routes for anywhere you're driving. Don't pick up hitchhikers.

Don't flash money around. Avoid identifying yourself as an out-of-towner. Don't, for example, go onto streets wearing a convention badge. Don't use automatic tellers if you're the only one there.

Don't open doors to strangers. Question anyone ostensibly making a delivery to your room. Check by phone to see if the front desk knows anything about this.

Leave your car in the best lighted section of your hotel parking lot, or give it to a doorman if there is one.

It's hard not to look like a tourist. No matter what you wear, your gait or body language gives you away. Especially on the street at night, try not to be conspicuously at play. Carry enough cash so that if someone does try to rob you, you have cash to surrender – but not more than you can afford to loose. Rely on credit cards.

It's ironic that in these times, when more and more people travel for relaxation, they have to spend a lot of time worrying. Some may wish to book only enclave vacations and stay within the confines of a hotel complex: but they will miss Florida's lively historical districts and outdoor opportunities.

Before traveling, be sure to make a note of telephone numbers you may need to call in the event of the loss or theft of traveler's checks, Eurochecks, credit cards, etc. It is also advisable to keep a copy of the address and phone number of the nearest consulate, as well as a photocopy of your passport with you.

In short, use caution and common sense when traveling.

Shopping

Stores are generally open from 9 a.m. to 9 p.m. Monday through Saturday, and Sunday from 9 a.m. or noon to 6 p.m.

For Europeans, this is a true shopper's paradise. Many things are much cheaper in the U.S. than they are in Europe, especially goods "Made in the U.S.A.," of course.

You will hardly ever encounter an unfriendly salesperson in the U.S. American shopping malls, some of which can house hundreds of shops, as well as department stores, restaurants and cafés, are like cities unto themselves.

Besides the usual arts and crafts and souvenir buys, electronics goods (TVs, stereos) tend to be cheap, as do CDs, videos and music casettes. Computer goods and peripherals, cameras and accessories, and select clothing can also be much cheaper. Some electrical goods, in fact, can be up to 30 percent less expensive than in Europe (check to make sure these can be switched to 220 volts!).

Televisions and VCRs are not much use to Europeans, as the American system (NTSC) is not compatible with the European (PAL and SECAM). Although some are multiple system. For the same reason, NTSC videos cannot be played on European systems.

Cameras, on the other hand, can be excellent bargains here – and you don't have to worry about whether it's the right system or voltage. All brand name cameras and accessories are noticeably cheaper in the States than in Europe.

When buying clothing, the biggest bargains are those made in America, like Levi's or Lee's, for example. American designer wear is also much cheaper here than in Europe.

A U.S. tradition is the Factory Outlet Store, where clothing and other goods with slight flaws, or last years fashions, can be purchased directly from the factory at a big savings.

Telecommunications

Florida has ten area codes for different regions of the state. These are 305, 352, 813, 407, 561, 727, 850, 904, 954, 941.

For long distance calling within one area code, dial 1 + telephone number. For calls outside the area code dial 1 + area code + telephone number. For operator assistance, dial 0.

For collect calls, calls billed to a credit card or to a third number, or person-to-person calls, dial 0 + telephone number, or if outside the area code, dial 0 + area code + telephone number.

For international calls, dial 0, or for direct dialing, dial 011 + country code + city code + telephone number. Direct dialing is less expensive than operator assisted calling. Additional discounts on direct dialed calls are available from 5 p.m. to 11 p.m., and even lower rates are in effect from 11 p.m. to 8 a.m., as well as all day Saturday and Sunday until 5 p.m.

Numbers with an 800 area code are toll-free – i.e., free of charge – within the United States. Often these are given with letters, for example, 1-800-HOLIDAY. The letters correspond to the numbers on the telephone.

900 numbers, on the other hand, are not toll free; in fact, they can be downright expensive!

Time

Most of Florida is in the Eastern Time Zone (EST), which is GMT minus five hours. The Apalachicola River in the Panhandle forms the border between the Eastern Time Zone and the Central Time Zone (CST), which is EST minus one hour.

Daylight Savings Time in the U.S. is from the last Sunday in April to the last Sunday in October. Remember: Flight arrival and departure times are always given in local time!

Tipping

Tipping is expected for most, if not all, personal services, including airport porters, bellhops, doormen (50 cents to $1 per bag); cab drivers (15%-20% of taxi fare); hotel maids ($1-$2 per day); food servers, barbers and hairdressers (15%-20% of total bill).

TOURIST INFORMATION

In addition to the numerous information sources listed throughout this book in the *Guideposts*, the following entities can provide you with information on current rates, seasonal schedules, facilities and services.

Attractions: Florida Attractions Association, P.O. Box 10295, Tallahassee, FL 32302, tel. (850) 222-2885.

Boating Registration and Regulations: Department of Natural Resources, Office of Communications, 3900 Commonwealth Blvd., Tallahassee, FL 32399-3000, tel. (850) 488-1195.

Camping: Florida Campground Association, 1638 North Plaza Drive, Tallahassee, FL 32308-5323, tel. (850) 487-1462.

Chambers of Commerce: Hundreds of individual chambers dispense free area information. A list of all local Florida chambers is available from: Florida Chamber of Commerce, P.O. Box 5497, Tallahassee, FL 32301.

Diving: Information from the Department of Commerce, Division of Tourism, Office of Sports Promotion, Collins Building, Suite 510, Tallahassee, FL 32399-2000, tel. (850) 487-1462.

Fishing and Hunting: Game and Freshwater Fish Commission, 620 South Meridian St., Farris Bryant Building, Tallahassee, FL 32399- 1600, tel. (850) 488-1960. Florida imposes the following fees on visitors for freshwater and saltwater fishing: $30 yearly, $15 for seven days. Licenses are available at county tax offices or bait and tackle shops, with a service fee of 50 cents to $1.50 added. The fine for fishing without a license can be as high as $500.

General Information: Department of Commerce, Division of Tourism, 126 W. Van Buren St., Tallahassee, FL 32399-0200, tel. (850) 487-1462. Available information includes free domestic or international travel planners and maps.

Golf: Florida State Golf Association, P.O. Box 21177, Sarasota, Florida, tel. (941) 921-5695.

Historical Sites: Department of State, Bureau of Historic Preservation, R.A. Gray Building, 500 South Bronough St., Tallahassee, FL 32399-0250, tel. (850) 487-2333.

Hotels and Motels: Florida Hotel/Motel Association, P.O. Box 1529, Tallahassee, FL 32302, tel. (850) 224-2888.

National Forests: U.S. Forest Service, Suite 4061, 227 North Bronough Street, Tallahassee, FL 32301, tel. (850) 681-7265.

Parimutuels: Department of Business Regulations, Parimutuel Wagering Division, 401 NW 2nd Avenue, Suite N 1026, Miami, FL 33128, tel. (305) 377-7015.

Polo: Palm Beach Polo and Country Club, 13198 Forest Hill Boulevard, West Palm Beach, FL 33414, tel. (561) 793-1113.

Professional Baseball: Major league baseball has come to Florida with the advent of the *Florida Marlins*, a National League franchise; 100 NE 3rd Avenue, Fort Lauderdale, 33301, tel. (305) 779-7070.

Eighteen of the 26 major league teams do spring training in Florida cities during February and March. Department of Information, Baseball Commissioner's Office, 350 Park Ave., New York, NY 10022, (212) 371-7800.

Professional Basketball: Miami Heat, Miami Arena, Miami, FL 33136-4102, tel. (305) 577-4328; Orlando Magic, P.O. Box 76, Orlando, FL 32802-0076, tel. (407) 896-2442.

Professional Football: Miami Dolphins, Joe Robbie Stadium, 2269 NW 199th St., Miami, FL 33056, tel. (305) 620-5000; Tampa Bay Buccaneers, 1 Buccaneer Place, Tampa, FL 33607, tel. (813) 879-BUCS; Florida Panthers, Miami Arena, Miami, tel. (305) 577-4328; Jacksonville Jaguars, 1 Stadium Place, Jacksonville, tel. (904) 633-6000.

Professional Hockey: Tampa Bay Lightning, 1 Mack Center, 501 E. Kennedy Boulevard, Suite 175, Tampa, FL 33602, tel. (813) 299-2658.

State Forests: Department of Agriculture and Consumer Services, Division of Forestry, 3125 Conner Boulevard, Tallahassee, FL 32399-1650, tel. (850) 488-6727.

State Parks: Department of Natural Resources, Office of Communications, 3900 Commonwealth Blvd., Tallahassee, FL 32399-3000.

Tennis: Florida Tennis Association, 801 NE 167th Street, North Miami Beach, FL 33162, tel. (305) 652-2866.

NORTHWEST FLORIDA

Director of Tourism, Escambia County, P.O. Box 550, Pensacola, FL 32593, tel. (850) 438-4081; **Apalachicola Bay Chamber of Commerce**, 45 Market Street, Apalachicola, FL 32320, tel. (850) 654-9419; **Wakulla County Chamber of Commerce**, P.O. Box 598, Crawfordville, FL 32327, tel. (850) 926-7849; **Pensacola Area Chamber of Commerce**, P.O. Box 550, Pensacola, FL 32593, tel. (850) 438-4081; **Tallahassee Chamber of Commerce**, P.O. Box 1639, Tallahassee, FL 32302, tel. (850) 224-8116.

NORTHEAST FLORIDA

Jacksonville Convention and Visitor's Bureau, 206 Hogan Street, Jacksonville, FL 32202, tel. (904) 353-9736; **Flagler County Chamber of Commerce**, P.O. Box 689, Flagler Beach, FL 32036, tel. (904) 439-2943; **Gainesville Area Chamber of Commerce**, P.O. Box 1187, Gainesville, FL 32602, tel. (352) 372-4305; **Jacksonville Area Chamber of Commerce**, P.O. Box 329, Jacksonville, FL 32201, tel. (352) 353-0300; **Suwannee County Chamber of Commerce**, P.O. Box C, Live Oak, FL 32060, tel. (904) 362-3071.

St. Augustine & St. Johns County Chamber of Commerce, P.O. Box O, St. Augustine, FL 32085, tel. (904) 829-5681.

CENTRAL COAST

Tourist Development Council, Volusia County, P.O. Box 2775, Daytona Beach, FL 32015, tel. (904) 255-0981; **Cocoa Beach Area Chamber of Commerce**, 431 Riveredge Boulevard, Cocoa Beach, FL 32922, tel. (407) 636-4262; **Daytona Beach Area Chamber of Commerce**, P.O. Box 2775, Daytona Beach, FL 32015, tel. (904) 255-0981; **DeLand Area Chamber of Commerce**, P.O. Box 629, DeLand, FL 32720, tel. (904) 734-4331; **Titusville Area Chamber of Commerce**, 2000 South Washington, Titusville, FL 32780, tel. (407) 267-3036; **Vero Beach Chamber of Commerce**, P.O. Box 3947, Vero Beach 32960, tel. (407) 567-3491.

CENTRAL FLORIDA

Tourist Development Council, Orange County, 7600 Dr. Phillips Blvd., Orlando, FL 32819, tel. (407) 345-8882; **Kissimmee/St. Cloud Convention & Visitors Bureau**, P.O. Box 2007, Kissimmee, FL 32742, tel. (407) 847-5000; **Greater Seminole County Chamber of Commerce**, P.O. Box 784, Altamonte Springs, FL 32701, tel. (407) 834-4404; **Kissimmee/Osceola County Chamber of Commerce**, P.O. Box 1982, Kissimmee, FL 32741, tel. (407) 847-3174; **Ocala/Marion County Chamber of Commerce**, P.O. Box 1210, Ocala, FL 32678, tel. (904) 629-8051; **Orlando Area Chamber of Commerce**, P.O. Box 1234, Orlando, FL 32802, tel. (407) 425-1234.

CENTRAL FLORIDA WEST

Tourist Development Council, Pinellas County, Newport Square 109A, 2333 East Bay Drive, Clearwater, FL 33546, tel. (813) 530-6452; **Greater Sarasota Tourism Association**, 655 North Tamiami, Sarasota, FL 33577, tel. (941) 957-1877; **Tampa Convention & Visitors**

Bureau, Hillsborough County, P.O. Box 420, Tampa, FL 33610, tel. (813) 228-7777; **Pinellas Suncoast Chamber of Commerce,** St. Petersburg/Clearwater Airport, Suite 239, Clearwater, FL 33520, tel. (813) 531-4657; **Madeira Beach Chamber of Commerce**, 501 150th Avenue, Madeira Beach, FL 33708, tel. (813) 391-7373; **St. Petersburg Area Chamber of Commerce,** P.O. Box 1371, St. Petersburg, FL 33731, tel. (813) 821-4069; **Sarasota County Chamber of Commerce**, P.O. Box 308, Sarasota, FL 33578, tel. (941) 955-8187; **Greater Seminole Area Chamber of Commerce**, P.O. Box 3337, Seminole, FL 33542, tel. (813) 392-3245; **Greater Tampa Chamber of Commerce,** P.O. Box 420, Tampa, FL 33601, tel. (813) 228-7777; **Ybor City**, 1513 8th Ave., Tampa, FL 33605, tel. (813) 248-3712; **Greater Tarpon Springs Chamber of Commerce**, 528 East Tarpon Ave., Tarpon Springs Ave., Tarpon Springs, FL 33589, tel. (813) 937-6100; **Venice Area Chamber of Commerce**, 257 N. Tamiami Trail, Venice, FL 33595, tel. (941) 488-2236.

THE SOUTHWEST

Tourist Development Council, Manatee County, P.O. Box 321, Bradenton, FL 33506, tel. (813) 722-3900; **Tourist Development Council**, Charlotte County, P.O. Box 1398, Englewood, FL 33533, tel. (941) 474-7713; **Tourist Development Council**, Lee County, P.O. Box 2445, Fort Myers, FL 33902-9990, tel. (941) 335-2631; **Everglades Area of Chamber of Commerce**, P.O. Box E, Everglades City, FL 33929, tel. (941) 695-3941; **Metropolitan Fort Myers Chamber of Commerce**, P.O. Box CC, Fort Myers, FL 33902, tel. (941) 334-1133; **Naples Area Chamber of Commerce**, 170 North Tamiami Trail, Naples, FL 33940, tel. (941) 262-6141.

THE SOUTHEAST

Tourist Development Council, Broward County, 201 SE, 8th Avenue, Fort Lauderdale, FL 33301, tel. (954) 765-5508; **Tourist Development Council**, Monroe County, P.O. Box 866, Key West, FL 33041, tel. (305) 296-2228; **Tourist Development Council**, Dade County, 555 17th Street, Miami, FL 33139, tel. (305) 673-7070; **Tourist Development Council**, Palm Beach County, 1555 Palm Beach Lakes Boulevard, Suite 204, West Palm Beach, FL 33401, tel. (561) 471-3995; **The Lower Keys Chamber of Commerce**, P.O. Box 511, Big Pine Key, FL 33043, tel. (305) 872-2411; **Greater Boca Raton Chamber of Commerce**, P.O. Box 1390, Boca Raton, FL 33432, tel. (561) 395-4433; **The Coconut Grove Chamber of Commerce**, 3437 Main Highway, Coconut Grove, FL 33133, tel. (305) 444-7270; **The Coral Gables Chamber of Commerce**, 50 Aragon Avenue, Coral Gables, FL 33134, tel. (305) 446-1657; **The Fort Lauderdale/Broward County Chamber of Commerce**, P.O. Box 14516, Fort Lauderdale, FL 33302, tel. (954) 462-6000; **Islamorada Chamber of Commerce**, P.O. Box 915, Islamorada, FL 33036, tel. (305) 664-4503; **The Key Biscayne Chamber of Commerce**, 95 West McIntyire Street, Key Biscayne, FL 33149, tel. (305) 361-5207; **The Florida Upper Keys Chamber of Commerce**, P.O. Box 274-C, Key Largo, FL 33037, tel. (305) 451-1414; **The Greater Key West Chamber of Commerce**, 402 Wall Street, Key West, FL 33040, tel. (305) 294-2587; **The Greater Marathon Chamber of Commerce**, 3330 Overseas Highway, Marathon, FL 33050, tel. (305) 743-5417; **Greater Miami Chamber of Commerce**, 1601 Biscayne Boulevard, Omni Complex, Seventh Floor, Miami, FL 33132, tel. (305) 350-7700; **The Miami Beach Chamber of Commerce**, 1920 Meridian Avenue, Miami Beach, FL 33139, tel. (305) 672-1270; **The Northwest Dade County Chamber of Commerce**, 45 Curtiss Parkway, Miami Springs, FL 33166, tel. (305) 822-1911; **The Palm Beach Chamber of Commerce**, 45 Coconut Row, Palm Beach, FL 33480, tel. (561) 655-3282.

AUTHORS

Pam Brandon is a former magazine editor who has spent the last eight years in the tourism industry. She now is a freelance writer based in Central Florida. For the *Nelles Guide Florida* she worked as a correspondent and contributed the chapter "Orlando and Walt Disney World."

Patricia and Edgar Cheatham are a travel writer/photographer team specializing in Florida. Their work appears in *Delta Sky*, *Vista USA*, *Travel-Holiday*, *Home & Away*, and in major North American daily newspapers. They wrote "Theme Parks" and "Golf and Tennis Resorts."

Steve Cohen is an author and photographer specializing in adventure travel. He wrote the section entitled "The West Coast."

Janet and Gordon Groene are a writer and photographer team who have scouted Florida in their own boat, motor-home, airplane, canoe and hiking boots. They wrote "History of Florida," "Florida's Spicy Cultural Mix," "Daytona Beach," "Gainesville" and "Northeastern Florida."

Herb Hiller is a back-roads traveler and freelance writer, author of *Guide to the Small and Historic Lodgings of Florida*, and editor of the *Ecotourism Society Newsletter*. Together with Laurie Werner he wrote "Miami," "Miami Beach," "Fort Lauderdale and Broward County" and contributed "Northwestern Florida," "Florida Trails," "Everglades Day Trips" and "Bed and Breakfast Inns."

Carol and Dan Thalimer have specialized in the southeastern United States. They write travel features for an Atlanta newspaper, and for *Travel Agent Magazine* and *Athens* (Georgia) *Magazine*. To this guide they contributed "Cape Canaveral."

Ute and Andrew Vladimir are a Coconut Grove, Florida based travel writing team. In addition to guide book writing, their work appears in many U.S. newspapers. They wrote "The Florida Keys," "The Everglades" and "National and State Parks / Underwater Parks."

Laurie Werner is a New York based writer who is fascinated by the dichotomy of typical Florida public relations hype and the sometimes less than bright realities found in the Sunshine State. Her work appears in major U.S. newspapers and magazines. She is the co-author of "Miami," "Miami Beach," "Fort Lauderdale and Broward County." She wrote "Palm Beach" and contributed all features in this book.

PHOTOGRAPHERS

Explore the World

NELLES GUIDES

CALIFORNIA
LAS VEGAS, RENO, BAJA CALIFORNIA

U.S.A.
THE EAST [...] AND SOUTH

MEXICO

AVAILABLE TITLES

Australia
Bali / Lombok
Berlin and Potsdam
Brazil
Brittany
Burma → Myanmar
California
  Las Vegas, Reno,
  Baja California
Cambodia / Laos
Canada
  Ontario, Québec,
  Atlantic Provinces
Canada
  Pacific Coast, the Rockies,
  Prairie Provinces, and
  the Territories
Canary Islands
Caribbean
  The Greater Antilles,
  Bermuda, Bahamas
Caribbean
  The Lesser Antilles
China – Hong Kong
Corsica
Costa Rica
Crete
Croatia – Adriatic Coast
Cyprus
Egypt
Florida

Greece – The Mainland
Greek Islands
Hawai'i
Hungary
India
  Northern, Northeastern
  and Central India
India – Southern India
Indonesia
  Sumatra, Java, Bali,
  Lombok, Sulawesi
Ireland
Israel - with Excursions
  to Jordan
Kenya
London, England and
  Wales
Malaysia - Singapore
  - Brunei
Maldives
Mexico
Morocco
Moscow / St. Petersburg
Munich
  Excursions to Castles,
  Lakes & Mountains
Myanmar (Burma)
Nepal
New York – City and State
New Zealand
Norway

Paris
Philippines
Portugal
Prague / Czech Republic
Provence
Rome
Scotland
South Africa
South Pacific Islands
Spain – Pyrenees, Atlantic
  Coast, Central Spain
Spain
  Mediterranean Coast,
  Southern Spain,
  Balearic Islands
Sri Lanka
Syria – Lebanon
Tanzania
Thailand
Turkey
Tuscany
U.S.A.
  The East, Midwest and South
U.S.A.
  The West, Rockies and Texas
Vietnam

FORTHCOMING

Poland
Sweden

Nelles Guides – authoritative, informed and informative.
Always up-to-date, extensively illustrated, and with first-rate relief maps.
256 pages, approx. 150 color photos, approx. 25 maps.